life is
just what
you
make it

donny osmond

and patricia romanowski

life is just what you make it

my story so far

HYPERION

new york

To Debbie and our children

ISBN 0-7868-8971-3

Original hardcover design by Kathy Kikkert

FIRST MASS MARKET EDITION

10 9 8 7 6 5 4 3 2 1

introduction

It happened one night at a gas station, somewhere around Fresno, California. All I wanted to do was gas up our motor home, drive my wife Debbie and our two little boys, Don and Jeremy, to a nice motel, and get some rest.

It was 1984—somewhere in the middle of what I euphemistically call my "lost years"—a difficult decade neatly bracketed by the end of the original *Donny and Marie Show*, in 1979, and my number-two "comeback" hit, "Soldier of Love," in 1989. What was I doing in Fresno? Working. Why? Because a decade after all the gold records and sold-out world tours, the Osmond family was just beginning to emerge from a financial debacle that had all but wiped us out. Here in the United States, public demand for Osmonds was greatest for Marie and me, so out of necessity and obligation, we found ourselves playing dates our agents tried to make sound better than they really were. Take tonight's, for example. Maybe no one thought we'd notice that the scene of this evening's presentation was a high school gym.

I don't want this to sound bitter, because I'm not. And, odd as it might sound, I wasn't really bitter then, either. I was, however, disillusioned, frustrated, and confused. Where was my career headed? What was my next step? Would I ever get another chance?

While the gas tank was filling, I slid into the driver's seat of the motor home and looked at my boys and Debbie, the only woman I ever loved. *This is what it's really all about*, I reminded myself. *The show's over. Let it go.* I willed myself to forget about the high school gym, but I couldn't stop thinking as I stared out into the night, *I'm just twenty-six. I'm too young to be a has-been.*

I was jolted from my thoughts by an unfamiliar voice from the distance: "Hey! There's Donny Osmond!"

Startled, I looked up and saw coming down the block a car full of teenage boys. They were hanging out the windows, shouting my name, and laughing loudly. It didn't surprise me that they weren't Donny Osmond fans; most teenagers back then weren't, and most guys never were. And these weren't the first to insult me, either. After more than twenty years in the business, I'd mastered the art of gracefully sidestepping confrontations, of refusing to rise to the bait. Donny Osmond in a fight? What would people think?

Okay. Just get out of here, I told myself. *Just a couple more minutes.*

"Hey! Donny!" one of them shouted, laughing. "How was the show?" Then he let loose with a stream of vulgarities, words my little boys didn't even know existed. If I'd been there alone, I could have ignored it. But my wife and my young sons were hearing it, and my jaw clenched and my heart began to race. It was the wrong time, the wrong place.

Debbie knows me so well, she read my mind. "Don't do a thing, Donny," she said evenly. "Just bite your lip, and let's get out of here."

I knew Debbie was right, and if the tank had been filled, I'd have probably driven away and never looked back. But years of grinning through the teeth jokes, pretending to laugh along as disc jockeys warbled "Puppy Love" in my face—almost a lifetime of not being taken seriously—came crashing through. Debbie surely saw it, because as I grabbed the door handle, she cried, "Don't do it, Donny! Don't you dare!" I have a temper, and Debbie was clearly—and rightly—afraid for me. "You don't know what those guys are going to do. Please don't!"

I knew I wasn't making the smartest decision, but I didn't care. As badly as I wanted to make them stop yelling at me, I also cared what they thought about me. This probably sounds confusing, but here's how I saw it then. I wasn't a failure because they were calling me names, but I would have felt like one if I hadn't at least tried to change their minds.

"I just want to go out and talk to them," I replied tersely, as I watched their car stop. I tried to be cool, but the instant the door slammed behind me, I lost it. Striding across the pavement and jabbing my finger at them, I shouted, "Hey, you! I want to talk to you!"

An enraged Donny Osmond heading for them was clearly not what these guys expected. After exchanging startled glances, they furiously rolled up the windows in a panic.

"Roll down those windows! Now!" I screamed. "I want to talk to you!" I felt as if I were somewhere outside myself watch-

ing this other Donny express all the rage and hurt I could barely acknowledge existed—and in language I'd never uttered
before. I was disappointed in myself, and I instantly regretted
that Debbie, Don, and Jeremy had to witness it. In that moment,
however, it felt pretty good.

The driver, who was getting a lot more than he and his
friends had bargained for, opened his window a crack and sheep-
ishly said, "Yes, sir?" If I hadn't been so angry, I probably would
have laughed.

"How dare you scream at me and insult me! Who do you
think you are? Do you have any idea what it's like to have the
name Donny Osmond?" I shouted as I paced back and forth by
the driver's side. "All I've tried to do is entertain people. And look
at what you guys are doing to me! It's not fair, and I'm sick and
tired of it!" Okay, I'm not printing every word I said here, but I
think you get the drift.

The windows lowered a few more inches, and one of the
kids softly replied, "Gee, Donny, we had no idea."

Just as I suspected, these were really decent kids who
assumed that I deserved to be insulted just for being Donny
Osmond. I didn't go out merely to defend myself; I wanted to
make them understand. "You know, I've got my wife and my children in that mobile home. And they're hearing you say these terrible things about me, and it hurts us all. You understand?"

They nodded, and we talked for another five or ten minutes. One of them said, "We're so sorry, Mr. Osmond."

"Yeah," another added, "you're kind of a cool guy."

Kind of? Okay. I let it pass. "Okay, guys, just think twice
before you open your mouths like that again."

"Yes, sir!"

"Take care, dude!"

I admit feeling vindicated as I strode back toward the mobile home. I'd really surprised myself. For once, I put the real Donny Osmond ahead of the image. I'd let a total stranger know how I really felt instead of automatically giving the "correct" answer, or worrying more about their feelings—or anyone else's—than my own.

I was patting myself on the back a bit, thinking, *Four down, several million more to go*, as I eased back into the driver's seat. I turned to Debbie, expecting her approval, or at least a smile. She fixed me with a no-nonsense look I've come to know very well, and said, "Don't you *ever* do that again!"

Well past midnight, long after Debbie had fallen asleep, I lay awake in bed thinking about what had happened and where I was in my life. After more than two decades in show business, I was at a crossroads with a compass but no map. I knew where I wanted to go, but I had no idea how to get there.

For the first time in my life, I really had time to look back and reflect. Where had all the time gone? At an age when most kids still had nap time on their class schedule, I was singing with my brothers on national television. When most teenage guys were nervously plotting how to ask that one special girl to the junior high dance, I was standing before thousands who were crying, tearing their hair, and screaming, "Donny! I love you!" I could have gotten a date, I guess, but I never had an opportunity to go to a school dance.

Instead, my brothers and I kept churning out hit records and touring sold-out stadiums and first-class showrooms around the world. We performed for royalty; we amassed a literal fortune. In 1972 we were awarded more gold records than any other act in the world. When the record sales began to cool, we made what seemed like a wise decision. Our family threw everything we had—emotionally and financially—into producing four seasons of *The Donny and Marie Show* and creating an elaborate, multimillion-dollar, state-of-the-art studio complex in Utah so that we could do it from "home." Three years later, in 1979, the show ended, freeing Marie and me to pursue independent careers. Being a little bit country turned out beautifully for Marie. Being a little bit rock and roll, however, hadn't worked nearly as well for me. A couple of career setbacks and the collapse of the family "empire," as the press liked to call it, and here I was: in my mid-twenties, unable to shake a gnawing feeling that it might be all over for me.

I'd recently located my family to the Los Angeles area and dedicated myself to getting my singing career on track, so far, to no avail. Despite my string of eight Top 20 hits on my own, plus seven with my brothers, and three with Marie, not to mention a pair of Number Ones in there, nobody in the record business believed I'd ever hit the charts again. Or if they did believe I could, they weren't willing to take the risk with me. Countless record executives told me in so many words, "I know you could make a great record, Donny. But breaking through your teeny-bopper image? Impossible." Still, I couldn't bear the thought of giving up, at least not yet.

Actually, the decision to give up wouldn't come for another three years, after I'd poured my heart into making an album it seemed no one wanted to hear. In December 1988, I had almost resigned myself to starting a home security business and leaving the Donny I thought I knew behind forever. I knew I'd miss him, but somewhere in my heart, I could easily imagine my relief at just letting him go. My friends, my family, and even I wondered why I hadn't hung it up already. Debbie alone stood by me as I struggled to rewrite the script I'd been handed as a child.

Then a funny thing happened. The minute I stopped chasing the dream, it caught up to me. Between December 1988 and March 1989, Donny Osmond went from a has-been to one of the comeback stories of the decade. With "Soldier of Love" and "Sacred Emotion" I didn't "reinvent" Donny Osmond as much as I finally revealed him. Like a blessing, others finally saw the Donny I knew always lived inside the image.

Of course, this is real life, so I did not live happily ever after. My next album disappeared with barely a trace, and I was seriously looking into becoming a professional race car driver when I was offered the lead in *Joseph and the Amazing Technicolor Dreamcoat*. My six years with that show brought me to a place of artistic and emotional fulfillment I'd sought for so long. In the midst of that, though, I also faced the possibility of never standing on a stage again.

After decades of performing for millions, one night while playing Joseph, I found myself onstage suddenly gripped by fear and panic so overwhelming, I honestly believed I was dying. Afraid that I was suffering a complete nervous breakdown or worse, I struggled blindly to unlock the secret behind this unnamed terror that revealed a Donny even I didn't know: fearful, suspicious, angry, out of control.

One morning at six A.M., I phoned my manager, Jill Willis, in Minneapolis, where I was performing. I was crying so hard, she barely recognized my voice. All I could say was, "I've got to go home. I've got to go home."

I might have retreated to Utah, where I felt safe, and disappeared forever, because in that crisis, that's all I could see for myself: just getting away. I had to get away. Fortunately, I was saved by a brilliant psychologist, Dr. Jerilyn Ross, who immediately diagnosed social phobia, a little-discussed but extremely common, often debilitating anxiety disorder. Anyone can develop such a disorder, but my innate perfectionism, my obsessive need to please others, and my inability to always express myself honestly made me particularly vulnerable. Ironically, two symptoms of social phobia are believing that everyone is looking at you and believing that people are criticizing you. For most people, these thoughts have no basis in reality. For me, however, these thoughts had a painfully real component that complicated my treatment. I was forced not only to treat my social phobia but to pay more attention to those parts of my inner life I'd almost unthinkingly sacrificed to the job of being "Donny Osmond."

As I learned more about my problem and heard accounts of people whose fear rendered them prisoners in their own homes for decades, I felt myself understanding how they felt. It frightened me to realize just how well I understood them. I knew I didn't want to go down that road, but I also feared that without help, I easily might. I'd worked too hard building my own life to let it all go again.

During these years I lived another lifetime, and I truly grew up. With the support and love of my wife, my children, and the rest of my family, I survived and even learned to laugh along with the people I'd always feared were laughing at me. I learned again to appreciate and to treasure the values and the faith my parents instilled in me. And I saw renewed time and again the family closeness and love we all so often spoke of through the years yet rarely put to the test. I struggled to receive the gift of perspective, the ability to face the personal issues I'd always felt more comfortable avoiding. I learned that life is what you make it.

Now, if that all sounds too sweet, too much like the "old" Donny, let me share some of the other title ideas I kicked around: How about *One More Joke About Big Teeth and the Old Lady Gets It?* Or *I Survived Donny Osmond—and You Can, Too?* Or, *I Suffered for My Art—Now It's Your Turn?* And perhaps you'd like to hear my roaring speed-metal version of "Puppy Love"? (No, I am not kidding.)

The other thing I learned is that success is, among many other things, fleeting, capricious, and often in the eye of the beholder. In 1998 I was doing prerelease publicity for the animated film *Mulan,* talking about my role as the singing voice of the heroine's teacher and eventual love interest, Captain Li Shang. From the industry's point of view, Donny Osmond was "back"—again. Interviewers inevitably mentioned my career as a child star and a teen idol, my late-1980s "comeback," and my famous family, but it was also refreshing to feel they accepted me for who I am today.

An animated feature like *Mulan* is typically years in the making, and so a couple of years had passed between the time I recorded "I'll Make a Man Out of You" and the premiere. Before that, my children—by then Don and Jeremy had been joined by Brandon and Christopher—thought no more of *Mulan* than they did any other part of my career. They've lived most of their lives away from Hollywood, and after growing up surrounded by a famous aunt, famous uncles, and some famous cousins as well, show business didn't impress them much. Some dads went to the office every day; their dad went to a stage or a studio. Ho-hum.

One of the most exciting nights of my life came in spring 1998, when Debbie and I brought the boys to the Hollywood Bowl premiere of *Mulan*. The industry buzz was hot then, and it was very gratifying to be part of a hit movie. But nothing beat watching my sons' expressions as they heard my voice booming from a five-story-tall animated Shang. When the film ended and the applause died down, they turned to me, beaming. They all agreed: "Dad, you're *really* a star now."

Now, not everyone who saw *Mulan* believed that I had "finally" made it. I teach Sunday school to a group of kids whose parents danced to "One Bad Apple" in grade school. Most of them, mercifully, have no recollection of me in a Donny cap or my Captain Purple cape and tights. One morning after church, I was walking several of the students who live in my neighborhood home.

"You know, Mr. Osmond," one boy said. "I saw that *Mulan* movie and heard you singing in it. And it was really, really good."

"Why, thank you, buddy," I replied, smiling.

"And you know what?" he added brightly, obviously thrilled to be giving his teacher advice. "You really should do more of that stuff. You could be a big star someday!"

chapter 1

I guess the beginning is always a good place to start.

I was born on December 9, 1957, in Ogden, a small community in the northeast corner of Utah. My family lived in a four-bedroom house at 228 North Washington Boulevard. We had a large plot of land, with apple, peach, and cherry trees, raspberry bushes, and room enough to keep rabbits and a cow. Several years ago, I went back to visit that little house, and nothing was the same. But for me as a child, this was a magical and very special place. It was in this house that I'm convinced I saw Santa's sleigh alight from the winter sky (and I know this is true, because I heard the sleigh bells and my brother Jay saw a reindeer lick our window). In the sandbox right outside the kitchen window, I passed some of the best afternoons of my life. But when and where I was born are just details. The real story of my life begins with the family I was born to, the Osmonds.

My parents, George Virl Osmond and Olive May Davis, met shortly after World War II. My father served during the war, and earned the rank of sergeant. He met my mother in Ogden, where she lived with her parents and brother, after he received an honorable discharge because of health problems. Although my parents were of similar backgrounds and beliefs, their family experiences could not have been more different. My mother grew up in a loving home, the daughter of schoolteachers. In contrast, my father had a far less happy childhood. His father died when he was a baby, and neither of his two stepfathers loved him. In fact, as a young boy, Father was forced to sleep on an unheated porch and live on milk and bread. He was barely a teenager when he had to leave his home and find his own way in the world, alone. It's a great tribute to my father and says a lot about him that those painful early experiences did not darken his view of the world. However, the uncertainty of his early life made Father a person who would always be uncomfortable with disorder and driven to let the world see only the best in himself and in his family.

As my parents got to know each other, they discovered that they shared the same dream: to have a large family. Mother recalled a large neighbor family she knew as a child and how she enjoyed being invited over to join in the fun. Today she laughs to think that five children seemed like so many; little did she know that she would become the mother of nine.

My parents' desire to raise so many children is deeply rooted in our church, The Church of Jesus Christ of Latter-day Saints. Our church members are more commonly referred to as

"Mormons," and while that's a widely used term, it's technically incorrect. There are two popular misconceptions about our church I'll lay to rest right here: Yes, ours is a Christian church, and, no, we do not practice polygamy. (The fact is, only a relatively small number of church members did so prior to the late 1800s when the Church decreed the practice unacceptable.)

More important to my story are the positive values our Church taught, and at the center of it all is a view of the world that looks beyond today and considers what I like to call "the big picture." From the time we were very young, Mother and Father always talked very openly about our faith and its teachings. They told us about how theirs was not just a marriage made here on earth, but a celestial marriage, a "sealing" together for eternity. And as their children, we are sealed to them and to one another forever, as our future spouses, children, grandchildren, and succeeding generations all will be. Our religious beliefs influenced everything in our lives. For example, I will always refer to my parents as "Father" and "Mother," because Father considered "Dad" and "Mom" disrespectful. "You don't say, 'Our Dad who art in Heaven,'" he reasoned.

I admit that this is the "short course" on my religious beliefs. It would take many books to explain it all, and I'm not here to proselytize. But a basic understanding of our values goes a long way toward understanding how our lives would unfold. We grew up knowing that life in this world passes in the blink of an eye. Over the years, people have marveled at how my parents managed to raise what is often considered an oxymoron: a loving, happy show-business family. Many factors played a part in my parents' ability to succeed as parents while their children succeeded in a very rough, sometimes shady business. At the core of it was our belief that life's material rewards are ephemeral. There's a saying I've seen quoted in many places and in many different contexts: "No success can compensate for failure in the home." This was uttered in the late 1960s by a former president of our Church. It expresses precisely the guiding principles my parents and now my siblings and I try to follow in our own families.

By any measure, my parents are conservative, but that didn't prevent them from seeing life as a great adventure. I've never known them to hesitate to turn a new corner or take an uncharted road. They are indefatigable optimists. Mother had the faith to endure any setback with her ardent belief that, as she often said, "This too shall pass," a sentiment that I admit did not always console me. Another, which I think betrays her down-to-earth outlook, is, "Tragedy plus time equals humor." Mother has a free, infectious laugh like no one I've ever known.

My parents' unwavering faith in the future was tested early in their marriage when they learned that my two eldest brothers, Virl (who was born in October 1945) and Tom (born almost exactly two years later, in October 1947), were hearing impaired. For reasons no one knows, Virl was born with a substantial hearing loss, and Tom has practically no hearing at all. Though heartbroken, as any parents of a disabled child would be, Mother and Father stood firm. They ignored the advice of experts who urged them to lower their expectations for Virl and Tom and to consider institutionalizing them. They were told that this would be best for my brothers, since they probably would never learn to speak. They tried to persuade my parents to accept Virl's and Tom's limitations.

But my parents believed that Virl and Tom could learn to

speak and to thrive in a hearing world. They never said it would be easy, and at times it wasn't. Mother learned everything she could about teaching her sons, then she relied on her own mother's intuition and common sense to devise very clever, innovative ways of helping them. My parents transformed a room in our home into a schoolroom, complete with blackboard, desks, and books, so that Mother could instruct them at home. It was a special place where we could do our homework and where Mother, who was a natural teacher, could help us with our studies. (Every home we lived in after that included a similarly appointed room.)

The point is that my parents never gave up. And they taught us never to give up either. Father had a saying that I'll never forget: "Don't aim for the moon, aim for the stars." It's a philosophy I think we all took to heart, because it encouraged us to set our sights higher and reflected the confidence our parents had in us. There were many wonderful gifts we all received from Father and Mother, but perhaps the greatest was their faith in us. They were the first people to tell us that we could achieve anything we set our sights on, and they created a supportive home environment in which we thrived.

As the seventh child, I joined a family already in full swing: my brothers Virl, twelve; Tom, ten; Alan, eight; Wayne, six; Merrill, four; and Jay, more than two and a half. I don't recall too many specific incidents from those very early years, only a general impression of a household brimming with activity and love. With so many of us, my ever-practical, highly organized parents relied on schedules and routines to keep the household running. Both Father and Mother are very hardworking, industrious people. Father turned his hand to insurance, real estate, and advertising sales for a radio station, in addition to serving as postmaster and being very active in our church. Mother helped keep his books, handled the clerical duties, and was quite knowledgeable about business as well.

Mother and Father made sure we were always involved in some constructive activity and always learning, if not by example or through lesson, then by osmosis. Mother loves collecting inspirational and insightful quotations, bits of wisdom that she would write on a kitchen wall painted with blackboard paint. (Never one to fall behind the times, Mother now posts these on her website.) On this board, she would also write out multiplication charts and complex sentences, that she would diagram the old-fashioned way, with the parts of speech branching out on diagonal lines (which I could never figure out). My earliest memories of Father all involve him teaching us the practical lessons of life: how to care for animals and the garden, how to organize, how to build and repair things.

When I think of home then, I think of the security I felt, being watched over by two loving parents and six older brothers. In the tradition of the teachings we followed, older siblings had authority over the younger ones. This was a great way for kids to learn responsibility, but from my low spot on the family totem pole, I sometimes felt as if I had eight parents, not two. Although in later years, Virl and Tom remained largely out of the spotlight (they performed with us only occasionally; both dance and play instruments), at home they assumed their rightful place as our older brothers. Virl is twelve and Tom ten years older than I, so we were never close in a buddy-buddy way, but I love and admire them. I always considered Virl the most handsome in our family, and I looked up to him because, in my young eyes, he was so accomplished and responsible. I admired Tom for his courage and determination. In addition to our close physical resemblance, Tom and I share a degree of fearlessness.

I remember once when I was about eight and we were living in California. Father and Mother took Virl and Tom somewhere and left us home alone with Alan, or Big Al, as we call him, in charge. Suddenly we heard sounds at the back door, like someone was trying to break into the house. Alan immediately phoned the number where my parents were, and they raced home. In the meantime, it was up to Alan to hold the fort.

"Everybody go get knives!" Alan, our fearless leader, commanded, and we scrambled for the kitchen drawer to arm ourselves. It sounded like a good idea at the time, but it's hard to imagine how the sight of seven kids wielding butter knives would have deterred anyone. We gripped our weapons tensely as the scratching sounds grew more persistent. We stood poised to attack when, thank goodness, Father and Mother pulled up. The burglar heard them and tried to run for it. Without knowing whether the intruder was armed, Tom leapt from the car and chased him away. Until then, this was the most dramatic moment of my life. When Tom returned, he was my hero.

Another time I'll never forget, I was sitting in the third, rear-facing, fold-down seat in our station wagon. My parents avoided a lot of bickering by giving us assigned seats, and as one of the youngest kids, I was relegated to the "cheap seats," you could say. I don't recall the incident, but somehow Father incurred the wrath of another driver who, assuming he wouldn't be heard, let loose with a stream of profanities. Of course, Virl and Tom were trained to read lips, but when Father asked them what the guy had said, Tom replied, "You don't want to know," and we all laughed. We knew those words existed, but we could never, ever say them.

Although my brothers and I were all pretty well behaved and polite, we were still boys and not immune to the lure of adventure and even trouble. We didn't have many store-bought toys, and so we all became adept at finding ways to amuse ourselves. Being the baby of the family—at least for a few years—I was often the guinea pig for my older brothers' experiments in "fun." I vividly recall once being led up to the attic, where Virl, Tom, and Alan had created a "spook alley," a makeshift "haunted" walkway they'd strewn with mousetraps. At only two or three, I was oblivious as I happily toddled along, only to start screaming as the snapping traps went off. Thank goodness my little toes were safely ensconced in my feety pajamas.

My other clear memory of that moment is Alan, ever the "producer" of our family, gleefully crying out, "It works! It really scared him! It works!" Alan never stopped dreaming up jaw-dropping stunts, and fortunately for him, I'm up for anything that involves danger. The result has been some very spectacular, heart-stopping moments over the years. Some twenty years after the spook alley incident, Alan would produce a Fourth of July stadium show at Brigham Young University, where I made my entrance circling the stadium, strapped to the outside of a helicopter. Do you think it's possible to love your little brother and still harbor a death wish for him?

I was adventurous, accident prone, and curious. Sometimes too curious. I was about three when I had my first intimate, shocking encounter with electricity. It would not be the last. For as long as I can remember, electricity always fascinated me. One day when no one was looking, I picked up a live extension cord socket and put it in my mouth. I got some nasty burns and scared everyone half to death. Miraculously, I suffered no permanent damage… I don't think. But that didn't stop me, and neither would any of the other major shocks I'd receive in the coming years. A few years later, I would amuse myself by threading a piece of copper wire into the socket end of an extension cord and plugging it into an outlet. Why? The resistance in the copper wouldn't blow any fuses, but the current coming through the outlet would heat up the copper sufficiently to start a small fire. At the sight of flames, I would start laughing, quickly yank the cord from the outlet, blow out the fire, and then try it again. I know what you're thinking—*Strange kid, huh?*—and I can't entirely disagree.

Another time, I gave everyone a scare when I almost choked to death on a button that went down my windpipe. Wayne, always a sensitive soul, became so overwrought at the sight of me turning (what else?) purple, that he panicked and ran out into the field screaming, "Save him! Save him!" The only problem with Wayne's "rescue plan" is that no one was outside to hear him. Fortunately, Mother just happened to look out the window, saw Wayne screaming, and ran to find me just in time. Now, in my defense, I wasn't the only child engaged in unusual behavior. Marie used to dress up Jimmy like a girl, and in later years Merrill would amuse us by sashaying around the house like a runway model. Jay created play characters out of paper clips, Alan wrote poetry, and Wayne spent an awful lot of time building model airplanes. Me? Well, there was that night in the backyard when I was convinced star men were communicating with me from a distant planet. Accidents, misadventures, and inno-cent adventures in cross-dressing aside, we were a typical, nor-mal family.

One of the first lessons you learned in the Osmond house-hold was self-sufficiency. With so many children, Mother could hardly be expected to wait on each of us, so mealtimes often demanded fending for yourself. She would prepare a big pot of stew, and you had to get to the table and help yourself if you didn't want to be scraping an empty pot. My parents kept track of us by having us count off, just to make sure no one had got-ten left behind somewhere. This was especially useful on car trips and other family outings, but it also became a mealtime rit-ual, especially since the dinner table didn't always accommodate everyone and some of us would eat in the kitchen. So every night at dinner, Father would order, "Count off!" and starting with Virl, we'd shout out, in descending age order, "One!" "Two!" "Three!" "Four!" "Five!" "Six!" "Seven!" "Eight!" and so on. Mother was ten and Father was eleven. It probably sounds a touch mili-taristic, but when we did it, it came out in a happy flurry: "Onetwothreefourfivesixseveneightnineteneleven!"

Whatever we did, we did it together as a family. I later real-ized that there are many people who say they believe that fam-ily should come first, but I've never met anyone who put that belief into practice quite the way Father and Mother did, and still do. In fact, whenever anyone would suggest to my parents that they might enjoy an evening out alone together, they would decline. They believed that if they couldn't bring us along for the fun, there wouldn't be any.

The very idea that they would want to take a break from us—then seven boys—was simply alien to them. They never took a vacation without us, they never went to dinner without asking for a table for nine, or, later, ten or eleven.

Because we didn't socialize much with our friends outside of school and church, my siblings and I just assumed that this was how all parents were. With two decades of fatherhood behind me, I can really appreciate the sacrifices they made for us. Each moment they spent with us reinforced our belief that we were important to them and, most of all, that they truly enjoyed being with us. Both Father and Mother credit our faith for the strength of our family, and certainly our beliefs were a major factor in how we grew up. But sometimes I think the emphasis on our faith obscured the fact that Father and Mother are two unique, extraordinary people who would have raised a strong, loving family regardless of what they believed.

Everyone had chores to do, but because I was the youngest (at least for a little while), I didn't have as many responsibilities around the house as my older brothers did. The area we lived in was rural, so we had a cow that my older brothers cared for and milked each day. One day Virl called me over to where he was milking the cow and said, "Donny, open your mouth wide!" I must have been about three, and being typically anxious to please, I did. Virl squirted the warm, raw milk straight from the cow's teat into my mouth.

"Argh!" I screamed, spitting out the rich, grassy-smelling, thick stuff. To this day, I still can't drink whole milk without feeling queasy.

We lived a rural lifestyle of self-sufficiency and thrift. We churned our own butter, for example, and Mother sewed most of our clothes. Cleverly, she made a jacket or a pair of pants in several different sizes, so that they could be handed down and we would all still match. My parents always kept a large garden, and Mother preserved the harvest every fall. Jars of tomatoes, peaches, and anything else she could can lined the shelves and provided food until the following fall. I loved to spend hours working out in the garden, and would invariably make my way over to the cascading, leafy walls of pea plants, all neatly strung up off the ground and bending under the weight of their pods. I couldn't imagine anything better than sitting down on the cool ground under the row and eating a handful of freshly picked peas. To this day, Father plants a garden every year with a few special rows of peas just for me.

Our family lived by very traditional values, but my parents were probably a little ahead of their time in that they regarded each other as equal partners. Still, most of the nurturing came from Mother and most of the discipline from Father. Over time, my father has become more easygoing, more comfortable with showing us all his softer side. In our early years, though, he was a strict but fair disciplinarian. The rules in our home were clear and firm. To talk back or disobey our parents was simply unthought of. Telling someone to shut up, for instance, was considered a very serious offense. And no matter what we children might be arguing about, once my father stepped into the room and snapped his fingers, the argument was over and done.

Father had definite ideas about how things should be, and anyone who stepped out of line got a spanking and a firm lecture. Of course, today we view spanking differently, but in the time and place where we were raised, spanking was very much the norm and considered a means to a better end (no pun intended), an unpleasant but necessary part of good parenting. I truly believe Father spanked us because he loved us enough to be sure that we grew up with the right values and the right attitudes. As a young child, I couldn't understand how Father could hurt me if he loved me so much. He believed that emotional control was essential to success in life. And even when he was angry with us, he never lost his temper and never uttered a mean word to us or to Mother. He was always in control, and demanded the same of us. For me, the worst part of being disciplined was hearing Father say, "Now stop that crying," because I could stop the tears, but there were always those "leftover" sniffles. Eventually, I learned not to let even the first teardrop fall.

After a lecture or a spanking, I would lie on my bed crying and know Mother would come to comfort me. I always remember the touch of her soft hands, and the gentleness of her voice as she said, "Everything is going to be okay." As a child, I thought of Mother as coming to my rescue. In the simplest terms, my parents' division of labor could appear to be a "good cop-bad cop" arrangement, but it went much deeper than that. Although in moments like these, Father and Mother expressed their love for us differently, somewhere deep inside, I knew that it was the same love with the same purpose. Spanking was not Mother's way, but she deferred to Father on this issue. Sometime after I arrived, Mother's more psychologically oriented approach to discipline began to prevail. In some ways, Jimmy, Marie, and I had it a little easier than our six older brothers. Still, there would always be times when I obeyed more out of fear than willingness. And while there were fewer spankings, my parents' standards remained high and nonnegotiable.

We were taught to say "Yes, sir" and "Yes, ma'am," "Please," and "Thank you" to everyone, not just because it was the right thing to do, but as an expression of the respect and kindness we were raised to believe that every person deserves. When you're young, I think, you understand that your parents love you, but as people, they remain something of a mystery until you mature yourself. It wasn't until many years later that I realized that one reason my father insisted on this was because he sincerely cares how he makes other people—including strangers—feel. It seems like such a small thing, but the philosophy behind it shaped how we saw the world. It left no room for rudeness. In these simple teachings, my parents laid a foundation we would all build from—and at times take shelter in. I think this is why it still bugs me when I hear myself or my family described as "goody-goody." In a time when everyone laments the loss of civility and basic kindness, I find it difficult to understand what there is to criticize about practicing the most basic courtesy.

I don't think any child could grow up in our home and not love music. Father and Mother both sang, and Mother had played the saxophone in a dance band. In an interesting parallel, Father, who never had a lot of friends growing up, became something of a star in his social circle by being a great dancer. Mother taught all of us to play the sax. Because my parents couldn't afford more than one private lesson for every child, each of us received private lessons on a different instrument, then came home and taught the others what he had learned. This is how we each came to play several instruments.

As soon as we were old enough to carry a tune, each of us joined the others in singing during a weekly tradition that we called Family Night. Mother instituted Family Night, which was usually held on Friday, because she felt there should be a special time when we all put aside our daily routine and had fun as a family. It's interesting to note that years later, our church would adopt and promote Family Home Evening as a good way of keeping the home life family-centered. Ours was not a home where we kids would be considered "spoiled" in any sense of the word, but for this night, we were treated like special guests. Sometimes our grandparents would join us for the special candlelight meal Mother prepared and served on the "better" dishes. Mother named a salad after each child in our family, and I always hoped we were having my favorite, Virl Salad (lime Jell-O with mandarin orange slices served with cottage cheese), or my favorite vegetable: pan-burnt scalloped potatoes. (I still like almost everything served on the burnt side. In fact, I often order my meat "cremated.")

Family Night was a time of real togetherness. We caught up on what was going on in each of our lives, and talked about family issues and upcoming events. We read from the Scriptures, and sang together. Then there was what Mother called "the floor show," when each of us had a chance to shine. As we grew a little older and more stage savvy, our "productions" got more ambitious. Later in the evening, we each grabbed our corduroy pillows (covered in different-colored fabrics, so we knew which was whose) and piled into the living room, where we got to stay up past our usual bedtime and watch TV. My favorite part was sitting with Father and having him give me a head massage, a cherished gesture of affection that I still look forward to. Of course, we never managed to keep our eyes open as long as we wanted to, and one by one, Father carried the younger ones off and tucked us into the army surplus bunk beds that lined the room all of us boys shared.

Family Night remained an important part of our lives as we grew older, and through the years we held it, no matter where we were, no matter what else we might have been doing. Despite the hectic tours and demanding schedules, this one special night was always set aside. Whether it was in our living room in the 1950s, a TV studio in the 1960s, or a London hotel suite in the 1970s, we made the time to be a family.

One outgrowth of our Family Night floor shows was my brothers' original singing act. For as long as I can remember, my brothers Alan, Wayne, Merrill, and Jay were performing together as the Osmond Brothers Family Quartet. Father and Mother had taught them the rudiments of four-part harmony, and they were quick studies. Not long before I was born, they had started singing in church, and then around the time I arrived, they were becoming an attraction at local events, for civic organizations and the like. The fact that they were so young—ranging in age from three (Jay) to eight (Alan)—made their perfect, close harmonies all the more impressive.

My parents never let an opportunity go to waste. For example, Mother learned that a barbershop quartet from Utah that had just won a national championship was going to be in Ogden. She persuaded Father to take Alan, Wayne, Merrill, and Jay to meet them, and through this meeting, they made the acquaintance of Dr. Val Hicks, a barbershop authority who taught them the art of true barbershop harmony. Without further formal training, my brothers quickly mastered the style. Being brothers, their voices had a natural affinity, but beyond that, they were great, "natural" singers. My brothers were so good that in 1960, a national barbershop organization unofficially proclaimed them the future 1970 champions. They were far too young to qualify for the 1960 competition, but apparently the judges saw enough to project where they might be a decade later, when they could compete (which they never did).

Looking back now at pictures of them, it's easy to see why they made Mother and Father so proud. In their matching outfits—homemade jackets, vests, and bow ties, bowler hats perched jauntily on their crew-cut heads—they were so cute. It's no wonder they melted hearts wherever they performed. As word of their talent spread, the Osmond Brothers Family Quartet was offered as many bookings as they could take. They were also fortunate to be getting paying dates, because those covered the expenses of costumes, travel, food, and lodging.

More important—and one reason my parents were keen on their continuing to perform locally—was that it also provided money that could be set aside for each of my brothers' missions. Although it is not strictly required by our Church, young men and young women who have completed high school are encouraged to dedicate two years of their lives to missionary work by preaching the Word of God. (Older people, whose children are grown, are also encouraged to go on missions.) Church of Jesus Christ of Latter-day Saints children grow up looking forward to when they will be called on their missions. My own son, Don, left on his mission to England just this past year, and I could tell that he went with a mixture of emotions, but mostly with a great sense of purpose. Most missions last two years, during which a young person can be asked to serve virtually anywhere in the world. Families provide all the financial support for the young person on his mission. Contact with friends and family is kept to an absolute minimum. While a young person on a mission may write as many letters home as he wishes, telephone calls are limited to Christmas and Mother's Day. (I'm not sure why Father's Day is not included.) Having seen my two oldest brothers, Virl and Tom, and countless nieces and nephews upon their return from their missions, I can attest to the character-building influence of this bittersweet separation.

Mother stayed behind at home with Virl, Tom, Marie, and me, while Father drove our brothers to their engagements. Initially, these were local dates in and around Salt Lake City, but interest in these little barbershop prodigies soon grew. At that point, we weren't yet a true "show business family," so the rigors of rehearsing, traveling, and performing were endured around Alan, Wayne, Merrill, and Jay's schoolwork and Father's commitments to work and to the Church. However, no one ever complained.

With my brothers often gone, either in school or working, I became closest to Marie, who was born a couple months before I turned two. With her brown hair, button nose, and sweet brown eyes, Marie was a little doll. Being the only girl in the family, and having been born on Father's birthday, she held a special place in our family. I think all of us brothers were always naturally protective of her, but she soon showed how well she could hold her own.

In our earliest years, Marie and I were more like fraternal twins. We always played well together and rarely fought. It was easy for me to fall into the role of an older brother (finally!), and Mother recalls Marie always being happy to follow my lead. (Well, that was nice while it lasted.) But we were essentially peers, and my relationship with Marie has always been different from mine with my brothers. When you consider the age difference between me and Virl, Tom, Alan, and Wayne, and then the fact that the two brothers closest to me in age, Merrill and Jay, were often busy rehearsing and performing, you can see how a little guy could feel left out even in this "crowd." I admired my brothers, but Marie was my best friend.

As in all families, we each had siblings we felt closer to at different times. I always looked up to my older brothers—namely Virl, Tom, and Alan—because I was usually a follower, not a leader. Although I am very close to him today, in our early years, Wayne and I were not best buds. Because of my upbringing, I'm a little reluctant to point out one family member for being better at something than the others, but there's no denying that Wayne is the family intellectual. It's a quality we all grew to respect but for which we teased him mercilessly when we were young. In our ignorance, Marie and I would razz Wayne for using what we called "chemical words," which were really just words we didn't understand. Because he was the most articulate and could express himself so beautifully, Wayne was often called upon to lead the family in prayer, another distinction that didn't pass unnoticed by the rest of us.

Merrill was always the family cutup, a trait that sometimes obscured his more serious, creative side. Like Alan, Merrill knew his own mind and never hesitated to put forth his ideas. Where Wayne was a walking catalogue of corny jokes, Merrill was a more physical comedian, and his hilarious antics—like jutting his front teeth out over his bottom lip to create his Bucky Beaver face—would have us all laughing so hard it hurt.

Jay, the youngest of the performing Osmonds until I joined the group, had a wonderful imagination. Like me, he could entertain himself for hours with games he'd created. Jay was always the most athletic among us, the one who was always playing sports and later working out. Looking back now from a parent's perspective, I see Jay as the "middle" child—too young to hang on a social level with his older three performing brothers, and too often away from the younger ones still at home (Marie, Jimmy, and me) to bond with us either. Being the youngest in the group, Jay had to work a lot harder on his routines, and this became a source of friction sometimes between him and Father.

Of course, I loved my brothers, but by the time I was old enough to be included in their games (except as a guinea pig), they weren't around, and when they were, their free time was consumed by rehearsing. With Marie and me, somehow, it was different. Because we were the only ones at home for a few years (or so it seemed), we created our own little world within a world. The friends I remember best were Scott Bramwell and his sister, Kathy, who would come over and play with us in the sandbox under the kitchen window. My older brothers, who attended school for several years before their show business schedules necessitated home schooling and special private tutors, had their own childhood friends. In contrast, my so-called "normal" school experience would be brief but memorable and didn't add up to more than a few months of my entire life (a few weeks of second grade and of sixth grade, then a semester of college at Brigham Young University in the late 1970s). The only "school" I knew came in the mail or through tutors. The rigors of performing, and later fame, would make the relationships with peers most kids took for granted beyond my reach. That's probably another reason Marie and I bonded the way we did.

In those days, both in Ogden, then in California, where we moved in 1963, Marie and I spent days that seemed to go on forever. She was my buddy and my coconspirator. Something of a tomboy when she was young, Marie was always up for anything. We buried treasure—including, on one occasion, Mother's real jewelry (which it took the whole family to dig up). We experimented with painting the house—and ourselves—with peanut butter. We were good kids by anyone's standards, but that didn't mean that there weren't days when Mother wished we could be just a little bit better. One day, after she'd caught us doing something we shouldn't have done, Marie and I hid under a table. We'd watched enough television to know about a widely advertised, mild over-the-counter tranquilizer called Com-poz. Mother still laughs today when she recalls briskly passing the "hideout" and hearing a little voice from under the table observe, "I think Mother needs Com-poz."

My brothers hadn't been singing together publicly very long when people began asking my parents when they were going to shoot for the big time, go professional. One thing led to another, and in the summer of 1962, Father, Alan, Wayne, Merrill, and Jay traveled to Los Angeles for an appointment to audition for Lawrence Welk, a famous band leader and the host of one of the most popular musical television series, *The Lawrence Welk Show*. Despite his big band being known as "the champagne music makers," his style was so clean-cut and wholesome, you knew the bubbles that drifted across the screen every finale could only be soap. Mr. Welk's large "musical family," as he dubbed his musicians and singers, was a show business anomaly even back then.

One of the longest-running and most popular acts featured on his show was the Lennon Sisters, a singing quartet from Los Angeles who at their television debut in 1955 ranged in age from eight to fifteen. Joining Welk's musical family would have been the break of a lifetime. So Father and my brothers showed up at Mr. Welk's office with high hopes, only to be told he could not see them. They did, however, meet the Lennon Sisters' uncle, Jim Lennon, who helped my brothers get a job singing between fights at a Los Angeles boxing arena. A wholesome group of kid singers was not what most of the arena's patrons had come to see that night, and they certainly let my brothers know it. Despite the catcalls and the boos, my brothers completed their numbers and politely bowed at the end, but it was a difficult moment for everyone, especially Mother.

In various accounts of our family history, this story has been presented as a minor setback, and when you read what comes next, the missed appointment seems like just another of the many lemons from which we Osmonds made lemonade. In real life, things were rarely that simple. Mr. Welk's refusal to see my brothers was much more than a minor setback or a lost chance. While audiences loved my brothers' act, and they'd received enough accolades to make any parent proud, not everyone thought encouraging children to perform was a good idea. When my brothers were still singing locally, there were people—family, friends, and strangers—who criticized Father and Mother's wisdom in this matter. "Why are you doing this?" they would ask. The decision to test the "professional" waters was not one Father and Mother took lightly. And I'm sure that the rejection my brothers received on this trip confirmed their darkest fears. Maybe this turn of fate proved that everyone else was right. Maybe—despite their talent—Alan, Wayne, Merrill, and Jay had no business in show business. Maybe this was, as so many people said, a stupid idea.

With the prospect of returning home disappointed looming ahead, Father decided to not let the trip be an entire waste, so he took them to Disneyland. Still dressed in their matching outfits from the canceled audition, Alan, Wayne, Merrill, and Jay were walking through Disneyland when they caught the attention of the Dapper Dans, a barbershop quartet that serenaded visitors in the Magic Kingdom.

"Are you a quartet?" one of the Dans asked my brothers.

After one of my brothers replied, "Yes, sir," they were asked to sing a song. As I've heard it told, my brothers and the Dapper Dans took turns singing their elaborately arranged barbershop classics—all sweetly old-fashioned, romantic songs from the turn of the century—and before long, this impromptu "battle of the bands" drew its own enthusiastic crowd. Many years later, Mother learned that there was much more to this meeting than mere chance. Dr. Val Hicks, who had worked with my brothers and knew they might be going to Disneyland, alerted the Dapper Dans and told them to be on the lookout for the young quartet.

The Dapper Dans offered to introduce Father and my brothers to Tommy Walker, the gentleman who booked the live acts for Disneyland. My brothers made such an impression that soon Walt Disney himself saw the act and invited them to appear in the "Disneyland After Dark" musical segment of the top-rated *Walt Disney's Wonderful World of Color*. In fact, it was Mr. Disney who, upon seeing Jay accidentally "lose" his fake mustache midsong, encouraged them to keep it in the act. He thought it was hilarious.

I remember all of us crowding around the television in Ogden to see Alan, Wayne, Merrill, and Jay. I was very little then, but there was no question that this was a very, very big deal. And we were all so proud of them. This was the Osmond family's first brush with the big time, but it didn't seem destined to last. They returned to Ogden at summer's end with no further prospects. So Father was quite surprised to receive a phone call from Jay Williams, the father of singer Andy Williams. Jay Williams (whose sons were very popular as the Williams Brothers quartet going back to the early 1940s) had seen my brothers on Walt Disney's program, and was sufficiently impressed to offer them the chance to audition for his son's new hour-long musical variety series, which premiered that September on NBC. Interestingly enough, no one in my family had ever heard of Andy Williams, who over the previous six years had been riding a wave of mellow Top 10 hit singles, including the Number One "Butterfly." Alan later recalled that it was only after they tuned in to Andy's show one Thursday night that anyone in the Osmond household realized how important a break this offer was. With his cool, understated manner and his velvet voice, Andy was the epitome of friendly, Middle-American values. He was hipper than Lawrence Welk, but not as hip as Frank Sinatra or Dean Martin. Dressed in conservatively cut blazers and sweaters, Andy had an easy smile and modest demeanor as smoothly understated as his show's signature theme "Moon River." It was relatively sophisticated entertainment the whole family could enjoy (if you could stay up past ten on a school night).

Once again, Father and Alan, Wayne, Merrill, and Jay left for Los Angeles while Mother and the rest of us "nonperforming Osmonds" stayed at home. My parents devoted many long hours to helping my brothers perfect their singing and their choreography, which in the classic barbershop tradition consisted largely of moving subtly and gesturing in unison. The Osmond Brothers Quartet, as they were now known, was obviously talented and exceptional for amateurs, and they made up in youthful exuberance what they lacked in professional polish. They auditioned on the set of the show twice, and everyone—including Andy, crew, dancers, and singers—watched in amazement. Here were four clean-cut, fresh-faced boys singing a style of music usually associated with barrel-chested men in straw hats, striped shirts, sleeve garters, and handlebar mustaches. Alan, Wayne, Merrill, and Jay were kids who didn't sing like kids, but they looked like kids, and cute ones at that.

My brothers felt they had done well, but they left the audition confused because so many people on the set were smiling and laughing. They were convinced they'd done such a poor job that everyone was laughing at them. When Father got the call shortly after the second audition saying that they had the job, my brothers were jubilant. The Osmond Brothers Quartet was booked to make two appearances on *The Andy Williams Show*, beginning in December. Both appearances were taped at the same time, and we were all back together again just in time for Christmas.

As we opened our traditional Christmas Eve gifts—always new pajamas—and then descended the staircase Christmas morning in stair-step order, youngest first, there was no way to know that this would be our last Christmas in Ogden. I'd just turned five, and vaguely recall seeing my brothers' debut on *The Andy Williams Show*, though by now I've seen the tape of it so many times, I sometimes feel like I remember it. Moments like these make me wish I could travel back in time to catch the expression on Mother's face, though I don't need to have seen it to know how she must have felt. It was Thursday night, probably a bit past my bedtime. Everyone gathered around the television was "shushing" one another and jockeying for the best view. Every song, act, or commercial that didn't feature our brothers seemed to drag on forever.

Then, there they were: My brothers sang "Side by Side"—which has become something of an Osmond family theme song—and "Ding Dong Daddy from Dumas," in which Jay especially revealed the precocious charm that made the act such a hit. Singing through his missing front teeth, "I'm just a half-pint roving Romeo, but what I've got they'll never know!" while playfully swerving his hips, Jay instantly became America's favorite Osmond. The audience's wild applause and the avalanche of mail persuaded Andy Williams to make the Osmond Brothers Quartet regulars. When he offered my parents a five-year contract, they accepted, packed up the household, and moved us all to California.

At first, my parents rented an apartment in Canoga Park, and then they found a big, rambling two-story Spanish-style house in Arleta, a San Fernando Valley suburb north of Los Angeles, near Burbank. From a kid's point of view, this was a perfect house, complete with two verandas (the perfect position for dropping water balloons), banana trees to slide down (and fall from), walnut trees with branches strong enough to support massive tree house forts, and a big swimming pool with a diving board. Figs, pomegranates, peaches, pears, apricots, berries, apples, citrus, grapes, and avocados grew on the property, as well as a large vegetable garden Mother canned from every fall. Marie and I set up shop in the backyard, riding our magic towels and blankets we'd spread over the lawn and pretend were fantastic ships sailing in the grass "sea."

Through the years, we always maintained a home in Utah, which I always thought of as a getaway, a haven, a place to relax and recharge. Still, I essentially grew up an L.A. kid. Or as much of an L.A. kid as I could be. My family found a Church of Jesus Christ of Latter-day Saints chapel in Pacoima, which we attended. Although we'd moved to Los Angeles, we never "went Hollywood." Away from the studio or the stage, we all continued to live more or less as we had been back in Utah. From the outside, I guess it would seem like a big change, but we didn't experience it that way. In terms of ethics and values, my parents would continue to hold us all to the same high standards of behavior no matter what we accomplished. And financially, even though my brothers had hit the "big time," our family was nowhere near rich. In fact, between the cost of uprooting and maintaining our family and the additional expenses of rehearsals and lessons for the quartet, we lived basically as we had back in Ogden. While technically, Father never "managed" us the way some other parents run their children's careers, he was always with us, and that precluded his working more than one regular job, as he had in Utah. We still practiced the economics of big family life: the youngest among us wore hand-me-downs; my father continued to cut our hair at home; and while we lived comfortably, we were not—and never would be—extravagant.

From this point, Alan emerged as the leader of the group. My performing brothers, and later the rest of us, followed Alan because in addition to being the eldest of the singing group, he was a natural-born leader. Even at a young age, Alan had the ability to understand instantly what needed to be done and how to do it. Offstage, he snapped his fingers, just like Father. On-stage, he led the group so masterfully that most people watching him wouldn't even notice he was doing it. He had specific gestures and expressions Wayne, Merrill, and Jay (and later I) were always aware of, and at times we all used sign language to communicate when we were onstage. Alan cued and led the group through virtually every move they made and every note they sang. Years later, while watching a tape of my brothers singing "Side by Side" the first time they were on Andy's show, I caught those moments when Jay and Wayne, who stood in front of Alan, checked him in their peripheral vision. There's a fleeting millisecond when you can even see Alan giving Wayne, positioned right in front of him, a subtle nudge.

They—and later the rest of us—learned that whatever Alan did or said, went. This applied even if we thought Alan was making a mistake. Many times Father reminded us, "There's only one boss in the group, and that's Alan. If he's wrong, everybody be wrong with him. If you're going to look like a group, you'd all better do the same thing."

Fortunately for everyone, Alan knew what he was doing, and having a clear chain of command, so to speak, within the family and within the group helped us avoid the fighting and petty jealousies I've seen in other performing families over the years.

Behind the house was a very large garage that Father made into a rehearsal hall. I can still imagine walking inside it and feeling the smooth, brown-speckled linoleum tile and catching my reflection off the mirrored wall. On the opposite side ran a ballet bar, which I hated, and over the windows hung panels devised to further soundproof the garage for the neighbors' sake.

Here my brothers, and later I, would painstakingly work through our routines until we could execute them to perfection. By the time we showed up at the studio to tape, we were so well prepared, we rarely had to do more than one take. It wasn't long before we became known throughout the business as "the one-take Osmonds."

At five, I hadn't yet been bitten by the showbiz bug, but it was definitely buzzing around our house. Alan, Wayne, Merrill, and Jay were a big hit on Andy's show, and soon they had begun to incorporate into their numbers ever more elaborate vocal arrangements and choreography. For the time, my creative energies found their expression in the games Marie and I played. Shortly before Jimmy was born in 1963, Mother gave Marie a Barbie doll. Of course, she couldn't give Marie a new toy without giving me one, too, so she bought me a Ken doll. Yes, a Ken doll! When Mother handed me my doll, the first thing I said was, "What will my brothers think?" Then, as Mother recalls, my imagination took over, and I realized that Barbie and Ken could have lots of great adventures together. So while I would like to say I played only with my tough, macho G.I. Joe, the truth is, I was in charge of Ken. (But I do want to reiterate: I did own a G.I. Joe.) Marie and I scripted and directed all kinds of adventures for our plastic alter egos. Most of the time, they sailed off to foreign lands, where they could be anything—spies, warriors, tourists— whatever we could imagine, they would do.

I guess you could say we lived vicariously through them, because one of our favorite games to play was Barbie and Ken singing and performing in their own show. Scary, isn't it? I would tape records from the family record collection or songs from the radio, build little stages for our plastic, foot-tall "stars," and write their scripts. Marie was in charge of wardrobe (of which Barbie had plenty, since Marie was quite the seamstress even then), hair (hardly an issue for Ken), and choreography.

A couple of years later, Marie and I invented a magical place called the Donarie Hotel. The Donarie is, as you probably guessed, a merging of our names. Not only was it the first time I got top billing over Marie, but it was also the first time I got to be the boss, a position I really enjoyed. Marie was my secretary, and when Jimmy got to be old enough, he became our trusty assistant. (A couple years later, I wired up a fairly sophisticated intercom system I could use to buzz Marie to send for Jimmy to fetch me a sandwich.) We put Jimmy in charge of the Donarie Hotel's restaurant, which turned out to be another example of life imitating play. One of his first successful nonshow-business ventures was a restaurant. But long before that, Jimmy showed the first glimmer of the entrepreneurial instinct he's well known for today. At around the age of seven, he padlocked the refrigerator and charged the rest of us for food.

My parents' record collection perfectly captured popular mainstream tastes: Frank Sinatra, Perry Como, Mitch Miller, Johnny Mathis, the Kingston Trio, Ray Charles, Peter, Paul, and Mary, and Henry Mancini. I loved Mancini's *The Music from Peter Gunn*. (A couple years later I developed an intense affection for Herb Alpert and the Tijuana Brass's *Whipped Cream and Other Delights*, but the object of my interest was the album cover, not the vinyl.)

As I listened to these records, I was doing more than scouting material for the next Barbie and Ken show. (Now that I think about it, shouldn't it have been "The Ken and Barbie Show"?) Though just five, I was really, seriously listening. I'd been

singing, in church, with everyone else on Family Night, probably even with Marie in the backyard, but I was still a mere
Osmond, not one of the Osmond Brothers, as my performing
older siblings were now known. In addition to their spots on
Andy's program, Jay, Merrill, Wayne, and Alan had roles in a
short-lived Western series called *The Travels of Jaimie McPheeters*,
which starred a very young Kurt Russell in the title role. My
brothers played the children of an extremely religious family
who were fellow members of a mid-nineteenth-century westbound wagon train led by none other than Charles Bronson.
Although I never appeared in the series, I visited the set, which
happened to be on the same lot where we're shooting the new
Donny & Marie show. I'd seen enough to know that being a performer was hard work, very hard work, though at the tender age
of five, that didn't deter me. Frankly, I didn't know any better.
Around our house, performing was simply something everyone
did. And I wanted to do it, too.

So how did I get my first "big break"? Well, being an
Osmond didn't exactly hurt, if you know what I mean. We had
several of Andy Williams's records, and I fell in love with his
Number One *Days of Wine and Roses* (I still love the title song,
too, by the way), which included his slightly jazzy version of
"You Are My Sunshine." My parents were impressed enough
with my note-for-note imitation of Andy that they arranged for
me to audition for Andy's father.

How the Osmond Brothers became a quintet was a gradual
process that's a little hazy to me. Looking back, everyone seems
to agree that I had a voice and a desire to be with my brothers.
While I don't recall the audition that got me the "job," my
national television debut on Andy's show seems like only yester-

day. The show aired on December 10, 1963, the day after my sixth birthday, but I still had a few days left of being five when it was taped. The segment began with my four brothers sitting in their usual positions around Andy: Alan to his right, Wayne in front of Alan, Merrill to Andy's left, and little Jay down front.

"You mean you have a brother?" Andy asked Alan.

Alan replied, "Yes, sir."

"Is he here?" Andy asked. The camera then cut to me, impeccably dressed and beaming as I carefully made my way from where I'd sat in the studio audience with Father to the front of the stage. There I climbed the red-carpeted bleacher-style steps on which Andy and my brothers sat. Like my brothers, I was dressed in a black suit, white shirt, and red bow tie with matching handkerchief, my hair combed back smooth and neat. I climbed onto Andy's lap and smiled.

"What's your name?" Andy asked in his kind, avuncular way.

"Donny."

"Donny? You sing?"

"Yes, sir."

"How old are you?"

"Five."

Alan took out his pitch pipe, blew a note, then gave us the cue to start "Yes, Sir, That's My Baby." My brothers were still singing four-part harmony, but since there were now five of us, I sang Jay's or Merrill's part along with them. My scripted interjections—"I don't mean maybe," "She's a real good looker," and a Rudy Vallee-esque "Vo de o do"—drew laughs from the audience.

When the applause died down and Andy stood me back on my feet to rejoin Father, I felt like a different kid. During the number itself, all I was really cognizant of was the red light on the camera that, I'd been told, meant *that* camera was "on." (From the beginning, Jay made a running gag out of looking directly into the camera, something people found precocious and endearing.) I'd watched my brothers on television, so I understood that I would be on television, but I didn't quite grasp what that meant. As far as I could tell, I was singing for the few dozen people whose faces I could make out from the stage. To be truthful, I don't really recall what I was thinking about, beyond remembering my part and smiling. But for some reason, the moment the applause rose, I was taken aback. It sounded too loud to be coming from just the few people I could see down front. But more to the point, I could hear something in their response that struck a chord in me I really can't explain. I knew that I had done something they liked. Looking back, it's the first time the bug bit. It would be the next bite, only a couple weeks later, however, that clinched it.

That Christmas season, my brothers were making live appearances with Andy, as we would all do through the years we worked together. Andy and the Quartet were doing a Christmas show in Chicago, when people began asking, "Hey, where's that cute little Donny kid we saw on TV?" In a matter of days, Andy's assistant and I were boarding a westbound plane for Chicago. From my first-class seat, I stretched to look out the window. Watching the clouds whisk by as we took off, I thought to my newly-turned-six-year-old self, *This is so neat!*

Audiences always love a child singing a grown-up song with a grown-up delivery, and this was no exception. I sang "You Are My Sunshine" while mimicking Andy's suave pose and coolly snapping my fingers. With my vision obscured by the spotlights, it hadn't occurred to me that this audience was any larger than the one in Andy's television studio. As I came to the end, I anticipated a polite shower of applause and took my bow. So I was startled when the beat of silence after my last note was exploded by the dazzling flash from hundreds of cameras and applause so thunderous, I bolted from the stage. Frightened and confused, I stood in the wings, listening as the applause gave way to gales of good-natured laughter.

Then Andy said, "Donny! Donny, come out, take another bow." *Wow, this is for me,* I thought as I ran back out, faced the crowd, and bowed again.

Looking back, this was the moment when it registered that applause signified approval and acceptance. Perhaps when you're older, you have the ability to understand that the audience applauds because they like what you've done or how you've made them feel. As a child, though, all you can think is, *They like me.* After all, everyone who ever encouraged or cheered you on before then was someone you loved, someone who loved you unconditionally. It probably seems like a fine distinction, but one thing that separates many performers who begin as young children, like I did, and those who start later in life is how they interpret the public's approval. To my six-year-old mind, the applause wasn't merely a polite show of appreciation but an unconditional acceptance of Donny, the person. Many, many years would pass before I truly understood that the Donny they loved was the performer. I wasn't old enough to see or appreciate the conditions of that acceptance or the strings attached.

Now, if you're expecting a litany of accusations and resentments to follow, you might be disappointed. That night I started down a road that I've never regretted. In later years, I would question what I was doing, consider how my life could have been different—maybe even better—had I not experienced that first heady rush of applause. Strange as this might sound, and knowing what I know now, that night in Chicago still shines as one of the most exciting and happiest moments in my life. Because that was the moment when I knew exactly what I wanted to be.

chapter 2

I didn't come to show business with big dreams of bright lights and applause. I was too young for that. I never thought of myself as "getting into show business," because, to my way of thinking, all I did was to join my brothers in what was rapidly becoming the family business. Though still far too young to understand all the implications of becoming the fifth Osmond, my six-year-old's take on it was straightforward: I was the little brother who got to be part of the group, who passed the initiation into the best secret club around. Though not one of the big kids, I was counted in among them, and for me, that was good enough.

I could see how diligently Alan, Wayne, Merrill, and Jay worked, and how rewarding it was for them when they got it all right. I saw the early-morning rehearsals and the late nights spent hunched over schoolbooks. I'd witnessed the hours passed striving to perfect their harmonies or master a complicated step so that it appeared as easy as walking. We worked at it until the best in each of us emerged shining, despite aching feet, heavy eyelids, and sore throats.

To some people, this may sound harsh. But nothing mattered as much to us as seeing Mother smile from the wings or hearing Father say, "Good job, boys!" My parents weren't the stereotypical stage father or stage mother, pushing my brothers, and later myself, Marie, and Jimmy, into the spotlight. We all loved performing, and Father and Mother supported us in this as they did many other interests. They were always very sensitive to each child's abilities and ambitions. Just as they had encouraged Virl and Tom in their endeavors (with spectacular results; my two eldest brothers became Eagle Scouts), so they nurtured each of us. They cultivated Alan's natural leadership skills and encouraged his poetry writing (which evolved into songwriting), Wayne's intellectual interests and passion for aviation (he had a pilot's license before he'd earned a driver's license), Merrill's natural gifts as a songwriter and lead singer, and later leader of the group, not to mention his great sense of humor, and Jay's skill as a top drummer and gifted natural athlete. And we all helped one another. Anyone who was having trouble learning a new routine knew they could count on a brother to help. We never let one another down. In the early years, I received a lot more help than I could offer in return.

Virtually everything my siblings and I learned about performing was on-the-job training. My only experience with "outside" lessons came when, at age six or seven, Mother enrolled Marie and me in modern dance and ballet lessons. Beyond the fact that it would give Marie and me something we could do together, I'm not exactly sure why Mother thought this was a good idea. Picture me in a black leotard (on second thought, please don't), and you'll understand why I really didn't want to go. Mother assured me that everything would be all right, and I kept reminding myself of that as I entered the dance studio. I remember meeting the instructor, a nice lady named Evelyn, and being gawked at by about twenty little girls for whom my form-fitting leotard quickly became an object of fascination, whispers, and giggles. Now, I'm not trying to suggest there was anything unusual about me in a black leotard. But the response it provoked was more than I could handle. Every tiny ballerina's glance seemed to say, "What's he doing here?"

At home, before the next lesson, I pleaded with Mother. "Please, Mother, I can't go back there," I said, wincing at the memory. "It's just too embarrassing, in front of all those girls." She persuaded me to give it one more try, and after that last excruciatingly humiliating class, she agreed to let me stop.

I never outgrew my modesty. And more than twenty-five years later, I was no less embarrassed to be dancing onstage as Joseph, clad only in a skimpy white loincloth. But we'll come to that story later. With my black leotard safely consigned to the hand-me-down closet (lurking there for Jimmy, who, wisely, never put it on), I moved on.

I was never what you would call shy, but I never really fit in with my peers. This was true even before I became famous. Where some children in show business might have missed going to a regular school like other kids, I have to say I was actually kind of relieved that I didn't have to. Months before I started singing with my brothers, Mother had enrolled me in the Liggett Street School in Arleta. Based on the results of my aptitude test,

I was skipped through kindergarten and first grade, making me a five-year-old second grader. Because Mother had taught me so well at home, I arrived at school already reading and writing, but even if some of my academic skills were at second-grade level, my social skills left much to be desired. I looked forward to attending school, but once Mother let go of my hand and turned to walk away, I felt so scared.

Amid the typical school days commotion of kids talking and laughing as they rushed through the halls, a sense that I didn't belong crept over me. Everything I heard and saw there was brand new to me, and foreign. Everywhere else in my life, the rules were clearly spelled out. I always knew exactly what was expected of me, precisely how I should behave. But there, behind my assigned desk, surrounded by older boys and girls who seemed so confident, who looked as if they knew they belonged, the classroom felt like a movie I'd walked into in the middle. The first bell rang and the kids rose from their seats to line up at the door. I thought it was a fire alarm, and immediately blurted out, "What's the bell for?"

There was a long silence, then my classmates broke into giggles; a few even pointed at me. I never felt so stupid in my whole life. Another time the teacher caught me looking at someone else's paper. In my defense, all I was doing was trying to figure out something I didn't understand. I honestly didn't know that looking at a neighbor's schoolwork was wrong.

The teacher called me to the front of the class, handed me a piece of chalk, and said, "Now, Donny, write 'I will not cheat' on the blackboard one hundred times."

What? I thought. I was always extremely deferential to

adults, but I was so surprised, I spoke up. "What do I have to do this for?"

She looked at me as if I'd just asked the dumbest question in the world. "You were caught cheating," she replied impatiently. "Now here's the chalk. Get to work."

"But, I didn't know," I protested weakly, as tears filled my eyes. I was devastated. I'd tried to do my best, and I hadn't meant to do anything wrong. Why didn't she believe me? As I stood at the blackboard carefully writing my promise, some of the kids behind me whispered and laughed. All I wanted to do was escape.

As badly as I wanted to belong, there was always an obstacle in my way. A recess game of kickball—which I'd never heard of, let alone played—brought more humiliation and, ironically, my first school friendship. I'll never forget how my heart sank when, after I fumbled a play, one of the kids asked incredulously, "You don't know how to play kickball?" Then he said to his buddies, "Come on, guys, let's go."

Suddenly a boy named Philip took me aside and gave me a crash course in kickball. From then on, I stuck by him, because he was the only kid I met in school who never treated me like an outcast. But that was a rare exception. About six weeks after I enrolled in Liggett Street School, I bade it a not-so-fond farewell. It would be years before I returned to a regular classroom and that would be an equally brief stint in the sixth grade.

Since I'd joined my brothers, my education came under the jurisdiction of the State of California and took the form of private tutors. I was the type of kid who loved learning but not necessarily school. If the subject interested me or if the information was something I could apply—like math to electronics—I couldn't get enough of it. If a subject and I just didn't click, I applied myself as much as I needed to, no more.

Like all child performers, we were assigned a tutor who not only oversaw our educations but also made sure that we spent the required hours each day learning. It was an education, but I wonder how many former child stars would say they got a great education. By public school standards of the time, it was sufficient, but watching my own children grow up, what it lacked is very clear. It's ironic that I would eventually travel the world several times over, yet never took the field trip to the turkey farm or the dairy. Class projects, group activities such as assemblies, playing on or rooting for your school team, picture day—I still wonder what that would have been like. But most of all, I now see how important the social experience of school is for teaching children just how to live in the real world and deal with people. How much of that I missed would become clearer as I got older.

At that time, it was more important to learn to function in an adult world of schedules and commitments. All the education we needed then was found on Stage 4 at NBC Studios, in Burbank. This is where *The Andy Williams Show* rehearsed and taped.

Andy was a consummate professional, and in all the years we worked for him, our relationship was strictly employer-employee. We were taught that all adults were to be respected, and those we worked for deserved special consideration. To me, as a child, Andy was the star, someone I wouldn't dare impose upon or ask for a favor. But that was then; in the years since, Andy has become a family friend.

Through Andy, we got to see firsthand what went into

making a show the best it could be. He was surrounded by some of the top people in the business: orchestra leader and arranger Dave Grusin, choreographer Nick Castle, and regularly featured artists such as comedian Jonathan Winters. *The Andy Williams Show* was very much a product of its time. Debuting in fall 1962, it joined approximately a dozen other musical or musical variety shows hosted by stars, including singer Perry Como, Western stars Roy Rogers and Dale Evans, the legendary Jackie Gleason, and the undisputed kings of musical variety: Ed Sullivan and Lawrence Welk. Although *The Andy Williams Show*'s ratings never placed it among the Top 25 programs, it was three times awarded an Emmy for Outstanding Variety Series.

For most of their first season with Andy Williams, my brothers fit the bill for a straight barbershop quartet: great harmonies with just a touch of basic choreography—a few steps and some synchronized hand gestures. By the time I joined, Andy had begun having other, more adventurous ideas for using the Osmonds on his show. One of the first decisions was to give us a more visually exciting act, and that job went to the great choreographer Nick Castle. Singing had come pretty naturally to me, but when it came to dancing, it seemed like I just didn't have it. Before I joined the group, it was Jay who often needed extra time to learn his steps, simply because he was the youngest. Onstage, I'd always be aware of what Jay was doing and follow him. Rehearsing, I'd always refer to what I called a "mental movie" of Jay doing the steps. He would help me and cue me with a push or a look if I was off somewhere. Like many things in our family, even my role in the group was hand-me-down: I assumed Jay's part as the young lead. Yes, I was the Ding-Dong Daddy from Dumas.

I was up front now, and I felt the pressure. Steps and routines my brothers could copy on first sight eluded me, sometimes for hours, even days at a time. When rehearsals ended,
inevitably, Alan would put his arm around my shoulder and say,
"Don't worry. We'll work on it at home." I'd feel like I couldn't do
another step, but once home, the grueling rehearsals resumed.
My brothers coached me through my moves. When they'd done
all they could do, they would leave me out there alone, staring
at the reflection of myself in the tap shoes Father spray painted
bone, rather than the traditional white. (Always practical, Father
decided bone was better because it didn't show dirt.) I sometimes felt as though I lived in those shoes, and I grew to resent
the sound of the metal taps striking linoleum as I counted out the
bars and critically eyed myself in the mirror. It's a bittersweet
memory for me: Just six years old, and already striving to be
perfect.

Every night after dinner, we put in one more hour of
rehearsal, then Father would bring Mother, Marie, Jimmy, and
whoever else was around into the rehearsal hall and say, "Okay,
now show us what you've learned." I dreaded these "shows,"
because Father would sometimes make us perform with our
backs to the mirrored wall, so we couldn't refer to our reflec-
tions—or the others'. I would be so afraid of messing up that I
instinctively looked down at Jay's feet. To this day, choreogra-
phers have to remind me to look up when I dance.

We also worked with a wonderful vocal arranger and songwriter named George Wyle. It was George who helped us develop our five-part harmonies, which became something of a signature for us. Five-part harmonies are rare, because most people
find it difficult to sing with others without wavering in pitch

from their part. The real trick for each of us was to stay in tune while listening not only to ourselves but to the four other brothers as well. When this worked perfectly, we achieved the blend that became our trademark. It sounds simple, but it's probably one of the most challenging techniques a singer can master. My brothers and I became so adept at finding the perfect balance, our voices could be recorded using just one microphone.

No matter how much practice was needed to master any arrangement or routine, Alan, Wayne, Merrill, Jay, and I arrived on the set prepared. Whether the script called for us to be singing cowboys or vaudevillians, whether we were singing in an elaborate production number or delivering lines in a skit, we were ready. Soon Andy and everyone else on the show grew so accustomed to our getting everything right the first time, they scheduled less time for us. And then, to make it even more "interesting," Andy and the writers started thinking, *What can we give the Osmonds to do that they can't do?* It was a running joke that yielded dozens of new gimmicks: One week it was jumping on Pogo sticks, another it was tap dancing atop seven-foot grand pianos. Oh, and we had about a week to learn to play solos on our respective pianos. Could we all play the banjo? The sax? Absolutely. How about roller-skating next week? No problem. And then the Christmas special: Here's your ice skates, there's the rink. No problem at all. There was only one time that I remember disappointing Andy, and that's when he asked me—a seven-year-old boy—to render a skat-perfect rendition of an Ella Fitzgerald classic. Couldn't quite cut that one, though I certainly tried.

One day I came to work and saw the set builders constructing an elaborate scene that resembled something out of a fairy-tale book. The production number featured a "dream sequence" in a candy factory, so the set included peppermint stick parallel bars and giant lollipops. I remember thinking, *Wow, this is for us!*

We were so well rehearsed for each number that it seemed nothing could go wrong. And even if it did, as far as the audience could tell, it still didn't. The candy factory number was a good example of that. Before we started to shoot it, everyone was well aware that they'd lost so much time setting up the elaborate scenery that we had only a short time left to shoot it. In order to comply with California's strict child labor laws, we were always accompanied by a tutor with the authority to call the whole production to a halt if we spent one minute too many in front of the camera or in rehearsal. (I guess that now I can go ahead and tell this story: There were times when we skirted the regulations here and there. Years later, there was even one occasion when we said good-bye, pretended to go to our cars and be driven away when we really were hiding, waiting for the tutor to leave. Once the coast was clear, Father turned the car around and we returned to the studio to finish shooting for hours beyond what the law allowed.)

So, back to the candy factory. It was time to shoot the sequence, and we could feel the pressure as we launched into the number. In our red-and-pink polka-dot shirts and white overalls, we breezed through the medley. Everything was going great until near the end, when I jumped down from the giant lollipop parallel bars and hit my head. For an instant everything went black, but something told me to keep going. If you could see that segment today, you might catch me pausing for a split second but never stopping. I continued dancing even though the set spun around me. It's a tired, worn, and frayed show business adage, but the show really must go on. In our family it wasn't just an expression but the reality of our working lives.

Working on Andy's show proved a great training ground in every aspect of the business. For every minute we spent performing in front of the camera, there were hours of rehearsing and just waiting as the writers, director, choreographer, conductor, arrangers, musicians, costume, hair, and makeup people, and dozens of others attended to the crucial details. I listened closely as great musicians such as Henry Mancini (who also toured with Andy when we did) or Dave Grusin worked through arrangements, or the director consulted with the cameramen about how each shot would be approached. Simply by being there, by observing and asking questions, my brothers and I learned the tricks of every trade. While virtually all of it would be put to use in the coming years, working on a real show just fired my imagination for the long-running series of "productions" I attempted to stage at home.

Fancying myself Utah's answer to Flo Ziegfeld and the family garage my personal Broadway stage, I mounted some quite impressive shows. From Alan, I'd learned enough about electronics to wire up a fairly elaborate lighting system in the ceiling and used the family slide projector as a spotlight. I'd shine slides on Marie's or Jimmy's face for that psychedelic effect. A volleyball coated with Elmer's Glue then dipped in about a pound of glitter became a mirror ball suspended from the beams. I scripted the openings, the introductions, and the closings; I chose the music and wrote the skits. I rummaged through closets in search of wardrobe, and I rounded up the audience, which might consist of only one person.

Standing in the garage, minutes before the curtain, I thought everything was so cool. Then one night I got my first bad review. Halfway through, my whole audience in the person of Grandma Davis—yes, my grandma!—rose and said, somewhat unconvincingly, "Well, I've got to go now." I remember thinking, *Where?*

"You can't go!" I answered. "It's the middle of the show."

"Well, I'm a little busy," she replied. I was crushed. If Grandma Davis returned to her seat, it was clearly out of obligation. Here I was, singing on national television with my brothers, getting all kinds of fan mail, and yet I couldn't even get my own grandma to sit through one of my shows. I learned a valuable lesson: Just because someone loves you doesn't necessarily mean they'll love your act.

When we weren't rehearsing or shooting Andy's show, we often accompanied him on live dates. We worked all over the country in all kinds of places, from major theaters to state fairs. All the preparation aside, the truth is, anything can happen, onstage or off. I will never forget standing onstage at an outdoor show and watching as a moth flew into Andy's mouth while he was singing "Moon River." But what a professional he was! He just spit it out and kept on going. Other things that went awry weren't so funny. My brothers and I were traveling to a date in a small prop airplane when I happened to look out the window and see oil all over the wing. It was coming from an engine, and immediately after one of us told the flight attendant about it, the pilot shut down the engine. We later learned that the cause of the leakage was a broken piston that was literally flying around inside the engine. We were told that if the broken piston had moved just a little bit in the wrong direction, the whole wing would have been torn off the plane. Most of the time, though, traveling was fun. At least in the beginning, it was fun to explore the new hotel room, check out the little soaps, and order from room service. We weren't yet so well known that we couldn't go outside the hotel and have some fun. We were too young to find travel exhausting, and there were enough of us around so that we never got bored.

The exposure we received from appearing on Andy's show opened other doors. Not long after I joined the group, my brothers and I were cast in a television movie as members of the legendary vaudevillian family the Seven Little Foys. Eddie Foy Sr. was a stage star who in his later years toured with his seven questionably talented children. The Seven Little Foys were known as the worst act in the history of vaudeville. Set in the late 1920s, *The Seven Little Foys* is the semiautobiographical account of widower Foy's reluctant decision to give his children a "normal" life. One of those children, now grown, Eddie Foy Jr., played his father, and my brothers and I—joined by two young actresses—filled out the cast. A feature version of the Foys' story starring Bob Hope as Foy had come out in 1955, and James Cagney, who played the great American composer George M. Cohan, reprised the Cohan role in our show.

I loved making that movie. As a performing family, we fit the parts very well, but beyond our being performing siblings, the similarities between the Foys and the Osmonds ended. It would be hard to imagine a household more unlike our own: Eddie Foy drank, school was considered a nuisance, and no one rose early enough for church. The children kept the same hours as their father, and loved it. They were wise and cynical beyond their years; as the Foys, we got to utter wisecracks on the set we'd never dream of saying at home. I played the littlest of the little Foys, Irving. And while none of the children seemed destined for greatness (in real life, Eddie Foy Jr. enjoyed a long-running career in film and on the stage), baby Irving was the least "gifted" of all. Irving missed his cues, fell out of step, walked into the curtain, and wandered aimlessly around the stage, always eliciting laughs. For most kids, this would be easy, but by then I'd been trained to do everything correctly, so that when the director said, "Donny, you're playing it too well," I wasn't sure what to do. Featuring a few Cohan classics—"You're a Grand Old Flag" and "Over There"—the film closes with the family's visit with President Franklin Delano Roosevelt, who proclaims the Foys, "a fine thing for the image of family life."

Working with Andy also opened the doors for us overseas. Around this time, our family embarked on the first of three annual tours of Sweden (I didn't go with my brothers the first time, but in 1966 I joined them). We toured with Lasse Landau, a singer who can best be described as to Sweden what Andy was here in the States. We and a small band traveled in a van with our driver. A trailer hitched to the back carried all of our instruments, our lights, and our sound equipment. We performed up to three shows a day, each in a different city, on outdoor stages in "folk parks." The Swedish audiences were very warm to us, and it was exciting for all of us to visit a new country, learn new customs, and try to speak the language. We could introduce ourselves in Swedish and learned several numbers in Swedish.

Following tradition, the folk park shows always ended with the performers being presented with bouquets of flowers by little girls. We learned to take our final bows, then wait a few seconds for five girls to run onstage and give each of us our bouquets. One time, we bowed, then stood smiling at the audience, waiting for the girls. I doubt that we waited for more than a minute, but it felt like an eternity, and we all nervously glanced toward Alan for a cue. The audience was still clapping, but with every second, it sounded more forced and polite.

"Let's get the heck out of here," Alan whispered. "The applause is dying."

We ran off, our smiling faces turned to the audience as we waved good-bye. Suddenly the five girls rushed onstage, colliding with us and sending hundreds of blossoms flying through the air. We didn't know what hit us! The audience gasped then burst out laughing, as we jumped up and ran off as fast as we could.

In another folk park, we performed on a stage that was adjacent to a corral that held a donkey. We were singing a barbershop classic called "Aura Lee" (the melody of which you may know as "Love Me Tender"), and when we reached the line, "Aura Lee, Aura Lee, with your golden hair," the donkey chimed in as if on cue, "Hee-haw, hee-haw." I guess you could say he became "the sixth Osmond" for the day. We were cracking up and barely got through the song. Even today, none of us can mention "Aura Lee" without all of us laughing.

Those were great times, but at the age of eight, I found the stress of my first long trip away from home overwhelming. Being away from my mother, not having any space on our crowded bus to play with my toys, and having to help set up and break down the equipment for every show was more than I had bargained for. I was tired and homesick. It's not that I didn't know joining the group would mean my days would be consumed by schoolwork, rehearsals, and shows, not to mention chores around the house and other obligations. I did. But it was in Sweden that I realized that for all the teamwork and mutual support we offered one another, in some aspects, we were each in this all alone.

No one had to sit me down and explain to me why our work was important to the family, I knew. At the same time, I also knew what it meant to be eight and have neither the time nor the energy even to play. Looking back, it's clear that I didn't have much of an idea what a normal childhood was, but whatever normalcy remained was dwindling. I couldn't really articulate it then, but something about the pressure seemed unfair to me. I needed a shoulder to cry on, but there wasn't one.

Mother had always encouraged each of us to keep a journal, so I passed the little free time I had writing in mine. It was around that time that I started collecting matchbook covers from every hotel we stayed in. These I carefully stapled between the pages of my journal, then jotted down my thoughts and drew little pictures. My journal, which I've kept throughout my life, was more than a diary, though. It really became like my own little world, the one place, especially later on, where I could say exactly what I felt. On the bus, between shows in Sweden, I'd withdraw into that world.

I was writing my weekly letter to Mother, which we all did whenever we were away. All of my sadness and loneliness flowed onto the page. I did not save that letter, but I'll never forget it. The trouble it caused taught me that the comforts of home most children can depend on would not always be mine. In the letter, I told Mother how much I missed home and playing in my sandbox. In my childish scrawl, I expressed my surprise at how hard I had to work and how tired I was. Why did I write the letter?

Because, in my child's heart, I truly believed that Mother—who was always there to comfort me and who always made everything better—would read it, fly to Sweden, fetch me, and take me home. But that's not what happened.

We were staying at a hotel that either had once been or was built to look like a castle, which we thought was really cool. This particular day, we were all sitting with Father, taking turns reading aloud the letters we'd each written home. Each brother who went before me wrote of the places we'd seen and the people we'd met. They wrote about our hectic schedule and the many shows, but while everyone expressed how much they missed Mother, Virl, Tom, Marie, and Jimmy, no one complained. Except me.

Of course, Father didn't know what I'd written, and in my childish reasoning, he never would. When he turned to me and said, "Okay, Donny, let's hear your letter," I swallowed hard and began, "Dear Mother…" I had it all figured out: I'd read the good parts and skip over those I knew Father and my brothers would not approve of. I got through the letter, but I soon discovered that my little ruse was doomed. Unwisely, perhaps, I'd confided in Jay, who told Father what I'd really written. Considering that I'd lied to Father, I wasn't surprised to get a spanking, followed by a lecture on my duty to hold up my end and not complain. No matter what Father or anyone in authority ever said to me, I had been raised never to contradict or question them. Performing was my job now, my responsibility, to myself and to my family. For many years to come, this subject was closed. Not only was it never discussed among us, I didn't even allow myself to think about how I felt.

It was around this time that people who worked with us—like our manager, our choreographer, and our vocal coach—began encouraging us to step out from *The Andy Williams Show*, expand our repertoire, and update our image. Between 1962 and 1965, my brothers released four albums of barbershop, religious, and contemporary standards on MGM Records, as well as a couple of singles. In 1966, we recorded for Andy's label, Barnaby Records, and worked with Bill Cowsill, the father of another future family group, the Cowsills ("The Rain, the Park, and Other Things" and "Hair," to name just two), but neither of those two sides ("I Got Lovin' on My Mind" backed with a Tongan song called "E-Mollie 'A' ") did much to expand our following. While we were with Barnaby, we also cut a song by an unknown Canadian songwriter named Joni Mitchell, but it was never released. Legend has it that someone got hold of our demo and thought the song would be perfect for another artist. When Judy Collins subsequently recorded her hit version of "Both Sides Now," we uttered a collective "oops." To be honest, our version wasn't that great anyway.

Like most young singers and musicians of the time, we were all impressed by the Beatles and the new wave of rock and soul music. Luckily, our parents weren't the type who considered "our" music loud or stupid. Unless the lyrics were offensive or unintelligible, Father and Mother were very open-minded and encouraged us. The 1960s were an amazing time in pop music, because in an hour's worth of Top 40 programming, you heard the whole spectrum, from the British Invasion to the hard soul of James Brown. Musical worlds merged and collided in an explosion that produced not only great rock and soul music, but some of the best singing anywhere. In addition to anything else that could be said for them, the Beatles, the Temptations and other

Motown groups, the Beach Boys, the Association, the Byrds, and the Hollies were great singers who used complex vocal harmonies.

It might seem a big leap from barbershop to rock and roll, but we had been progressing in a more youthful, hip direction over the past couple years with Andy. When we sang four-part barbershop harmony, I felt like my voice never stood out, since I had to share a part with one of my brothers. The first time I sang five-part harmony, on "When the Red, Red Robin Comes Bob, Bob, Bobbin' Along," I remember thinking, *Wow, that's my own part!*

To his credit, Andy pushed us to move in new directions, so in addition to the barbershop material and the occasional hymn, we were also doing Motown, rock, standards, and show tunes. We listened to the radio constantly, so we knew what was happening, and we were all anxious to be part of it.

After we did a Beatles medley—complete with collarless suits and our hair combed into the requisite mop-top style—the Fender guitar company sent us a free set of guitars. They probably figured the promotion they'd get every time my brothers played them on Andy's show was well worth it. With Jay already playing drums, Alan on lead guitar, Wayne on rhythm, and Merrill on bass, the Osmond Brothers metamorphosed into a rock band. Of course, it didn't happen overnight. Alan, who had studied classical guitar, showed Wayne how to play and taught Merrill what he knew of playing bass. (Earlier, Wayne, who had taken drum lessons, taught Jay to play them. We'd always had drums in the house, because Virl and Tom used them so that they could physically feel the beat in music.) Later, I started playing keyboards onstage, but at first my stage duties were restricted to background vocals and go-go dancing (I did do a mean Pony, if I say so myself).

I first started playing keyboards—and I use the term "playing" loosely—because after everyone else claimed their instruments, that's all that was left. There was always a piano at home, which I played around on, but I never took formal lessons, and I still cannot read music. This was one instance where our "can-do" attitude got a little out of hand. Just because I could stand behind a keyboard and peck out a tune by ear did not make me a keyboard player, yet that's how I was presented and how I was expected to act. In the beginning, say, if we were performing with a band behind us, I sort of faked my way through. That charade ended the day Andy stopped us midsong and said, "Turn up Donny's keyboard. I can't hear him."

I froze behind the keyboard, because I knew once the volume was up, everyone would discover I didn't even know the chords. Somehow I got through the number, but I vowed I'd never be caught short like that again. From then on, whenever I came across a musician or an arranger who seemed knowledgeable, I'd ask them to show me a few chords, and the rest I figured out on my own. Out of necessity, I developed my own approach to the piano, which I never thought of as being so different from so-called standard technique until I began teaching my son Brandon how to play. What I teach him is very different from what he learns through his regular lessons. Now, when he and I write songs together, Brandon teaches me things.

One of our favorite numbers from those early rock-and-roll days was "Hang On Sloopy," a garage-rock classic. Coincidentally, "Sloopy"'s writer and the leader of the McCoys,

Rick Derringer, who'd had a big hit with it, played lead guitar on our next try at the charts, "Flower Music" backed with "I Can't Stop." For these, we'd moved to Uni Records, but again we were disappointed when it failed to crack the Hot 100.

That May, Andy Williams ceased production of his regular weekly show in favor of starring in a handful of specials each year. We would join Andy on many of those specials and continue to back him on recordings. We will always be grateful to Andy for all he did to launch the Osmond Brothers—and me, Marie, and Jimmy. But after five years, it was time for something new. Speaking for all of us, I don't think we could have worked any harder at making this transition into rock and pop. It meant that much to us. It was a little bit of a rude awakening for us, because for five years we'd worked quite comfortably in our niche. We were learning an important lesson, one that I would refer to years later: Television and rock-and-roll music don't always mix.

The 1960s being the heyday of the musical variety series, you could see rock-and-roll and soul artists performing their hits virtually every night of the week. But those were musicians who made guest appearances on television. Outside the box, they were considered credible, legitimate artists. Even then, however, there was something about receiving near-constant television exposure that made it impossible to be viewed by the public as a serious musician. I'll bet the executives of the record companies we first recorded for were surprised to discover that the household name we'd cultivated during our years with Andy didn't immediately confer us a place on the charts. Why this is so, I've never quite been able to figure out. But I think it may have to do with the fact that teenagers preferred their music stars to be somewhat unreachable, with an air of mystery. Perhaps being on television made us too familiar. Or maybe we just hadn't found the right sound.

Even if our career had never taken the turn toward rock, the Osmond Brothers would still have been working steadily. From the mid-1960s, we opened in hotels across the country for established performers, including Shirley Bassey (then hot with "Goldfinger"), Mickey Rooney, Phyllis Diller, Nancy Sinatra, Phil Harris, and Sergio Franchi. One thing I remember about these dates was that no matter how nice our accommodations inside the hotel, we always preferred to sleep in our silver "bullet" Airstream trailer in the parking lot. It had bunks, a kitchen, bathroom facilities; it was home.

Young as we were, we dreamed of returning to these very stages as headliners, and we seemed well on our way. But there were those bumps and setbacks you can never anticipate. For example, we had one disastrous engagement, at the Fairmount Hotel in San Francisco. The cool response we got from the nearly empty room gave new meaning to the Zen riddle about the sound of one hand clapping. We heard, maybe, four hands clapping, if that. For the rest of that run, the people onstage outnumbered the audience. Not a good thing. To make matters worse, I accidentally walked onstage one night with my fly down.

In May 1967, we got our first live review from *Variety*, the show-business trade magazine. From then through the 1970s, we performed at least one, sometimes two, extended engagements in Las Vegas or Lake Tahoe each year. Eventually, we played practically every major hotel on the Strip. During one of these early dates, we opened for comedian Jerry Lewis. There was one number we did together where my brothers and I would try to deliver a serious rendition of "Danny Boy" while Jerry played the part of a zany conductor. He tried so hard to crack us up, but we didn't give in. The audience found the bit hilarious, and it was the beginning of our association with Jerry.

That engagement is memorable for another reason, though. It was the first time Wayne, Merrill, Jay, and I performed without Alan. After one performance, which Alan watched from the wings, he boarded a bus and headed for basic training in the National Guard. Of course, he wasn't the first Osmond to leave home; both Virl and Tom served two-year missions during the mid-1960s, in Edmonton, Canada, and became the first hearing-impaired missionaries in the history of our church. We were all proud of Virl and Tom, and proud of Alan, too. Although the Vietnam War was raging, Alan's being a reservist lowered his chances of going into battle. We knew he'd return to us in about six months, when his training was complete. Still, it was an emotional time for everyone, because we would miss our brother Alan. On another level, I worried that his absence would spell the end of the Osmonds.

Because Wayne was now the oldest performing member, the responsibility for the group fell to him. Wayne was always extraordinarily intelligent; there was nothing he couldn't learn once he put his mind to it. He had the tenacity and the discipline for the job, but, I'm a little embarrassed to admit, Merrill, Jay, and I didn't give Wayne the same respect we gave Alan. In the "natural order" of the group, Alan and Merrill emerged as the strongest personalities, the leaders. Wayne, Jay, and I mostly followed them. Why? Who can explain the dynamics of a large family? Suffice it to say, we were all different, with our unique strengths and personalities.

In hindsight, I can see that Wayne was a good leader, but we didn't always make it easy. More than once during the six months Alan was gone, Merrill, Jay, and I gave Wayne a hard enough time that he had to tell Father, "They're not listening to me."

With Alan in charge, Father rarely had to step in, but with Wayne he intervened more often. Despite Father telling us all, "Wayne may not always be right, but he's still the leader," our attitudes did not improve enough. I think Father meant well, but this was not exactly the vote of confidence Wayne probably needed. Being the group leader was never an easy job, because that's where the buck stopped. No matter who made the mistake onstage, the leader too was held accountable. I once heard Wayne say, "I didn't ask for this. I didn't want this position."

It was only natural that Merrill tried to assume some of the leadership responsibility. Of the five of us, Alan and Merrill probably had the most in common. They shared a passion for songwriting and for creating the eye-catching effects and stunts that set our shows apart. Within the next couple of years, when he emerged as the lead singer on most of our records, people outside the group often assumed Merrill was the leader and treated him accordingly. But even prior to that, he had no problem with sticking out his neck, taking a chance, trying a new idea. He was simply more comfortable taking charge, and over time, he did.

In the fall of 1967, after returning from our third tour of Sweden, my brothers and I joined Jerry Lewis on his hour-long

Tuesday-night series. *The Jerry Lewis Show* was aimed at a younger audience than Andy's show, and Jerry reprised all the crazy characters he'd developed in films and his comedy act. In fact, it was on Jerry's show that we first performed our "Motown Special" medley—"My World Is Empty Without You," "I'm Gonna Make You Love Me," and "I Can't Get Next to You"—which became a cut on our first pop album.

In addition to singing on the show, my brothers and I were often enlisted to play roles in the skits. My favorite was playing Ralph Rotten Jr. to Jerry's malicious, coldhearted, social outcast Ralph Rotten, a new character Jerry developed for the show. Everyone hated Ralph except his son, whose devotion to his universally reviled father called for him to imitate his arch accent, hunched back, dragging foot, and ragged Victorian attire. I was just nine years old then, and my "training" for the part consisted of Jerry saying, "Okay, Donny, now follow me" and me mimicking his every gesture.

I cannot recall a rehearsal when we didn't have the whole cast laughing. If Jerry took off his coat and hung it on a hook, I took off my coat. If I couldn't find a hook, Jerry would shout in his high, manic voice, "Hey, you! You didn't follow me!" and chase me. Another recurring bit involved Jerry grabbing my neck and shaking me while I played along by jerking my head wildly as if it were about to fly off. Jerry thought that was really funny, so whenever I'd come onstage, before the tape rolled, he'd start "shaking" me senseless, or so it appeared, sending the entire crew into hysterical laughter. For some reason, Jerry also liked to bite my nose.

As we had with Andy, my brothers and I kept a professional distance from Jerry; he was our boss, after all, and we would never presume otherwise. That said, however, I've always felt that Jerry took me under his wing because I reminded him of one of his own sons. I laughed through many of my lines, and almost lost it altogether in scenes like one where Ralph holds his "little" boy in his lap like a baby. Jerry, like comic legends Milton Berle and Bob Hope, had the rare ability not only to make an audience laugh but to laugh along with them. Watching Jerry, you knew that he knew that you knew it was ridiculous. But that made the wilder bits—like Ralph Jr. spitefully tying a nosy social worker to a giant Roman candle and blasting her off into space—even funnier.

While working on Jerry's show, we were still performing in Las Vegas and recording—on our own and with Andy Williams. As a kid my burning desire was to be the first singer on the moon. I imagined myself soaring through the heavens in a spaceship and landing on the moon, where I'd sing for everybody there, whoever or whatever they might be. I hadn't ironed out all the fine details of my scheme, but I believed in it nonetheless. (Give me a break; I was just a kid.) Oddly enough, I got to fulfill at least part of that dream, even if not in person and not entirely on my own. A medley of songs, including "Aquarius" from the rock musical *Hair*, that we recorded with Andy was included on an audio tape that Apollo 11 astronaut Neil Armstrong left on the lunar surface after his historic moon walk, on July 20, 1969. Okay, I wasn't the first or only singer to make it to the moon, but at least I got there.

Jerry's show lasted for two years, and by the time it ended, in spring 1969, the Osmonds were more determined than ever to give our music career precedence. That summer we played Caesars Palace, in Las Vegas, for the first time. Through 1973, we would play Caesars once, often twice a year. In fact, it was at Caesars that I celebrated my twelfth birthday, in 1969, and there that six-year-old Jimmy made his Vegas debut, with a rousing version of "I Got a Woman." Jimmy had made his national singing debut with us on Andy's show at age three with Bobby Vinton's hit "Red Roses for a Blue Lady." Blond and cherubic, Jimmy was adorable. Many people don't know this, but Jimmy was the first Osmond to score a hit record. In 1970, our whole family toured Japan, where we not only performed concerts but got a chance to star in a commercial for the country's leading soft drink, Calpis. Although we were all in the commercial, Jimmy had the punch line—"Cal-u-pee-su-da"—and the Japanese people fell in love with him. The soft-drink commercial ran for several years, during which Jimmy Boy, as he was affectionately known there, laid the foundation for a long-running and highly successful career. In 1970, the Osmonds released two singles in Japan ("Young Love Swing" backed with "Sha La La" and "Chance" backed with the traditional "Greensleeves"), but Jimmy's two ("My Little Darling" backed with "Peg o' My Heart" and "I Found a Little Happiness" backed with "Jimmy's The Happy Robbers") were the bigger hits. With Mother, Jimmy, and Marie now traveling with us, I didn't feel as homesick. Wherever we were, we'd stake a claim somewhere in our hotel suite and play our games. Lots of chains have hotels all over the world, but I think the Donarie was the first hotel to actually tour the world.

Las Vegas has changed a lot in the past decade, but back in the 1960s and 1970s, it was probably the last American city you would associate with the term "traditional family values." The Strip's neon blazed all night, and the drinking and gambling never stopped. I know that Las Vegas had a reputation as Sin

City, U.S.A., yet my siblings and I moved through that world without being touched by it. Sure, there were some very interesting moments. None of us had really seen anyone drink alcohol before, and the sight of inebriated adults slurring their words and walking unsteadily was something new. I was too young to understand what gambling was about, though my parents taught me that it went against our teachings. On those occasions when we passed by or walked through the smoked-filled casinos, the tension around the gaming tables was palpable.

I will never forget the time we were playing the Sahara Hotel. Shirley Bassey headlined, and we opened for her, preceded by a burlesque revue. I was sitting backstage, in front of a mirror, when a very scantily dressed showgirl from the revue stopped beside me and began adjusting the bottom half of her skimpy costume in a way that practically made it a show in itself. Only nine or ten years old, I was embarrassed and thinking, *What are you doing, lady?* I was so stunned at the sight of a nearly naked woman, I couldn't move. What surprised me most was not what I saw but the showgirl's nonchalant attitude. I'd never seen anything like that before. In fact, I don't think I even knew there *was* anything like that. It was eye-opening, to say the least.

Although we were exposed to people whose values and lifestyles were unlike our own, we also knew that it wasn't our place to judge their choices. Our religion teaches that we are all born with agency, the ability to choose for ourselves which principles we will live by and how we will act. On the issue of people who don't share our beliefs, the answer is simple: Live and let live. Las Vegas has a sizable population of Church of Jesus Christ of Latter-day Saints members, so our beliefs were not foreign to the people who ran the hotels, and they were respected. Then, as in later years, it was obvious that people who knew us and understood our values protected us as well. If, for example, we met another star in his dressing room, you can bet all the drinks and the drugs were cleared out before we arrived. Contrary to what you might expect, no one offered to give us drugs or procure girls for us. Even though we knew that other performers may not have agreed with—or even laughed at—our beliefs, they respected us enough to abide by them in our presence, a courtesy I always appreciated.

That August, MGM released "Movin' Along," the first rock song written by Alan that the Osmonds recorded. Once again our hopes rose, and once again they fell. We had left the barbershop act behind, but without a hit record or regular television exposure, it would be difficult to establish ourselves as a rock band. I guess because of how our career had evolved since that fateful day at Disneyland, we continued believing that if we just worked hard enough, our chance would come. But after we left Andy's show in 1967, the opportunities that did come our way didn't always yield the desired result. Don't get me wrong: We were grateful to be playing Las Vegas and the big hotels, but the adults we performed for—while appreciative—were not the audience we needed to court to break a hit. Because of where we were professionally, we couldn't go back and start from scratch the way most unknown bands would, since we weren't just a band but an entire family on the road. Economically speaking alone, it was unfeasible to play Vegas showrooms one minute, then open shows for established rock acts the next. The only way for us was to get that hit. The question was, how?

We were in Las Vegas, at the Circus Maximus Restaurant in Caesars Palace, opening for Nancy Sinatra on a bill that included Mac Davis and Darlene Love, who was part of the Blossoms. Without our own hits, our act included a little bit of barbershop and a heavy dose of contemporary hits and Motown songs that showcased the five-part harmonies. Only a few months before, we'd all fallen in love with a song by the British group the Hollies, "He Ain't Heavy, He's My Brother." Musically and lyrically, it was a perfect fit, and it soon became a permanent addition to our set list.

Despite our lack of recording success with MGM, its young president, Mike Curb, had taken a personal interest in us. He believed that all we needed were the right song and the right sound, and I will always be grateful to Mike for making us his personal cause. A singer and songwriter himself, Mike came to music with a deeper understanding than perhaps some other label executives, and he knew everyone there was to know, including an independent songwriter, producer, and studio owner from tiny Muscle Shoals, Alabama, named Rick Hall.

Rick had put his FAME Recording Studio on the map with a dazzling series of R&B hits that included Aretha Franklin's "I Never Loved a Man (the Way I Love You)," Wilson Pickett's "Mustang Sally" and "Land of 1000 Dances," Percy Sledge's "When a Man Loves a Woman," and dozens more by such soul stars as Clarence Carter, James and Bobby Purify, and Joe Tex. During the late 1960s and 1970s, artists ranging from the Allman Brothers to Mac Davis, Paul Anka to Little Richard, traveled to FAME to work with Rick and his amazingly talented studio musicians.

Mike believed the Osmonds' future waited in Muscle Shoals. Now all he had to do was convince Rick Hall. One day in 1970, Mike met up with Rick in Los Angeles and invited him to Las Vegas to see an act and consider producing it. When Rick asked Mike who the act was, he replied, "I'm not going to tell you now, because if I tell you, you'll probably say no."

That piqued Rick's curiosity, so he flew with Mike to Las Vegas and caught our show that night. Like most people, Rick remembered us from Andy's show, serenading America with "Ragtime Cowboy Joe" and "When the Red, Red Robin Comes Bob, Bob, Bobbin' Along." He later admitted being surprised and impressed to see us now, in our white hip-hugging one-piece Bill Belew jumpsuits (which bore an unmistakable resemblance to those worn by his most famous client, Elvis Presley) and grown-up (i.e., a little bit sexy), soulful choreography. But what really pushed Rick into our corner was hearing us sing "He Ain't Heavy." As he recalled nearly thirty years later, "It was like hearing a five-headed man harmonizing with himself." He told Mike he'd see us all in Muscle Shoals. Real soon!

That fall we all traveled to Muscle Shoals, Alabama, a small, unassuming town of about five thousand. While we were there, we lived in a trailer home, which was nothing new for us, since we continued to travel in our silver Airstream trailer. The fact that our "home" was parked smack dab in the middle of a cow field, now that was different. FAME (which stands for Florence Alabama Music Enterprises) Studio, on Avalon Avenue, wasn't anything fancy, either. With its walnut, recreation-room wood paneling, and location somewhere close to the middle of nowhere, it appeared surprisingly modest in view of the great music that came out of it.

But it wasn't the place that made the magic you heard on those great records, it was the people—Rick and the stellar songwriters and musicians who created a signature sound that whipped guitar-driven rock into a thick R&B base. I was just twelve when we went to Muscle Shoals, and the first thing that impressed me was how different this recording session was. Rick Hall is simply a genius at bringing together the right songs, the right musicians, the sounds. His easygoing, Southern manner put us all at ease immediately. Anticipating our arrival, he had called on his writers for material, and I watched as my older brothers sifted through demo tapes of potential songs. They knew what they were looking for: a hit.

In the years since we first broke onto the charts, much has been made of the comparisons between the Osmonds and the Jackson 5. I'd be lying if I said that the Jacksons' three consecutive Number Ones in 1970—"I Want You Back," "ABC," and "The Love You Save"—went unnoticed by any of us. We loved those records and were Jackson 5 fans from the start. Granted, our early hits did have a Motown-style R&B base, but we were not "imitating" the Jackson 5—or any other group, for that matter—as much as we were simply trying to sound current. The influence of Motown's chart-dominating style can be seen all over popular music of the time, and if we were "guilty" of being white boys who sang "black," we were certainly not alone. All over the dial and up and down the charts, white singers everywhere were bringing a stronger soul influence into their work. Through all the years that my brothers and I have been slammed for "appropriating" a black sound (and the fact is, there's virtually no style of American popular music that does not harken back to African-American music traditions in some way, including barbershop and country), I noticed the same critics never attacked other artists—and I could name hundreds of great white singers—for singing "black." Maybe the similarities—five brothers with the youngest pushed out front, the cute lyrics, and bouncy melodies—made it easy for cynics to pigeonhole us as "Jackson imitators." That was never our intention.

My brothers and I came to Muscle Shoals with the idea that we would be recording as five lead vocalists. We'd never thought in terms of any one of us being a front man. In our live act, we took turns with the leads, depending on the song. Merrill's voice was especially well-suited to the contemporary material we covered, so Jay no longer dominated the lead position as he had in our barbershop days. However, this was not a reflection on Jay's talent. In the coming years, he did an amazing job singing lead on our biggest international hit, "Crazy Horses," as well as "My Drum," from *Phase-III*, and "One Way Ticket to Anywhere," from *The Plan*.

We arrived in Alabama uncertain what role any one of us would play. Rick immediately made it clear that we could have one, possibly two voices out front, but that was all. Each of us took a swing at a song called "One Bad Apple," but Rick—who'd spent years behind the board producing Aretha Franklin and Wilson Pickett—was something less than impressed. We were too stiff, too tentative, and—I admit it—too white. The years of striving to remain "the one-take Osmonds" had taken a toll on our sense of spontaneity and trust in our own instincts. Standing on a soda crate so I could reach the mike, I listened as Rick exhorted me to "give it more feeling" and "sing it from your gut." For a second, I flashed back to those times when a vocal coach or choreographer could stop me dead in my tracks simply by saying, "Donny, let loose."

"Come on, Donny, sing it the way you really feel it," my vocal coach exhorted one day.

I froze. "Okay, tell me what to do," I answered.

Up until this point, the goal of singing together was to achieve a perfect blend, with no one really standing out beyond singing a particular part or a lead. The style Rick pushed us toward was totally opposite, because it required that each voice stand out in the mix. I think I can speak for all of my brothers when I say that letting go and really singing from our souls was something we all wanted to do. We just needed someone who could peel back the layers, and that person was Rick.

So we each sang "One Bad Apple" over and over and over and over. Finally Rick chose Merrill to take the lead with plans for me to take a few select lines on the chorus. Rather than sing it all together live, as we would do onstage, Rick recorded Merrill singing the song all the way through and then me singing it all the way through, too. Then he cut our parts in. At the time FAME was an eight-track studio, so mixing called for a technique called "bouncing," where several tracks are "condensed" onto one of the eight so that everything fits. A couple of times in bouncing, a good performance got erased or lost and we'd have to rerecord it. Another time, Rick was working with the irreplaceable product of our efforts—the master tape—of one of our early hits. In those days, you had to literally, physically cut pieces of tape and splice them back together. Rick was in the process of editing when a crucial piece fell into the garbage can. Before Rick realized the piece was missing, we'd all tossed what was left of lunch—greasy, fast-food sandwiches smothered in a mysterious, gooey special sauce—on top of it. When we realized what had happened, we panicked. We covered the studio floor with trash, and crawled on our hands and knees, picking through the goop before the precious tape was found. Through the whole episode, Rick never lost his cool. Nothing ever seemed to fluster him. He calmly wiped the tape clean, finished the edit, and that became our master.

Productive as it was, our time in Muscle Shoals was not without a few tense moments. Mike and Rick were determined to get a hit on us, and to that end, Rick called on some of his top writers who usually wrote songs with more adult themes. I don't know how much Rick and the people at FAME knew about us or our religious convictions, and in their defense, it's a pretty good guess we were probably the first performers to record there who didn't even drink caffeine. Father and Mother both reviewed the lyrics to every song we considered, and they were direct but kind in expressing their objections to anything that they considered too suggestive. Despite the fact that the biggest hits of the time included the Doors' "Touch Me," the Rolling Stones' "Honky Tonk Women," and Led Zeppelin's "Whole Lotta Love," it never occurred to my family that we would have to compromise our values to succeed. My parents believed there could be rock and roll without the sex and the drugs. Mike Curb, a rare political conservative among record company executives of the time, believed so, too. And so when Rick presented us with song lyrics that crossed the line, my parents stated their case.

Years later, Rick remembered explaining to my parents that his songwriters might be offended if asked to make the changes they suggested, and pointing out to them that changing a typical R&B-style lyric like "I want to get it on with you" to "I want to get to know you better" took all the "guts" out of the song. They stood their ground.

My mother recalled that once in the studio, Mike Curb said of a song, "You know, this song is definitely going to be a hit.

There might be something in the lyrics you don't like, but it will be all right. It isn't that bad."

To be fair, my parents listened to a demo tape, then asked Mike, "Could we talk to the writer?" Although Mike was worried that the writer would take the song back, he relented.

This story has been in my family so many years, I don't think anyone recalls if it was Father or Mother who said this to the writer, but it could have come from either of them: "Look, we want to have clean lyrics in our songs. And this one has a few suggestive things in it, so we wonder if they can be changed. We know it will be a hit song, but if it can't be changed, then we'll just have to turn it down."

Sometimes the writer could accommodate us and fix the lyrics so that we could record them (as with "Love Me for a Reason"); other times, they could not or would not, and that was that. One time, a writer listened to my parents, and with tears welling up in his eyes, said, "You know, if my father were alive and he heard these lyrics, he'd probably feel the same way."

Now, this isn't to say that there weren't a few songs in our repertoire you could read something into if you were so inclined. Our follow-up to "One Bad Apple," "Double Lovin'," was never one of Mother's favorites. But as she recently remarked with a laugh, "Some of the lyrics in it bothered me, but you can't always have your way and be a prude." Amazingly, though, we got our way in this area more often than not.

We left Muscle Shoals feeling that we were definitely in good hands and returned to Arleta. I was certain the first single would be a song called "Flirtin'." I liked "One Bad Apple" but wasn't crazy about it; in fact, it would be about twenty years before that song finally grew on me. In December we taped our first television special, a half-hour show called "He Ain't Heavy, He's My Brother."

On January 2, "One Bad Apple" became our first single to appear on the *Billboard* Hot 100—at number seventy-eight. Six weeks later, on a Sunday, my brothers and I were getting ready for church, all worrying that we wouldn't get home in time to hear Casey Kasem's weekly countdown show. We were big fans of Casey's and kept up with the countdown every week, but this week was different. After five weeks of climbing steadily up the chart, "One Bad Apple" had risen to number three.

Where would it be this week? we all nervously wondered.

We got home from church, burst through the door, and ran to the radio. We'd missed most of the countdown and tuned in just in time to hear Casey announce the number-three record: Lynn Anderson's "Rose Garden."

I'll never forget the looks on my brothers' faces as we each silently figured the odds. If "Rose Garden" was at number three, then where was "One Bad Apple"? Maybe, we all feared, it had begun its inevitable drop back down the chart and we'd missed it. Disappointment descended over the living room as Casey announced, "And now the second most-popular record in the country today: 'Knock Three Times,' by Tony Orlando and Dawn."

I remember staring down at the ugly gold shag carpeting, afraid to meet my brothers' eyes as "Knock Three Times" droned on. When it seemed like the song would never end, Casey came back on to announce, "Right after this, we'll play the Number One record in the United States!"

We looked at one another anxiously as we endured what felt like an eternity of commercials. And then the big moment.

"This is Casey Kasem—" We held our breaths.

"And the Number One record: the Osmonds and 'One Bad Apple'!"

With the first "Yeah...," the five of us jumped up and screamed so loudly, I can't believe the neighbors didn't call the police. Wayne was so overwhelmed, he just kept running up and down the stairs and screaming, and Mother, Father, and everyone else in the house were screaming, too. If anyone had looked in our window, they'd have thought we were all crazy, and for a few minutes I guess you could say we were. We'd finally done it, and it would be many years before we doubted out dreams again.

chapter3

And that's where the roller coaster ride began. In less than a year, the Osmonds went from a singing group with a trail of failed singles behind it to rock stars who were, in the words of *Billboard*, "a U.S. phenomenon akin to the Statue of Liberty." Now, none of us would ever agree with *that* assessment, but it was typical of some of the hype we five clean-living but hard-rocking boys from Ogden, Utah, inspired.

So much happened so quickly, there sometimes seemed barely enough time to live through it once, let alone stop and think. By the time next Christmas rolled around, the Osmonds had sold more than eleven million records and were packing stadiums around the country. This was a moment we'd all been working toward for so long, sometimes it was hard to believe it was actually here. Not that we had hours to sit and ponder it all.

The same week "One Bad Apple" dropped to number four after five weeks at Number One, CBS broadcast our first television special, a half-hour musical variety show that featured George Burns and other stars. Our debut album, *Osmonds*, was in the Top 15, and our calendar was quickly filling up with concert dates, recording sessions, rehearsals, and appearances.

Father, Mother, Virl, Tom, Marie, and Jimmy all truly shared in our success, because each had contributed to making it happen. Beyond the money and the gold records, our success had a far deeper meaning for all of us. It was especially sweet for my older brothers, because they, particularly Alan, had a vision for our group, an idea of where it could go and what we could achieve. Not to dwell on the negative, but by 1971 we'd all heard enough about the "big mistake" we supposedly made by leaving Andy Williams, by going rock and roll, by taking risks. If I didn't say that vindication was sweet, I'd be lying.

Of course, back in the 1970s, that was a side of our story we didn't dwell on. That explains why we were often unfairly described as an overnight sensation. I don't think the public ever understood how many years of hard work, sacrifice, and even failure we'd endured to reach this moment. And pursuing that rock-and-roll dream did entail taking a risk. We probably could have gone on forever as a contemporary middle-of-the-road showroom act and made a great living touring Vegas lounges (in contrast to the so-called big rooms where we would later headline) and the upscale hotel showrooms. Television appearances and outdoor festival and state fair dates were always coming along. And, as we'd seen from Jimmy's phenomenal success in Japan, the world was full of overseas markets where we conceiv-

ably might have found acceptance as a bona fide rock band more
easily than here at home. If we'd wanted to play it safe, we could
have started treading water in 1970 and kept doing that forever.

Appealing as that prospect might have been, my brothers
and I wanted desperately to write and to sing about things that
mattered to us for an audience of our peers. We wanted to perform material inspired by the artists we listened to and loved,
and between my brothers and me that list encompassed virtually everything from Led Zeppelin to Stevie Wonder to the
Beatles. "One Bad Apple" gave us the chance to make the
Osmonds a true rock band. It was like a blessing. We were showbiz veterans, relatively old dogs who suddenly found themselves
given a new bag of tricks. And yet we were so young: Alan was
twenty-one, Wayne, nineteen, Merrill, almost eighteen, and Jay
just a few weeks from turning sixteen. Me? I'd just turned
thirteen.

This level of acclaim was new to all of us, but because I'd
joined the group last, the experience would always be somewhat
different for me. Sure, I worked my tail off like everyone else,
but even though they were my brothers, our individual histories
as performers were different. To a great extent, I was spared the
long car trips to shows, the big disappointments my brothers
faced as children before things really took off. Although Father
never ceased being a stern taskmaster, most of my professional
training and coaching—and the criticism you must endure to
progress in your craft—came from people who were paid to correct me, not my parents. Because I was working or on the road
so much, I didn't have the day-to-day responsibility for Marie
and Jimmy that my older brothers had for me and those who

came after them. Although today I feel that much of my childhood was lost, in some ways, I don't believe I had to grow up as
quickly as my brothers did.

I wasn't a kid anymore, but age and experience kept me
from ever being a true peer. Within the Osmonds quintet, I
would always be regarded as the little brother, the one who
could sleep in the Greyhound bus's overhead luggage rack if
space got too tight. I would always defer to the decisions my
older brothers made for us all. I had a mischievous streak and a
temper that sometimes got me into hot water, but at heart, I was,
like Father, someone who cared very much—sometimes maybe
too much—about what other people thought of me.

Where success usually drives artists away from their families, it only brought ours even closer. The Osmonds were more
than a group made up of family members; we were a family
enterprise. Although Father was never technically our manager,
he oversaw everything relating to us. On a practical level, along
with Mother, he made sure that we ate right, rested enough, and
were well taken care of. More than that, they created a sense of
home around us, so that whatever hotel we fell asleep in—even
if I was so exhausted, I didn't know what town we were in—we
were secure. Money didn't change us, and our daily life remained
simple, considering everything. On the road, we usually ate our
meals in our rooms or on our rented Greyhound bus.

Marie also traveled with us and helped Mother with some
of the mundane, unglamourous chores, such as collecting the
box office receipts and checking on unsold tickets. The irre-
pressible Jimmy had a spot in the show singing rock-and-roll
oldies, like "I Got a Woman." Zipped tightly into his form-fitting
jumpsuit, Jimmy came on like a little ball of fire and threatened

to steal the show more than once. Having Marie and Jimmy around to play with created an oasis of childhood that my ever-increasing professional responsibilities threatened to wash away. Virl ran our growing fan club, and Tom provided the printing for all the fan club magazines, concert programs, and other things. In fact, Tom's work with the fan club led to his launching his own printing company, TOPS (Tom Osmond Printing Service).

During these years, before Jimmy traveled regularly with us, Jay and I usually shared a room, and we became very close. Jay still spoke up at times, even to Father, when none of us would have dared. Alan, Wayne, Merrill, and Jay got the respect and the attention of our managers, promoters, and others we worked with. Their advice was solicited, their opinions regarded. Me? I pretty much did whatever I was told, regardless of how I felt. My willingness always to go along with the program became a point of friction between me and some of my brothers at different times. Added to the fact that I was now "the kid" in the act, I'm sure there were moments when Jay's feelings must have been hurt. Once, shortly after I joined the group, Jay complained to Father about all the attention I was getting. Father gave him a spanking. Although Jay was always cool and never said anything to me about how he felt until just recently, looking back I regret unknowingly making him feel pushed aside.

As our repertoire had evolved over the years, lead singing duties were more fairly spread among us. People always seem to be curious about how Jay, for example, may have felt about being pushed out of the spotlight, first by Merrill on our early hits, and then by me. Father, Mother, and each of us always responded to any question about professional sibling rivalry with what almost became a family motto: "We don't care who's out front, as long as it's an Osmond." And that was true, though, looking at it from the perspective of a father, I know there had to be times when feelings were hurt. Yes, we were one for all and all for one, but we were still just kids. Fortunately, Jay and I grew closer through the years and can now look back on those times and laugh.

At the time, I didn't think too much about how things were changing around us. If Rick Hall felt that Merrill's voice had more commercial appeal for the singles, fine. If the people we worked with wanted to push me out front, get some mileage out of my being the youngest, that was fine, too. I didn't mind the extra attention; in fact, I loved it! Back in early 1971, though, things were still relatively tame. I had yet to have my shirt torn off by a mob of fans or feel our limousine rock under a tidal wave of hysterical girls; that comes a little bit later. I learned to love that, too.

Even though we had literally grown up in show business, nothing we'd done before could have fully prepared us for the media onslaught that followed. In the beginning, we were those nice Osmond boys who grew up on television, America's electronic front porch. In our early years, most of what was written about the Osmond Brothers came in the form of a live review or two in *Billboard* or *Variety*, usually of an appearance in Las Vegas. Fortunately, we had always received very positive live reviews, because in the show business world that revolves around stage shows as opposed to record charts, the performance is all that counts. On Andy's and Jerry's television shows, and playing Las Vegas to a predominantly adult audience, being young and fresh-faced worked to our advantage.

"One Bad Apple" brought us the younger audience of kids

that we really wanted. With that came a different media with a different agenda, or at least a different idea of what was acceptable and cool. Perpetually in our corner were the teen magazines like 16 and *Tiger Beat*. Catering to young girls' innocent fantasies, these publications pounced hard and never let us out of their soft, cuddly clutches. Under covers that screamed, "Win a Dream Date with [fill in your "fave," "fab," or "grooviest" teen idol]," was a text-and-pinup universe where we could do no wrong, where five or six shots of me eating an ice-cream cone justified a two-page "feature," and where Alan's, Wayne's, Merrill's, Jay's, and my favorite colors, least favorite foods, favorite TV shows, and most prized possessions were news. Because the teen magazine readers were the same girls who bought our records, it made sense to grant the writers and photographers access to interview and photograph us.

For the most part, it was a very congenial relationship, but every once in a while, the editor of 16, Gloria Stavers, went a little too far, in Mother's opinion. There were several occasions—like the time Gloria used my attending a baby shower as an excuse to write a suggestive headline imploring readers to join me in the shower—when Mother and Gloria went head to head. It didn't take a genius to see that Mother and Gloria were from vastly different worlds with different values. Long after our teen idol days had passed, I learned just how different they really were. At the time we were unaware of the fact that 16 lavishly promoted stars—including the Doors' Jim Morrison—with whom Gloria was on, shall we say, very intimate terms. Despite Gloria's frequently imploring us during photo sessions, in her low, sultry voice, "Sexier, sexier," we stood our ground. And, as you probably guessed, my brothers and I were not in that "select" group of stars whose relationship with her became more than just professional.

In the other corner was the so-called "rock press," a new form of journalism that drew clear, sometimes confusing lines marking the cool from the uncool. To those writers, at least those here in the United States, we were clearly in the second camp. Their view of us seemed to boil down to: too sweet, too straight, too many teeth. These were the critics who referred to us as "Jackson 5 imitators" and judged us by our image rather than our music. To them, our music was a whitewashed, counterfeit soul, a criticism the radio stations and record buyers who made "One Bad Apple" number six on the R&B—a.k.a. soul—chart obviously didn't agree with. Throughout the 1970s, the leading rock magazine, *Rolling Stone*, covered us in feature stories and even put me on the cover in 1976. But in all those years, it deemed only one of our albums—our first—worthy of review. In a May 1971 issue, critic Lester Bangs wrote in his review, "The Osmonds are truly an inspiring island of family solidarity in this fragmented world of fraternal enmity and filial rebellion. Everything they do is the epitome of good taste and clean funk....And they know they don't need to go 'underground' to be 'earthy'." Reading it nearly three decades later, I still couldn't tell you if he liked us or not, though I can't shake the feeling that his compliments were backhanded. (In England, as you'll see, it was an entirely different story.)

Then and at many other points in our career, we had the opportunity to change course, to play down our beliefs, and to pretend we led more of a rock-and-roll lifestyle. But we never did. And, believe me, we were well aware of the criticism, and, to be honest, some of it hurt. Clean-cut, wholesome, well mannered—we were everything the press said we were. Perhaps compared to some other rock stars, we weren't normal, but then I guess that all depends on how you define "normal." When writer Albert Goldman (who years later would take his poison pen to Elvis Presley and John Lennon) reviewed our show for *Life* magazine the following year under the headline, "A Plague of Wholesomeness," we shrugged it off. And maybe we brought a little of it on ourselves. When I read in the liner notes to our first album that I "never [had] a bad thought toward anyone," I could understand some people's cynicism. Still, we learned early on that we never could please everyone, and the price of pleasing certain people was too high for us.

But were the Osmonds really that unusual in the early 1970s? The conventional wisdom tells us that the 1970s were one long sex-and-dope party. And history has reduced the decade's later years to a shorthand synopsis of disco, platform shoes, and hair that looked like it was styled in a wind tunnel. But the decade was about much more than that, and if you look closely, our success isn't so hard to understand. In between the highly politicized, psychedelicized late 1960s and the hedonistic, discofied late 1970s, the pop culture took a breath, and young people began asking some questions. Where a few years earlier, they might have asked, Why shouldn't I have casual sex, do drugs, or drink? Some were now asking, Why should I? The sex and drugs and rock-and-roll lifestyle that so many rock stars then promoted had begun to claim casualties, most notably the drug-related deaths of Jimi Hendrix, Janis Joplin, and Jim Morrison. Music fans, especially the girls who became fans of the Osmonds, David Cassidy, and other "teen idols," wanted something new. They were not alone. The same year the term "silent majority" was coined, the Best New Artist Grammy went to brother-and-sister duo Karen and Richard Carpenter, whose hits included "Close to You."

The 1970s brought profound changes in families. Divorce was hitting an all-time high, and I don't think it's coincidence that young teenagers growing up in such tumultuous times embraced famous families, both make-believe, like the Bradys and the Partridge Family, and real, like the Cowsills, the Jackson 5, and the Osmonds. To some of our fans, our being a family was as important as our music. Even before we hit the charts, we'd received thousands of letters from kids who wrote of their unhappy lives. These heartbreaking letters were like a window into a realm of family life I would never experience and that I could barely imagine. Even at that young age, I felt a very profound sense of obligation never to let those fans down, never to let them think that what they believed about my family and me was not true.

I have a wonderful family, but I admit that in those early days there was some gilding of the lily. Of course, we argued among ourselves, as all siblings do, but we never really talked about that. Of course, we worked extremely hard, but we somehow managed to make it sound so easy. In our defense, I have to say that the image we put forth was essentially true though incomplete. Almost every article focused on my family's success and rarely mentioned the difficult times.

If we were concerned only with how the world regarded us, it might have been simpler. We never forgot that we represented not only ourselves and our family but the Church. Belonging to a church as misunderstood and unjustly maligned as ours, we were particularly mindful about how we were perceived. In fact, it was reported to us that we eventually became the most widely recognized living members of The Church of Jesus Christ of Latter-day Saints in the world. Once we began touring widely, we made a point of attending church wherever possible and giving talks, which we call "firesides." Many people became aware of the Church, in part because of the example our family put forth.

With success came an ever-growing burden of responsibility to say, to do, and to be what was expected. No one told me how to behave or what I should and should not say. No one had to. At a very early age I'd learned to analyze anything I might do or say publicly in terms of what other people—the fans, the media, fellow church members, my family—might think of me. For instance, if out in public, I'd always order a 7-Up or ginger ale—something light-colored or clear—because I worried that someone might assume a dark-colored soft drink was a cola that contained caffeine. I lived with a near-constant low-level anxiety that I might make a mistake that would threaten not only my career, but also my brothers', not to mention the livelihoods of many people who worked with or for us.

So we paid close attention to what was written about us, and performance reviews meant a lot. Early on, Father made a point of getting the papers and going over the reviews with us. Of course, by then, we'd each have heard from Father or the other brothers about mistakes we made, spots in the show that could use improvement. Being the youngest, I sometimes felt that I took more than my share of criticism from my brothers. Maybe any little brother would have felt the same way. It was not my place—either in the group or in my family—to point out their errors, no matter what I thought. And it never would be.

Though we'd worked with countless stars, for the first time we were working with stars our own age. In late April 1971 we met the Jackson 5 for the first time while we were performing at the Canadian National Exhibition, in Toronto. It was our first appearance in Canada, and one of our first large stadium dates. Even before we actually met the Jackson 5, my brothers and I felt an affinity for them, because we had so much in common. We knew and loved their music, and Michael and I were practically the same age. When we got to know them better, we found out that the similarities between their family and ours border on the eerie. Check this out: Both of our families have nine children, Michael and I are both the seventh child in our respective families, and Mother and Mrs. Jackson share the same birthday. Michael has a younger sister and a younger brother, Janet and Randy. I have a younger sister and a younger brother, Marie and Jimmy. We both came from strict homes, and we were both raised in faiths most people consider outside the mainstream (the Jacksons were Jehovah's Witnesses).

The real connection, though, was our mutual understanding and respect. Watching the Jackson 5, I could imagine the hours of rehearsal and hard work that must have gone into sustaining the illusion of ease they brought to the stage. And I admired and respected them all, but especially Michael, in ways few other people could. Even before we met, I knew that Michael and I would have a lot to talk about.

Before we could get to socialize, however, there was the matter of the show. The Exhibition Grandstand was sold out, and the Jackson brothers watched us from the wings as we received one ovation after another. It was one of those magical shows where the harmonies blend perfectly on every note, and each step hits its mark. The crowd was up and screaming our names, clapping, and singing along. Every move we made seemed to send a ripple of electricity through the audience. I remember glancing toward the wings during a number, singing my heart out, catching Michael's eye, and thinking to myself, *If I ever do a great show, it's gotta be now!*

After the show, we went back to the same hotel and hung out together. My first memory of being with Michael is just the two of us, a pair of soft-spoken, well-mannered, thirteen-year-old boys sitting on the floor, in the corner of a hotel room, playing games, and just having a great time. We didn't talk about the shows or the business or how it felt to be famous. We didn't treat each other as competitors but as peers. All of us innately understood, I think, that we were the only people who could really appreciate what the others were going through. For those moments we got to be what we could never be most of the time: kids hanging out with kids who were just like them. Except for the few future occasions when we crossed paths, we never had that kind of rapport with any other performer again. It was during this visit that the Jacksons told us that their father, Joseph Jackson, loved our harmonies, which were different from the gospel- and soul-based vocal arrangements the Jacksons used. Every week, their father would make them watch us on *The Andy Williams Show.*

That June, our second single, "Double Lovin'," peaked at number fourteen. That same month, Mike Curb launched my solo career with "Sweet and Innocent," which hit number seven.

The perky midtempo "Sweet and Innocent," written by Rick Hall and Billy Sherrill, appeared on both the Osmonds' first pop album and my solo debut, the imaginatively titled *The Donny Osmond Album*. (Another track I've always loved, "Flirtin'," was also on both debut albums.) Considering how my solo career took off, this would seem the most carefully planned strategic assault on teenage girls in history, but it was nothing like that at all. No one ever sat me down and said, "Donny, my boy, we're making you a teen idol. Now, here's the plan: You'll record sweet remakes of tender, romantic songs young girls will love. You'll be so cute and lovable that they'll want to tear you to pieces. They'll join fan clubs by the millions, paper their bedrooms with your picture, buy your records by the millions. Every girl in the world under a certain age will dream of marrying you. Also, be sure to remember that every boy your age will hate your guts. Oh, and by the way, no one will ever take you seriously as a musician again. Sign here."

It wasn't like that at all, though if it had been, what a different ending this book would have. Given the industry climate then, with Michael Jackson being touted as the next James Brown and David Cassidy's TV alter ego Keith Partridge cutting a velvet-vested swath through teenybopper hearts everywhere, it didn't take a degree in rocket science to figure this might work. In the years since, I have been made painfully aware that my so-called "teen idol" career is considered by a persistent, vocal minority as a blight on the history of rock and roll, an evil plot, a horrible mistake. One rock magazine proclaimed my birthday one of the darkest days in rock history; another found my parents remiss for neglecting to drown me. You know, some people just take all this way too seriously.

In my defense—which I've had many years to perfect—let me remind you, I was just a thirteen-year-old singer who made some hit records. And let me take this moment to apologize to all the boyfriends whose pictures I replaced on their girlfriends' walls. I'm really, truly sorry. Well, not really.

Back in late 1970, when we recorded *Osmonds* at Muscle Shoals, Mike Curb thought it would be a good idea for me to record "Sweet and Innocent" as a solo track. My parents and my older brothers trusted Mike Curb to make decisions about our recordings, and, judging by our success, our trust was well placed. I was too young to realize that both Mike Curb and my brothers felt that as a unit, the Osmonds were courting two different audiences. One consisted of the younger girls, or "teeny-boppers," as the media dubbed them. The other was an audience of my older brothers' peers—teenagers, boys and girls. At the same time as we were recording songs written by other writers, Alan, Wayne, Merrill, and Jay were honing their skills as writers and producers. My father had purchased a sound board from a radio station, and we had managed to rig up a surprisingly impressive little studio at home. Long before the public heard our songs "Hold Her Tight," "Down by the Lazy River," or what some now regard as a lost heavy-metal classic, "Crazy Horses" (which 1990s recording artist Beck recently described to a *Rolling Stone* reporter as "a great song . . . [where] the music's really rocking and legitimate"), my brothers were thinking about and experimenting with those heavier, harder sounds. Our second album, *Homemade*, contained two songs cowritten by Alan and Merrill ("If You're Gonna Leave Me," "Sho Would Be Nice") and one by Wayne and Merrill ("Carrie"). So when Mike Curb presented us with "Sweet and

Innocent," my brothers told him that they didn't think that it fit the rest of the album.

"You know, what we ought to do is have Donny release his own album," Mike suggested. "Do you have a problem with that?"

"Heavens, no," Alan remembers saying. "Then we'll put ours out, and we can keep our integrity with our peers."

I don't think my brothers planned to jettison me off into a solo teenybopper orbit, but they did realize that two very different commercial impulses were pulling at our group. I don't think anyone screamed for me when we played Las Vegas, but when we started performing larger concerts for the kids who bought our records, something strange happened. Nearly every time I stepped out front or had a solo spot, the girls, who were already going wild, went even wilder. That's not to say they didn't scream for my brothers, because they did. Each of us had our own contingent of fans who thought their guy was the cutest, even seven-year-old Jimmy. But there's screaming, and then there's screaming. This was earsplitting, bone-piercing, wall-cracking *screaming*. It was screaming so loud that Alan and Wayne both lost a degree of hearing on the side that faced the audience. It was screaming so relentless that there were times you couldn't even hear the music. It was chaos—wild, unpredictable, sometimes even a little bit dangerous.

To their credit, Alan, Wayne, Merrill, and Jay recognized and welcomed the "audience within the audience" that paid special attention to me. While it may not have been obvious on our records and in our television appearances, each brother took his solo turn in the spotlight. Among us, there was no one "star." We were confident that even though they were presented together, the public would see the difference between the heavier rock style my brothers and I were leaning toward and the lighter pop I was given to record alone. And I say "given" deliberately, because I chose none of my solo material and in some cases, hadn't even heard of the song, let alone heard anyone's prior version of it, before I sang it. Later, onstage, Alan would introduce my solo spot by saying how I'd "found" these songs—a nice touch though it wasn't true.

At the time I made these records, they were just songs, material I was asked to record. At thirteen and fourteen, I didn't give it too much thought. If only I'd had a crystal ball to see myself singing "Puppy Love" on national television in a dog costume…well, maybe it's better that I didn't.

"Sweet and Innocent" vaulted *The Donny Osmond Album* to number thirteen over that summer, and was quickly followed by a cover of "Go Away Little Girl," a Carole King–Gerry Goffin ballad that had been to Number One for Steve Lawrence in 1963 and number twelve for the Happenings three years after that. Like "Sweet and Innocent," "Go Away Little Girl" addressed the unrequited, forbidden attraction of an older boy for a younger girl and the singer's struggle not to yield to temptation. This was a dilemma I had yet to face in my own life; in fact, I hadn't even kissed a girl. But I must have sounded somewhat convincing, because that September "Go Away Little Girl" was Number One for three weeks. From this point on, my solo singles and the Osmonds' raced up and down the chart like a relay team. As we always said, as long as it's an Osmond . . .

That October, as "Go Away, Little Girl" began to drop down the chart, the Osmonds' third hit single, "Yo-Yo," raced up to number three, and in November my second album, *To You with Love, Donny*, debuted. "Yo-Yo" was a Joe Simon song that I'll never forget recording. We spent what felt like hours recording and rerecording the synthesizer-ish "doo-yoop" background vocals on the bridge between two choruses. I remember thinking—and not for the last time in my career—*Is this how we have to sing to get a hit?* Despite my early reservations, I still think it's a pretty cool record.

Homemade was the last album we recorded at FAME. There's no question that the Osmonds and Rick Hall's studio was a winning combination, but there was a downside, too. Working with a genius "full-service" producer like Rick—with his great musicians and songwriters—left little room for my brothers to develop as writers and producers. They were anxious to test their wings, so on a creative level, the break with FAME, amicable as it was, was probably inevitable. Artists in the music industry speak a lot about "creative control," because the more control you exert over your career in that arena, the greater your control of its business and financial aspects. And the greater your control, the stronger your independence. We found ourselves, again, at a fork in the road where we could either stick with the route we knew or take the detour—and the risk—and have an adventure. Again, we chose to risk it.

By the end of 1971, we had amassed four gold albums (the platinum award did not yet exist), four gold singles, a pair of Number One singles, and the distinction of being among the top-selling artists of the year. However, even after the money began pouring in, we lived relatively frugally. No fancy restaurants, no clothes-buying sprees, or other extravagances. When it comes to food, I'm a guy of really simple tastes, and after a few memorable forays into the world of gourmet eatin', I adopted a restaurant strategy I still fall back on now and then: Club sandwich, please. No matter where you are in the world, a club sandwich is still a club sandwich.

By then, our family had moved from the big Spanish house in Arleta to an apartment building we called the Manning Apartments, on Manning Avenue, just off Santa Monica Boulevard, in the Westwood area. Conveniently located across the street from a Church of Jesus Christ of Latter-day Saints temple, the eight-unit complex made a perfect home away from home, which is how we saw L.A. Father has always been very conservative when it comes to finances, and he'd had enough experience with real estate to view our home unsentimentally, as an investment. So even though the hit records had pushed our income up into the millions, Father decided that we would not live like millionaires.

Rather than invest our money in one luxurious home, Father thought it made more sense to purchase an apartment building that we could renovate to accommodate our family. When we moved, he figured, we would simply repatch the walls and return it to its original condition. We broke down walls to combine three of the apartments into one large home for Father, Mother, and all the unmarried children. When my brothers and I were not working on a new album or performing, we were home, knocking down walls, running electrical wires, hanging sheetrock, painting, plastering—you name it.

The other five apartments were left intact, the thinking being that once Alan, Wayne, Merrill, Jay, and I married, we would each live with our families at Manning. In our family, thinking ahead to our wedding days was not really "long-term" planning. By this point, both Virl and Tom had started their own families, and by late 1974, Alan, Wayne, and Merrill were married too. Despite common show business wisdom, none of their marriages had an adverse impact on our career.

While other stars lived in exclusive communities, behind guarded gates, we Osmonds tried to live just like everyone else. The location of the Manning Apartments did not remain secret for long, and the number of fans waiting outside for us sometimes grew so large that some neighbors came right out and asked us to leave. Sometimes there were up to seventy-five fans just waiting, for hours, out front. One group of about ten fans we called the L.A. Gang had some members who actually slept outside.

The landlord across the street was so vocal in his dislike of the fans that they retaliated by sprinkling soap powder in his bushes. The next time he watered his yard, soap suds billowed out of the ground, carpeting the beds with white bubbles. He was furious, and while I have to say my family and I did not approve of the prank, I can't say we didn't have a few good laughs over it.

Times were different then, and it was nothing for me or anyone else in my family to step outside, sign some autographs, and talk with fans. We later erected an electric gate at the garage, so that we could at least get into our cars without having to stop and visit. But fans can be surprisingly bold, and there were hundreds of times we would carefully pull out of the drive only to have fans surround the car and bang on the windows.

It was only the beginning of our fame—the start of what the press labeled "Osmondmania"—but I began to feel the walls closing in on me. I remember coveting Michael Jackson's home in nearby Encino, with its large, private backyard, manned guardhouse, and imposing front gates that kept the fans at bay. The freedom to step out of my front door and onto my lawn without someone calling my name or approaching me was lost. No matter how famous you are or how much the public loves you, everyone needs that time, that space, in his life to just be. These sound like very small things, but until they've been taken away from you, you have no idea how much they mean. None of us, including Father, Mother, and my siblings who didn't perform, would ever be rude to a fan. At the same time, I began to feel like a prisoner in my own home.

It wasn't long before I avoided going outside and looked forward to our time in Utah, where there was space to get away, physically and emotionally. The family had three homes up north: a ranch, the farm in Huntsville, in the mountains just north of Ogden, and the Riviera Apartments. Father purchased the Riviera, a very large, multibuilding apartment complex in Provo, Utah, near the Brigham Young University campus not long after we moved into Manning. We renovated one of its buildings into a home for our family and part of it served as our business offices.

I loved the Riviera, because that was where I built my famous (at least to teen magazine readers) "007" bedroom. My fascination with electricity had only grown, though now it had been channeled into more constructive pursuits than self-electrocution and fire-starting. When my parents asked me how I wanted my new bedroom to be decorated, I don't think this is exactly what they had in mind, but they let me do it. And it was so cool. I'd always been fascinated by James Bond movies and television shows such as *Mission Impossible* and *The Man from U.N.C.L.E.* Beyond the fact that Bond, Napoleon Solo, and

Mission's electronics genius Barney Collier were cool guys, what really appealed to me was the secret, private control centers where they could hide from the world. And if anyone needed a secret hideaway, it was I.

My room was small, so everything was designed to work in a minimum of space. For example, my workbench was against one wall with my bed above it, so I wired the bed with motors and pulleys, so that at the touch of a button, the bed disappeared into the ceiling and my workbench was clear. I could stop the bed at any point between the floor and the ceiling, so that if I wanted to lie on the bed and it was six feet off the floor, I'd hop in my little "elevator"—which now that I think of it kind of looked like the pole elevator Batman used on TV—and up I'd go. If I wanted to read a book, but my bed was in "midair," another button would elevate an adjacent bookcase. Time to get dressed? You'd push a button, a door in the ceiling opened, and my clothes descended on a closet rod.

I worked closely with a guy named Dave Steed, who was an expert on motors, and learned a lot from him. Still, I did the actual wiring of all the components, which led to one of my most terrifying electrical mishaps. When it comes to any project, I've always had the ability to become so totally absorbed that I forget what time it is and can work myself to exhaustion if I don't watch out.

One day I was wiring the motors for my bedroom. I was up in the attic, too tired to go back down to the basement to switch off the breakers to shut the power off before I started working with a live 220-volt line. I figured I could wire it in "hot," because I'd done it before. That's not to say it was a smart thing to do; it wasn't. As I was crawling in the attic, I slipped and accidentally grabbed a live 220 line and could not let go. Time seemed to slow down as I felt the sixty cycles surge through my body, causing me to jerk violently. As if that wasn't bad enough, I happened to be between two ceiling joists, so the electricity sent my head banging back and forth between them. Believe it or not, getting your brains scrambled between solid wood beams has its upside: The force of my head hitting the joists tore the line from my hand and freed me.

Now, I must have suffered some temporary brain damage, because once I caught my breath, I went ahead and finished wiring it in hot anyway.

Did I give up playing with electricity? Never! My favorite hangout was Central Utah Electronics, in Provo. I could spend hours there, just roaming the aisles, checking out the cool tools, components, and testing equipment. I also loved to assemble Heath kits, with which you could build literally anything electrical. In fact, a year or so later, my parents gave me a Heath kit color television, which I assembled in about six days without ever once getting out of my pajamas. I was a boy obsessed.

Around that time, Ed Greene, our recording engineer at MGM who was as crazy about electronics as I was, gave me a five-inch-thick book of schematics, or plans, for building almost anything you could imagine. I spent days readings books like that, until before long I was designing my own circuits. My brothers would encourage me to go out, perhaps sit in with a local band with Jay, or play sports, but I couldn't stand people watching my every move when I was just living my life. In the whole world my favorite place to be was alone in my bedroom, sitting at my workbench, and listening to the radio as I puzzled through the resistors, capacitors, and the integrated circuits, the lines and the switches to harness the power and just make something happen. There my world was quiet, safe, orderly, and my time was really my own.

Of course, the time spent in Provo never felt long enough. I also loved going up to our farm in Huntsville, where the army bunks my brothers and I had slept in as children were stacked. In the room I shared with several of my brothers, about twenty of Wayne's beautiful model airplanes hung from the ceiling. I was starting to pay attention to girls, and in my bottom bunk, in the springs of the bed above mine, I slid pictures of girls I liked. They weren't my girlfriends or anything like that (I couldn't date until I was sixteen), but they were girls that I actually knew and had spoken to before we became so famous. At a time when I was receiving tens of thousands of girls' pictures in fan mail every week, I found comfort in looking at these. I guess because they were so real to me.

Like all pop stars, our history is largely written on the records, those vinyl artifacts that we mistakenly regard as the definitive record (no pun intended) of who an artist is and what he means. Records are great, of course, but in the big picture of most performers' work, the time spent in a studio is actually very small compared to that consumed by performing live. The bulk of what we did professionally in those years revolved around touring: rehearsing, living on the road, putting together the most exciting show we could imagine.

When music historians write about the Osmonds' records, they usually compare us to the Jackson 5. In terms of our live performances, however, the more apt comparison would be to mainstream artists who presented more elaborate stage productions than most current rock acts did. In Las Vegas, Elvis Presley's show had raised the bar for everyone who followed. It wasn't enough just to perform well. Your show had to be visually exciting while at the same time conveying a level of intimacy that would also carry over in big 10,000- to 20,000-seat arenas. The eye-catching jumpsuits, tightly choreographed steps, and, later, the lasers, karate routines, dancing waters, dry ice fog, and other special visual effects we employed over the years were meant to dazzle—with a vengeance.

Around mid-1971 we made a leap to the larger arenas, coliseums, and auditoriums where the seating capacity might exceed 10,000. Everyone in show business measures you by your numbers—record and ticket sales, chart positions, and so on—but these concerts, and the pandemonium that often surrounded them, were the living and breathing force that drove the machine.

In early December, with my "Hey Girl" just peaking in the Top 10, my brothers and I recorded our first live album at the Forum, in Los Angeles. We had been on the road almost constantly the whole year, and still found the time to record our third album, *Phase-III*, the first without Rick Hall, and lay the groundwork for our own label, Kolob. I say "we," although my older brothers were more deeply involved in the business and creative decisions than I was. For the next several years, "life" meant life on the road. For most artists, the bulk of income comes from touring, and through the mid-1970s, live shows and record sales went hand in hand. Today, you can tour for months without seeing an uptick in record sales; conversely, you can sell a million records without ever setting foot on a stage to perform live. Back in the early 1970s, however, it was a totally different scene, and record companies looked to their artists' touring to drive record sales. This is why virtually every major act had to release a live album at some point in their career, and the sooner the better. (Today, in contrast, a live album is an afterthought, or something that comes much later in your career.) With our third album, *Phase-III*, slated for early 1972 release, we got ready to record a live album on December 4, 1971, from two shows before crowds of approximately 20,000 at Los Angeles's Forum.

In some ways, these were the two most important dates in our careers so far. The pressure was really on, and every time someone mentioned how expensive it was to bring in the people and the equipment to record the album, it went up a notch. By the time the big day arrived, my brothers and I were sick. Literally. Every single one of us had a cold, the flu, or just didn't feel well. If this had been a show like any other, maybe we would have canceled it. But while we sat at home feeling miserable, dozens of technicians were running wires, hooking up sound boards, and testing lights. Thousands of fans were lined up and pressing toward the Forum's doors. The merchandising people were stacking up the programs, the scarves, the T-shirts, the buttons, and whatever other Osmond paraphernalia they had. The show was going on, and we were going with it—ready or not.

I remember thinking to myself, *We're all so sick. This will be a disaster!* But, as always, it was a thought I never voiced because I knew no one in my family wanted to hear it. We would, we all assured one another, make the best of it. And, believe me, we've each had our moments when we've hit the stage when we should have been hitting the pillow. Standing backstage, decked out in our white fringed jumpsuits, Alan, Wayne, Merrill, Jay, and I joined in a family prayer, as we did before every performance.

The arena literally shook as our backing band, the American Underground, started playing our introduction and thousands of screams pierced the darkness and rang off the high walls. It's so hard to describe those magical moments right before you hit the stage. Strangely, it's there that you first feel the connection with the audience. Standing backstage I always knew, for example, the precise second when the house lights went down because there would be a shift in the psychic atmosphere that you could almost feel. In that instant, while the stage was still dark, as I climbed the riser and got set behind my keyboard, I felt—for want of a better word—high, euphoric, intensely alive. Every now and then I'd flash on the thought, *This isn't really me up here*. But it really was.

Once we were in position and the screaming couldn't get any louder, the announcer shouted, "The Osmonds!"

The lights came up onstage and thousands of flashbulbs popped at once like flashing stars. Alan counted off, "One! Two! Three!" and we were suddenly "on." Not that we were different people onstage than we were off, but onstage we had a freedom that existed nowhere else for us. With our just-tight-enough jumpsuits unlaced to reveal the presence of chest hair (on those of us who had it) and soul-influenced choreography that was, I admit, designed to be sexy, we understood what the girls were all screaming about. And we knew exactly what to say and how to move to set off the next avalanche of squeals. I could wipe the sweat from my face with my purple scarf or—the best—lean forward into the crowd and tease the girls down front with the chance to touch my hand. If I was lucky, a couple would grab my wrist and pull me down into the crowd. That didn't happen as often as I liked, but I never stopped trying!

That night at the Forum, we opened with the "Motown Special" medley, which had become a staple of the live show, and proceeded through "Double Lovin'," "Sweet and Innocent," Wayne's solo turn on "You've Lost That Lovin' Feelin'," "Proud Mary," "Free," "Go Away Little Girl," Jimmy's solo spot ("Trouble" and "I Got a Woman"), a gospel medley, and "Down by the Lazy River," "Yo-Yo," and "One Bad Apple." All the while, the audience applauded and yelled, despite the fact that we felt our performance was off in every possible way. With one of us under the weather, the rest of us could always pitch in and cover for him. But with all five of us sick, forget it.

The tapes, which we heard several days later, confirmed our worst fears: MGM Records had just spent thousands of dollars recording one of the poorest shows of our career. Bizarrely, *Billboard* gave the same show a sterling review. Now what? Ditch the whole project? It was too late for that. The only way to save *The Osmonds "Live"* was to release a version without our live performance. We rerecorded our vocals in the studio, added them to the live backing, and layered it all over the near-constant screaming. I don't think any of us felt really good about doing this, and at the time I thought the finished product sounded fake, as if our vocals had been slapped on. Strangely, though, no one seemed to notice, and in mid-1972, the double *Osmonds "Live"* quickly became the second-highest-charting album of our career. (*Phase-III* was first, at number ten.)

I was fourteen the day in 1972 when I arrived at MGM Records Studio on Fairfax Avenue (now Cherokee Studios) assuming I'd be recording vocals for an Osmonds track. Instead I found an entire orchestra waiting for me and a piece of sheet music for a song I'd never heard before: "Puppy Love." MGM spared no expense and provided for my solo session perhaps the top arranger of the time, Don Costa, who was best known for his work with Frank Sinatra. "Puppy Love" had been written by Paul Anka, a former teen idol who'd managed to shed his teen idol shadow and become a respected songwriter and performer. I didn't give any of these things too much thought then; I had a job to do. I quickly studied the lyrics, and within a couple takes, it was done.

Coincidentally, it was released nearly simultaneously with the Osmonds' "Down by the Lazy River," and I don't think two songs that were more different ever had so much in common. Both records peaked on the charts in March 1972; "Puppy Love" at number three and "Lazy River" at number four. They were both certified gold on the same day, and they later became the first Osmond records to hit the British charts. It's interesting that in England and throughout Europe, the Osmonds were always accorded more respect as a rock band than they ever got here at home. I can't help but think that our being "introduced" overseas through the hard-driving, rocking "Lazy River"—which sounded nothing like the Jackson 5 or any other group—greatly influenced our futures there. And, I guess you could argue, my solo debut there being "Puppy Love" probably had a similar impact, though with a very different outcome over the long haul. The British people accepted us for who we were, and on a pop chart dominated by glitter-rock stars sporting mascara and feather boas, our wholesomeness was an advantage.

The Osmonds' relationship with Great Britain could not have had a more auspicious start. In May 1972, we flew to London, where we had been invited to perform at the invitation of Her Royal Highness, Queen Elizabeth. Precisely why we were chosen, considering we'd placed only two singles on the

British charts up 'til then, I've never really known. It was a great honor, and we were all very excited in the days leading up to the Royal Gala Variety Performance.

By then we were being managed by Ed Leffler, an American whose previous experience including working on the Beatles' U.S. tours. Around the time that Ed managed us, he also managed the Carpenters, and, some years later, Van Halen. Ed was a very direct, no-nonsense kind of guy, and he made sure that everything we did ran smoothly. This first trip to Great Britain stands out because it was probably the only one we made where everything pretty much happened as planned. We'd charted and our fan base was growing, but it had yet to reach the fever pitch we'd witness when we returned six months later. For this trip, we mainly had to concentrate on memorizing the correct protocol for after the show, when we would meet the Queen. We practiced standing in the reception line, and reminding ourselves that we were not to speak to Her Majesty unless she addressed us, and not to offer a hand in greeting unless she did so first. I actually remember little about the show except that it was an abbreviated set and well received.

We lined up in age order, as we always did: Alan, Wayne, Merrill, Jay, me, and Jimmy. Her Majesty approached Alan, and everything went perfectly, as it did with Wayne. Merrill's nerves got the best of him, and he unthinkingly ran his tongue over his lips to moisten them at the very instant the Queen stopped to greet him and the press photographers snapped. The next day, there it was for all the world to see: Merrill Osmond sticking his tongue out at the Queen! Of course, Merrill wasn't actually sticking his tongue out, and the British public saw the humor in it. But Merrill was mortified.

The show, which was taped and also featured performances by Liza Minelli, Lily Tomlin, and Roger Moore, aired several days later on British television. It established the Osmonds in Great Britain and also sent "Puppy Love" flying up the charts. Between June 1972 and January 1973, that single would reenter the British pop chart two more times. Now, I don't want to mislead you. Not everyone loved "Puppy Love." In fact, in March 1972, police raided L.A.'s top-rated Top 40 radio station KHJ after disc jockey Robert Morgan played "Puppy Love" repeatedly for nearly an hour and a half. And I don't think it was because he really liked it, either.

We returned from London and resumed a crushing summer concert tour. In Philadelphia, Alan collapsed from exhaustion, and we canceled or postponed a couple of dates. In July, a fire that broke out in our Memphis hotel destroyed Alan's only manuscript for the album that would become known as *The Plan*. That summer my "Too Young" and the Osmonds' "Hold Her Tight" were Top 15 hits, and September brought our own cartoon show (for which we provided the voices) and our first headlining date in Las Vegas. We were, officially, the youngest act to headline there, and the press was out in full force. I was fourteen.

By mid-1972, we were one of the most famous families in the world; my brothers and I were stars. Some stars crave the money, the cars, the girls, the attention. But for me then, the biggest perk of fame was simply the excitement of coming off the stage, my ears ringing, my heart racing. There was, it seemed, always the next plane to catch, so the security people would whisk us out of the auditorium and into the waiting limos for the mad dash to the airport. The police escort, usually on motorcycles—which was so cool—took off, and our driver followed. I'd sit in the back of the speeding limousine as it blew past the traffic jams our concerts invariably caused, flew through red lights, and raced along highway shoulders. I loved the looks on people's faces as they tried to peer into the tinted windows and see who was inside (though they usually guessed). I loved the speed and the possibility, however distant, of danger. Still in my perspiration-soaked stage costume, guzzling orange juice from a bottle my brothers and I passed around, I just kept thinking, *Man, it can't get any better than this.*

chapter4

One of the most memorable times of my life began in early November 1972, when we arrived in England for a brief tour. I was just a month or so shy of fifteen. It had been six months since our appearance on the Royal Gala Variety Performance, but our fan support showed no signs of wavering. "Puppy Love" had gone to Number One that summer, "Too Young" was nearing number five, and "Crazy Horses" was galloping up the chart, on its way to number two. Shortly before we arrived, "Puppy Love" reentered the charts, and shortly after we left, "Why" became a number-three hit for me. Jimmy kept the Osmond name alive with his December Number One, "Long Haired Lover from Liverpool." At the time Jimmy was the youngest person in the history of the British pop charts to reach the top. (As of 1999, he still held that record.) Mother gets the credit for finding the song and suggesting that Jimmy record it. Recently someone remarked to Mother, "You could have been a producer," to which she responded in her typically humorous way, "Well, I was. I produced nine of them!"

Our plane touched down at London's Heathrow Airport around ten in the morning. It had been a long flight. I remember my brothers and I freshening up and changing in the jet's closet-sized bathrooms so we'd look fresh and presentable for the press and the fans, who had been gathering in the terminal since five o'clock that morning. With the fan hysteria of Beatlemania in mind, one reporter described the scene as "the sort of welcome that most people thought was only to be found in the pages of pop history." Those who got there early enough got a special treat, since Elton John and the Jackson 5 arrived just hours before we did. In flight, we were told that the airport authorities were concerned about controlling the crowd, but fortunately there were no incidents. At least not this time.

We stepped off the plane to find about two thousand screaming, crying girls waving at us from everywhere—including the roof of the terminal's observation deck—and chanting the rallying cry of "We want the Osmonds!" Some of them had mobbed the Jacksons just hours before, pulling their hair and nearly choking Michael with his own scarf, so our security people took extra precautions. We smiled, we waved, then we ducked into the waiting limousines and took off for the Churchill Hotel, in London's West End.

I don't know exactly what I expected to find at the Churchill, but as we turned the corner and began making our way into the underground garage, we realized that whatever security plans were in place weren't going to be enough. A huge crowd surrounded the block-long hotel, and these girls were determined not to surrender their "posts"—outside the front entrance, around the staff entrance, and even around the receiving bay, where trucks unloaded food and other goods. And the Churchill staff really had its hands full, because just a few hours before we got there, the Jacksons checked in. Now, you have to picture this: The Churchill is one of the oldest, most exclusive hotels in England, if not the world. From the marble-columned lobby to the wood-paneled elevators, it is the epitome of old-world grace and elegance. So you can imagine the hotel's management's reactions as they tried to defend us—and the premises—from the fans and their ever more elaborate plans to get in to meet us. Some even broke windows on the ground floor.

I'd like to think that we were model guests, though I doubt the hotel staff would agree. Except for leaving the hotel to make appearances and perform, we and the Jackson brothers were virtual prisoners there. We couldn't go outside to play, and boys will be boys, and hotels will be boring. So what was wrong with a nice friendly game of touch football? Besides the fact we played in a hotel hallway, and overlooking the fine old chandelier that got in the way of the ball, nothing really.

One of the best parts of the trip was getting to hang out with the Jackson 5, who were in the middle of a European tour and promoting Michael's latest single, the film title theme "Ben." This ballad to a rat had gone to Number One back in the States, a development I watched with keen interest since "Ben" originally was written for me. Only a scheduling conflict—we were on tour and the track had to be ready in time for the film's release—kept me from recording it. The producer just couldn't wait, so he went to Michael, with brilliant results. I couldn't harbor any grudges about it, though, since we'd gotten our first hit off a song written with the Jackson 5 in mind. You see, the similarities between "One Bad Apple" and the Jackson 5's hits were in place long before we ever heard the song, because George Jackson wrote "One Bad Apple" specifically for them. If Motown president Berry Gordy, Jr. had not rejected the song a year before we recorded it—well, we can only imagine. Michael was secure enough to take it all in stride —though he did tell reporters that he thought we could have been a little more "original," and that even some of his relatives thought "One Bad Apple" was the Jacksons. Michael's father, Joseph, wasn't quite so forgiving, though. According to one of Michael's biographers, Joseph felt our being white and being members of The Church of Jesus Christ of Latter-day Saints added insult to injury. The few times I visited Michael in the years to come, his father always let me know that I was not especially welcome there. To his credit, Michael never let that deter him from inviting me over.

Michael and I were never really in competition, but that's not what our contingents of fans outside the Churchill thought. We stood at our respective windows, like a couple of half-pint world leaders, waving as the crowd below us cheered. I felt so sorry for the other hotel guests, because the noise never let up. When they weren't screaming our names or chanting "We want the Osmonds," "We want the Jackson 5," "We want Donny," or "We want Michael," they were singing.

"We love you, Michael, oh yes we do," one group sang as Michael waved from his window.

Then I popped my head out of my window, and cries of, "We love you, Donny, oh yes we do," rose from the street.

Then Michael waved again, and they sang for him. Then I

waved, and they sang for me. The whole time, the two of us were having a blast. We'd flip the lights on and off, just to hear the girls below scream over it.

Anywhere there's a crowd, there's always the possibility that things might get out of control or that someone could get hurt. Fortunately, we had a crack security team, headed by Don Murphet, one of the best in his field. Our security watched and worried about the girls hiding down in the underground garage (who were "dissuaded" from remaining with blasts from fire extinguishers) and the girls who outfoxed them and somehow found themselves on the floor we'd rented for our stay. Once a girl broke through all the security, but was so excited when she finally got to us that she fainted (and after all that work!). To say that these girls were determined barely describes the raw will and sheer nerve they applied to the pursuit, and you'd be a fool to underestimate them. We learned that lesson in 1971 at Miami's Diplomat Hotel, when a girl came up with a unique plan to get to us. She was going to rappel down the side of the hotel building from a balcony several floors above ours. Fortunately, we were able to talk to her from our balcony and convince her not to try it. But you always had to wonder, What next?

While our security team never left anything to chance, I still couldn't resist causing a little trouble. I've always had a mischievous streak, and had I lived a normal childhood, it would probably have found outlets in all kinds of typical boyish pranks. But cooped up on tour, there wasn't much I could do, so when I got the chance, I set to it with a vengeance. Many times fans found out where we were staying and would assemble in the parking lot below and chant, "Throw something down, throw us a souvenir!" I'd stand on a balcony high above a crowd of fans and watch as they screamed, "Throw us something, Donny!"

Well, okay. First, I would throw down the kinds of things they would expect: a few Donny caps, a couple of scarves, one or two handmade and personally autographed paper airplanes. From that height, all the fans could see was that something was falling toward them. From where I stood, they looked like a swarm of dots scurrying this way and that in their attempt to catch whatever I'd just pitched out the window. The funny part was, they never knew what was coming at them; they just knew they wanted it.

I did this in almost every city we played in, but I particularly recall one time. I'd thrown just about everything that wasn't nailed down and the girls were still begging for more. I surveyed the room for anything I could possibly give them. Then inspiration struck—in the form of three large, cold leftover pizzas. I remember thinking to myself, *This is not a good idea,* but by then I'd become so curious to find out what would happen if I tossed them, that I even rationalized that perhaps some of the fans might be hungry. Maybe this sounds a little cruel, and it probably was, but at the time, I just couldn't resist. I was just a kid. The girls all ran together as the pizza sailed through the air, but once it got close enough for them to see what it was, it was too late to get out of its path.

During this 1972 tour, we performed two shows at the Rainbow Theatre in London, and also did shows in Birmingham and Manchester. Fans screamed and carried on back in the States, but what the papers called Osmondmania was especially intense in England. The editor of the popular fan magazine *Jackie* stated that every time the Osmonds appeared on the cover, sales tripled. But media interest spilled beyond publications targeted at the teenyboppers—or, as some of our critics there derisively dubbed them, "weenyboppers." (What would they possibly think up next, I wonder, "eensie-weensieboppers"? It was so silly.) Even the nation's largest daily newspapers found something Osmond-related to write about. By then we'd all gotten used to seeing our names in print, and even the stories that invaded our privacy started to roll off our backs. But imagine how I felt when I saw the headline of the country's most popular morning newspaper screaming, "Donny's Voice Is Breaking!" Boy, as if I didn't feel self-conscious enough about this physiologically embarrassing portent of puberty. From day to day, I never knew which of the dozen or so arrangements of "Puppy Love" we'd be using that night. And then my older brothers, meaning well I'd like to think, could never resist reminding me after a show about the number of times my voice cracked. At the time, it didn't occur to me to remind them that they'd all gone through this, too. The only difference was that they didn't have four older brothers to tell them about it later. The hoopla over my voice change grew so ridiculous that Mother issued a statement to the press informing them that my voice was "getting lower," not breaking. One magazine called the fans' intense even irrational interest in me "Donnydementia," but from what I could see, it was not only the fans but the media that was out of control.

Back home in the States, part of my job as "Donny Osmond, Teen Idol," was to participate as the "prize" in contests run by the teen magazines. As they say, many entered, few were chosen, and from what the magazine people told us, millions wrote in for the chance to have a "dream date" with me. I know that some other artists looked down on these contests as tedious public relations chores, but I never did. I always genuinely liked my fans, and I'd reached the age where I really liked girls, so how could I lose? There was an added bonus, too: It gave me an excuse to go out on a date, although I wasn't really permitted to date for another year or so.

I had just come home from a very pleasant "date" with the winner of a *Tiger Beat* magazine "Win a Date with Donny" contest. Suddenly, a familiar, flu-ish sensation crept over me. I remember thinking to myself, *Oh, no. Not again,* because I knew what was coming next: at least twelve hours of excruciating stomach pain that would leave me doubled up on the floor, crying, screaming, and wishing I could die. Around the age of nine, I started experiencing these painful attacks every few months. Without MRIs or CAT scans, my doctors did their best to pinpoint the cause. Considering how well I bounced back after each attack, and taking into consideration the pattern of the attacks, they concluded that I had a lazy pyloric sphincter, which was allowing acidic digestive fluids from my stomach to go where they didn't belong, creating an ulcerlike condition. After guzzling all that barium and holding still for all those X rays, I was relieved to have a diagnosis if not a cure. And everyone was especially happy to know that the doctors had all ruled out appendicitis specifically.

I'd had enough attacks by then to recognize the signs: a vague, flu-ish feeling, cold sweats, and then the pain. It always seemed to start after I'd eaten a lot of meat, or, inexplicably, peanuts. I'd suffered attacks while we were at Muscle Shoals and in England, where they rushed me to the hospital in an ambulance and the press wrote that I was dying or, in a couple of irresponsible publications, that I was dead. (But how could fans solve the mystery of my mortal status? Why, play "Puppy Love" backwards, of course, some earnestly believed. And the sad part is, I'm not making this up.)

I have wonderful memories about the loving way Father cared for me. Whenever I was sick, Father stayed beside me, speaking to me gently and holding me as I screamed at the top of my lungs and lay on the floor with my legs drawn up in a fetal position, unable to move. In those moments, I saw Father's tender, compassionate side. Several times as I felt an attack coming on right before a show, Father would pray with me and I'd be able to finish my performance, though the pain would resume a few hours later. This might sound reckless. However, I'd been seen and tested by doctors all over the world, including Dr. Newman, my own doctor in Los Angeles, and no one could find anything wrong with me that couldn't be explained by the pyloric sphincter problem.

A few hours after my "dream date," I was in the basement recording studio we'd set up at the Manning Apartments when I started to feel this attack coming on. Father knew it would be several hours before the pain really took hold, so he said, "We're taking you to the hospital in the morning for blood tests." Perhaps because I'd just had a thorough checkup from Dr. Newman and we'd all been through the attack "drill" so many times before, there was no sense of urgency. But Father and Mother must have sensed something was different.

At the Beverly Glen Hospital, a nurse drew my blood and the lab discovered my white count was sky-high—a sure sign of massive infection. The problem was, if it was the appendicitis (the most likely culprit), the pain wasn't where it was "supposed" to be. All I remember after that is doctors and nurses frantically rushing around my bed, inserting intravenous lines into my arm, and then suddenly the sharp pain of a needle in my behind. After they wheeled me into the brightly lit operating room, a rubber mask was held over my face, and I heard someone say, "Now, count to ten."

The next thing I knew, I was awake in my hospital room and the intense pain I'd felt before was replaced by a gnawing soreness. Terrified, I raised the covers a few inches to see my entire abdomen wrapped in bandages. Immediately I knew they'd done something to my stomach, and I broke down in tears. Mother and Father heard me and quickly came into the room.

Holding me, Mother said, "We figured out what's been causing the problem all these years. They took your appendix out. They performed emergency exploratory surgery [which explains the large scar Marie forced me to show everyone on national television not too long ago], and the doctor was surprised to discover that your appendix was abnormally positioned behind your liver."

My parents were told that besides my appendix showing signs of repeated infections, it had clearly begun to rupture. "In another three hours," one doctor said, "Donny would have died."

Now that I knew my stomach attacks would never return, I tried to enjoy my involuntary vacation. The week or so I spent recuperating in the hospital was uncomfortable but surprisingly pleasant. It wasn't that often I had time off, so I tried to make the best of it. The hospital switchboard was flooded with calls (I enjoyed knowing that even from a hospital bed, I could still cause some trouble), and cards, letters, flowers, and gifts poured in. The pain of my incision made it difficult to breathe comfortably, and the one thing I couldn't do was laugh. One of my best friends, Larry Nielsen, who had a terrific sense of humor, came to see me and had to leave after thirty seconds because he made me laugh so hard without saying anything, I was crying in pain.

Among my other visitors were writers and photographers from the teen magazines. After all, they had a surefire angle: Donny was "dying"—what a scoop. By the time they arrived, I was long out of danger. But that didn't deter them from asking me to reenact my ordeal, to create the impression that they'd been right there in the emergency room reporting the crisis as it happened.

Looking back now, what I did was so funny. Clearly, my life had taken a surrealistic turn, but at the time, I didn't really appreciate that aspect of it. I was just doing what was expected of me. I lay in my hospital bed, modestly revealing my bandages while the magazine's photographer and editor were "directing" me:

"Make it look like you're in pain," the editor instructed.

I closed my eyes and grimaced a little, but the photographer pleaded, "No, Donny. More painful! More painful!"

Okay, I can do that. I affected a look of anguish, squeezing my eyes tightly shut and opening my mouth as if I were moaning, only to hear, "No! No! Re-create the moment, Donny, make it look real! I want pain! Pain!" It's true, there is no business like show business.

Through early 1973, my brothers and I all worked together recording *The Plan*, the ambitious concept album that Alan first imagined a couple years before. (Because Alan's only manuscript had been destroyed in a fire, he had to rewrite the songs from memory.) Conceived as a rock opera based on our religious beliefs, *The Plan* remains the Osmonds project that still means the most to all of us, and we all take pride in its now being "redis-covered" by younger audiences, particularly in England and in Europe, as a "lost classic."

Our decision to release *The Plan* entailed the biggest com-mercial risk of our pop career. Although it was a spiritual work, except for "The Last Days"—which speaks explicitly about the end as revealed in the Book of Revelation—the songs could be interpreted other ways. Running the gamut, from the heavy-metal blues of "Traffic in My Mind" to the hit ballad "Let Me In," *The Plan* showed the Osmonds in a new light. "The Osmonds' *Sgt. Pepper*?" was how England's *New Musical Express* headlined its review, which gives you some idea how differently the Osmonds were perceived overseas. There, my solo career was viewed as a spinoff, a footnote of sorts to the Osmonds' harder rock and roll.

This was the first album for which Alan, Wayne, and Merrill had written every song. And I think it says a lot about my brothers' songwriting talent that they created songs listeners could enjoy whether they shared our beliefs or not. You didn't have to be religious to appreciate *The Plan* any more than you'd have to have followed Mehar Baba to understand the Who's *Tommy*. In that and other ways, I think Alan was brilliant.

For example, one of my favorite things about *The Plan* is its cover artwork, which Alan conceived. Printed in one of the few triple gatefold album jackets, with lyrics across two "pages" and a drawing depicting the seasons of mortal life across another two, the artwork was very much in step with the times. The "mural" begins with two strong hands coming down through the clouds and gently dropping a baby to earth (an allusion to our belief that we had heavenly parents in a spiritual existence prior to mortal birth) and ends with those same hands reaching down from heaven again, only this time to embrace the eternal soul of an elderly person who has passed away.

What was not so brilliant, however, was how the album was promoted. Not surprisingly, Alan felt very strongly about the work, and stated in interviews not only that it was about spiritual beliefs, but that its inspiration was the teachings of our church. Unfortunately, I think we miscalculated the public's response. First, we underestimated how much my teenybopper image had begun to candy-coat the group. And second, we didn't factor in that the public may not have been ready for a "serious" album from us on any subject, much less one that spoke specifically (if you knew it) about the Latter-day Saints teachings. Complicating matters were Mike Curb's departure from the label and a change in distribution.

Today, even most people unfamiliar with our beliefs would recognize and probably understand if not agree with this conception of eternal spiritual life. The album doesn't go into explicit detail about the theological teachings of our church. But if you knew what they were, you would hear the love songs, which—like most pop love songs—speak of stepping "toward eternity" and "goin' home," differently than someone who did not. Almost all of them—"Goin' Home," "Mirror, Mirror," "Darlin'"—could be easily read in both religious and nonreligious contexts. I regret that the promotion campaign left listeners no room to appreciate it as anything but a "religious" work, because I'm convinced that had *The Plan* been heard on its own terms, many things might have been different for all of us.

And it's not as if we didn't try. How completely sealed our

images were was driven home when Alan dropped by a Los Angeles, hard-rock FM—which in those days meant "non–Top 40"—radio station. Alan arrived at the studio with *The Plan* in an unmarked jacket and introduced himself by saying only, "I've got this group, and we've recorded these songs. I'd just like to see what you think about it."

The manager was in a rush, but he sat down and listened to one track, then another, then another until he'd played the whole thing. "This is great! Who are these guys?"

"Well, those are my brothers," Alan replied. "We wrote it, we played it. We're the Osmonds."

The guy's jaw dropped, then he replied, "Yeah, sure. Sure you are. Now what's your name?"

"Alan Osmond."

"You're kidding." After a second, he said, "Okay, I'm going to bring this in to my top disc jockey, and you tell him the same thing you just told me. Don't tell him who you are. Play him some cuts, then ask him if he'd play it on the air."

Alan did, and after the disc jockey heard it, he exclaimed, "Wow, this is great stuff! I'd put it on the air."

Then the manager said, "Okay, guess who it is. It's the Osmonds."

"You're kidding, right? Come on, give me a break." The manager introduced Alan, and the disc jockey said, "Okay, you know what would be fun? Let me play a couple of tracks and introduce the group as a 'mystery band' and let the listeners call in and try to guess who you are."

No one guessed correctly, but Alan was not the least offended by some of the guesses: Led Zeppelin, Grand Funk Railroad, Deep Purple, the Doobie Brothers (in their early, heavier incarnation). The problem was that not everyone got a chance to hear the music without first knowing it was us. Except for "Let Me In," *The Plan* was a little too ambitious for Top 40 play lists, and the Osmonds being the Osmonds made us a poor fit with FM's free-form, "underground" image.

Ironically, throughout Europe, where we were associated with "Crazy Horses," we were considered a hard-rock band. This was heartening, even if it left some fans confused. We still had some of what you could call "Las Vegas" style in our live show. For example, there was one segment where we did our "Motown Special" medley, another where Merrill performed a medley on banjo. I don't think any of us will ever forget one show in Paris, where the audience—made up entirely of hippies and Hell's Angels who'd come to groove to the heavy, mind-bending sounds of "Crazy Horses"—stared in disbelief as Merrill took out his banjo. In the few front rows we could see, people in the crowd were turning to one another, their expressions an odd mixture of disgust and confusion, as if to say, "What is this crap?" We were so embarrassed, but there was nothing we could do about it, since we didn't know "Stairway to Heaven" or "Smoke on the Water." All we could do is finish up the show and escape the stage before the beer bottles started flying. It's funny to look back and wonder how many of them that night thought they'd just gotten some bad drugs.

Looking back, we can all see how things might have been approached differently, but when it comes to the actual work on *The Plan*, no one would change a thing. At the time Alan said, "Let our careers go down the drain, but we'll know that we did an album that came from us—that we played on, that we wrote, that we believed in." As performers, our careers were secure. As recording artists, however, the public had spoken. *The Plan* was the first of the group's six albums released since 1971 that was not certified gold (despite including two Top 40 singles, "Let Me In" and "Goin' Home"), and the first to stall in the lower half of the Top 100, down at number fifty-eight. Considering that our previous album, *Crazy Horses*, had hit number fourteen, this was quite a drop. After next year's *Love Me for a Reason*, no album by the group would ever chart above the hundredth position in the United States again.

Back in 1972 during our trip to England I'd begun feeling uncomfortable about being pushed out in front. Especially after *The Plan*, I could see a widening gap between the direction the group was going and where my solo career was taking me. From a creative point of view, I simply could not compare the excitement of working with my brothers in our studio on our material to my standing alone to record another sugary cover tune I had no hand in creating. By mid-1973, even though I was feeling less enthusiastic about my solo career, it was as strong as ever. Through the end of the year, I scored four hits with covers coproduced by Mike Curb and Don Costa: "The Twelfth of Never," "A Million to One" and its flip side, "Young Love," and "Are You Lonesome Tonight." And all was not lost. Ever in keeping with our "As long as it's an Osmond" philosophy, we made room down front for our newest star, Marie, who that fall had a Number One country hit with her first single, "Paper Roses."

In the summer of 1973, we found ourselves with an entire month off. Father said, "Enjoy yourselves, guys." After spending so many years working constantly, I honestly didn't know what to do with myself. Relaxing and doing nothing was an art I wouldn't practice let alone perfect for many years to come. For me, spare time meant only one thing: a project.

When Virl and Tom were young, we had a machine called a color organ, which consisted of circuits that would turn on different lights depending on the frequency of a sound spoken into a microphone. Obviously, my brothers could not hear themselves well enough to know that they were pronouncing specific sounds correctly. Since each sound had its own frequency, and each frequency activated its own light, the color organ made it possible for Virl and Tom to "see" what they were saying. I remember as a child being intrigued by the machine. I always wanted to build one that we could use onstage, so that different instrumental and vocal sounds would trigger different lighting effects. I decided I'd create one for our stage show.

Probably for the first time in my life, I had my own area of expertise, and I felt so good when my brothers expressed their amazement at the intricacy of the schematic drawings I'd done. When they gave me the go-ahead, it was such a vote of confidence. Here I was, just fifteen and charged with designing the backdrop we would use onstage for the next tour. But along with their confidence came the realization that the pressure was on, and if I was going to do it, I'd better do it right. I redesigned a basic circuit I'd found in the reference book Ed Greene gave me, and ran down to Central Utah Electronics, bought all the parts, and settled down to work.

I was in my own little world, etching my own circuit boards and soldering each component onto them. Father and my brothers helped construct the six big boxes that would house the actual lights, while I worked on wiring the boxes and the controlling circuitry. It was June, and we were set to hit the road in July, so

I worked constantly. It was nice being the one everyone turned to with questions. For the first time in my life, I had the answers. I couldn't wait for the first show. I imagined the audience's amazement and my brothers' pride as my electronics genius was revealed to the world.

So, of course, my world almost shattered when the thing blew up! Like the mad doctor in a cheap horror movie, though, I couldn't let my creature die. I spent practically every moment when I wasn't onstage sitting in my makeshift workshop at the back of the bus, redesigning the circuits, trying to ignore my brothers' jokes. No matter what I did, however, almost every show included its own light box disaster: If the thing didn't overload the main supply breakers, the colored gels were cracking, exposing the bare 100-watt lightbulbs. I was so embarrassed. I shouldn't have been too surprised when before the next tour, professional electricians were called in to construct boxes for new special effects.

This time, Alan was the mastermind behind a system that employed flash pots, CO_2 cartridges, and special lighting effects that actually did work (the ones I had nothing to do with). All across the front of the stage, we placed flash pots, and Wayne was in charge of loading the squibs, or igniters, before each show. Our road manager, Masanobu Ono, or Mas as we called him, was in charge of igniting the flash pots on cue. We'd been incorporating bits of magic and other nonmusical elements into our show, and at one point, I performed a sleight-of-hand trick, turning a purple handkerchief into a cane. Then I'd turn around and the back of my purple cape would light up to form a brilliant capital D in flashing, chasing lights. It made for a hokey but dramatic moment during our indoor and nighttime shows. Outside in broad daylight, though, no one off the stage could make out the letter. As I dramatically spread my arms to show off the dazzling but largely invisible capital *D*, I secretly feared that I looked like a diminutive Liberace.

We'd planned on firing the flash pots precisely as choreographed, so that wherever I was standing, the pot would fire. Simple. Something got mixed up, because I was singing onstage right when suddenly—boom!—the flash pot across the stage went off. I ran over to stage left, and the flash pot on stage right went off. This happened a couple more times, and when I knew there was only one left to fire, I figured I'd play it safe and just stand next to it until it exploded. The cue came and went; nothing. A few more seconds; nothing. Thinking, *Great, a dud* (which happened every so often), I stupidly stepped right over the top of it and—BOOM! It nearly scared me to death, but my attention was quickly diverted by the next, unplanned pyrotechnic display—my cape was in flames, with me still in it! My brothers dropped their instruments and ran to me. Someone tore the cape off, and the five of us stamped on it until the fire was out. I'll never forget the pathetic little *pop* each light bulb emitted as the famous Donny cape met its dramatic, undignified, but well deserved end. (We actually tried to resurrect it for a few more shows, but the hem was tattered and burnt, and the lights didn't work.)

Most performers live in fear of the moment onstage when something goes terribly wrong. Some mistakes are noticeable only to your fellow performers or your stage crew. And most audiences are gracious and forgiving about the ones they do notice. Looking back, I think we let our quest for perfection and fear of failure onstage go a bit too far. Around this time, we found ourselves playing so many shows it just was not humanly possible to be in top form every time. Alan decided that the audience deserved always to hear us at our best, so we developed our "secret weapon," code name Beauford. I believe that Beauford is among the best-kept Osmond family secrets, and before I continue, my apologies to anyone who may feel cheated to learn that they may not have seen us as "live" as we appeared. Beauford was our ace in the hole, a taped version of our show that we could play through the sound system whenever the going got a little tough. Of course, today, many top performers use prerecordings in their "live" shows, to varying degrees. Some rely on tapes to recreate a instrumental track from their recording or background vocals if their singers are unavailable. More recently, others have admitted to lip-synching to recordings of their own vocals, without apology. I'm not passing judgment on any other performer, but back in the 1970s, using recordings so extensively in a live show was pretty much unheard-of. While I understood the reasons why we needed Beauford at times, I hated him (or it, or whatever you want to call it), because I worried that one day Beauford would rebel and expose our charade. Which he did.

Beauford backfired on us at the Houston Astrodome a couple years later. We were filming our concert for an upcoming episode of *The Osmond Family Show*, and one of Jimmy's numbers had him singing "Rhinestone Cowboy" as he made his entrance riding a horse. Of course, most of the singing you see on television is actually lip-synching to a prerecorded tape, and this was no exception. Jimmy was wearing his red, silver-studded Elvis-style jumpsuit, looking every bit a rhinestone cowboy himself. The music started and Jimmy's voice came over the speakers smoothly singing, and the illusion was perfect—until suddenly the horse reared up and started bucking, startling Jimmy, who was hanging on for dear life. All this time, however, his voice came through the speakers sounding as relaxed as if he were sitting in a rocking chair. It brought to mind a badly dubbed Japanese monster movie, and while we can laugh about it today, at that moment, everyone was thrown into a panic.

But that wasn't the worst of it. Later on, in that same show, my brothers and I were onstage singing when suddenly the unthinkable happened: Someone accidentally hit Beauford's rewind button. We were saved by Alan's quick thinking. He told the crowd, "I'm sorry. We're taping this for a television show, and since there's a problem, now we'll do it for you live!"

The crowd cheered, and before I had a chance to think about how we were going to do that since we hadn't rehearsed it, I saw Alan hit the play button again, and we were "live"—live Beauford, that is.

In the fall of 1973, we returned to England to find Osmondmania in full force. Interestingly, 1973 was our best year, chartwise, in England. The Osmonds hit number four with "Goin' Home" and number two with "Let Me In," ironically, both from *The Plan.* (In 1974, the number-twelve "I Can't Stop"—which we had released unsuccessfully prior to "One Bad Apple"—was followed by the group's sole U.K. Number One, "Love Me for a Reason.") I had two consecutive Number Ones in 1973: "The Twelfth of Never" and "Young Love," followed by "When I Fall in Love," which went to number four that fall.

After shows in Sweden and Denmark, we had arrived in London on a private jet to find ten thousand—compared to last year's two thousand—fans overrunning Heathrow Airport.

There were too many people on the balcony, causing a wall to collapse and fall fifteen feet onto people standing below. Fortunately, no one was hurt, but in the wake of the trouble, British authorities banned future announcements of our flight plans. This time we stayed at the Britannia Hotel (we were banned from the Churchill and after this visit, we'd be banned by virtually every major hotel in London), where again fans created havoc by darting through the lobby and trying anything to get to us. The plans laid by our management and promotion people to make the Osmonds a household name there had succeeded—almost too well.

On one level, I suppose I was too young to realize or understand the implications of it all or the danger. When girls would swarm our Bentley limousine, screaming, pushing, and rocking it until from the inside you almost felt like the car would either tip over or implode, Alan would start shouting, "Get off the car! Get off the car!"

They can't hear you, I'd think to myself. *Let 'em go!* I loved it.

The concerts then were so wild—and for the first time, dangerous. I don't think anyone sat in their seats, and within minutes, the crowd would be surging toward the stage with such force that our security people and the police had to "fish" fans out from in front of the stage to save them from being crushed. The problem was that the people in the most danger were those down front, but it was a classic Catch-22. The front was the most dangerous place to be, but the girls knew that once they got close enough to be "rescued," they would be pulled on to the stage and taken backstage, where they would be cared for. The prospect of getting up close to the stage, even if for only a few seconds, only encouraged more risk taking. At one performance,

girls were being pushed toward the stage faster than the security people and police could move them out of harm's way. We
had to stop the show. Alan—who usually did most of the talking
onstage—could not get the audience to listen to his pleas for
them to calm down. He turned to me and said, "Donny, you try
to calm them down."

I approached a mike and said, "Now, listen, everyone,
you—"

To say that plan backfired would be a gross understate-
ment. The crowd pressed forward like a tidal wave, and more
girls were trapped in the crush. Someone yanked me away from
the microphone and told me to shut up.

In the eyes of the British media, this was no longer
Osmondmania, but, as one leading newspaper headline put it:
"Osmond Terror." Who, us?

The situation reached a crisis, or at least a public relations
crisis, when a BBC news program featured a psychologist and
someone from Scotland Yard describing in lurid detail the madness gripping Britain's young women. What was kind of funny
about the show was that while the panelists were aghast and the
adults in the audience looked terribly, terribly concerned, all the
girls sat beside their parents with these faraway smiles on their
faces. To paraphrase the Doors' Jim Morrison, the little girls do
understand. They were out of control, a frail, gray-haired psychologist warned, driven by an irrational desire to be near their
idols. In the throes of this mania, these girls could do anything,
just anything.

The proposed solution: Get that little troublemaker Donny
out of England and ban him from returning. For someone who
enjoyed a little trouble now and then, this was a gift! Of course,

we were virtual prisoners in our hotel rooms then, so with nothing better to do, I found myself watching the program. Knowing what we were really like and how different we were in our personal lives than many other rock stars, we just couldn't believe they were talking about us. Obviously, the fact that public opinion was so divided and so intense was no laughing matter. But it just struck us as funny to think that I was being discussed as a national security threat. I'll never forget Alan turning to me and saying, "Donny, remember this moment for the rest of your life, because nothing like this will ever happen to you again."

For the most part, the fans were kept at a distance, but I had a few close encounters that reminded me how volatile crowds could be. Once in Manchester, England, fans mobbed me and tore my favorite shirt to shreds; another time, a girl became so confused and excited to get my autograph that she wrapped her arms around me and must have forgotten she had her pen in hand. I felt the sharp, stabbing pain as the pen cut into my cheek just millimeters below my eye. In another incident, two girls ran in front of our car, were hit, and suffered minor injuries. I'm sure the British people weren't pleased to hear one of the girls announce on a nationally broadcast talk show that receiving a phone call from me while she was hospitalized for her injuries made it all worthwhile.

We returned to England in 1974 to tape an unprecedented series of six television specials for the BBC, which aired over six days. These shows were a lot of fun to do, because we did so many different things. With so much air time to fill, we pulled out all the stops and went back as far as the Andy Williams days for numbers. There were production numbers like "Singing in the Rain," interviews with family members (including Father and

Mother), and performances by Jimmy and Marie as well as the Bay City Rollers and the Three Degrees. But this audience, which was made up predominantly of fans who'd gotten tickets through a lottery, screamed after every number, whether it was rock and roll or barbershop. We added Merrill's banjo medley with a little trepidation, in view of the "overwhelming" response it had received in Paris. But the girls in London screamed for that, too!

The following year, we toured again, and I'll never forget those shows because of the grand entrance I made at Earl's Court. This was probably one of Alan's most brilliant but daring ideas, and the minute I heard about it, I couldn't wait to do it. Imagine this: The show opens with the announcer shouting, "The Osmonds!" The lights go up, and the audience is surprised to see only Alan, Wayne, Merrill, and Jay onstage. In the split second it takes to register that Donny is "missing," flash pots go off onstage and suddenly I fly out from behind a curtain upstage and out over the audience tossing rose petals. If the audience was thrilled by this mini spectacle—and you knew they were because a scream of surprise filled the hall—it was nothing compared to the adrenaline rush of flying over all those girls, with their faces upturned toward me and their arms reaching for me.

My rig was very basic, so I was just swinging like a pendulum—out over the crowd and back. The problem was that at the bottom of the arc, I was so close to the audience that a girl of average height, standing on a seat, could easily jump up and grab my foot. Peter Foy, the famous rigger who "flew" Mary Martin in *Peter Pan* on Broadway, told us that if anyone or anything stopped or slowed me down during my "flight," I wouldn't have enough momentum to swing back to the stage. I could easily get stuck dangling over the crowd. This was something my family and everyone dreaded, but when I heard the backup plan for getting me back to the stage, I secretly hoped for the worst, because here's what would happen. Foy would immediately let go of the rope, causing me to drop into the crowd. The security staff and the plainclothes bobbies stationed along my "flight path" would throw big nets over me and anyone who'd managed to get on top of me. Then they'd start pulling girls off of me, one by one, until they found me. I don't think I've ever admitted this, but as I flew out, I'd stretch my foot as far as I could, just hoping some brave girl would jump up and trigger the emergency plan. I'm sorry to say, the emergency everyone else dreaded never took place, although I admit to often daydreaming about what it would have been like to have been "trapped" under all those girls.

England was only one stop on a very crowded tour itinerary that took up most of every year. I often woke up not knowing where I was or how I got there. Before long, I managed to make my sense of dislocation into a little game where I'd try to figure out where I was without having to ask someone or do the obvious things, like look at the phone number on the telephone or turn on the television. In the beginning, it was fun. But I'll never forget one day, years later, when it took me over half an hour to reconstruct my whereabouts. By then I estimated that I had performed for audiences in all forty-eight contiguous states and Hawaii, not to mention dozens of countries overseas. Life on the road can be maddening, and a teenage boy who spends weeks trapped in one hotel room after another is bound to suffer a little cabin fever. And for me, that meant trouble.

By now you've gotten the point that we were all very well-behaved kids. Despite that, there was—I probably should say "is" —a practical joker lurking inside me. And sometimes the boredom and fatigue made it impossible to resist the pranks I knew I'd suffer the consequences for later. My main target in those days was our manager, Ed Leffler. Why? Who knows? We had a good relationship, and we both appreciated a well-executed practical joke. One evening, I went to the front desk and got the key to Ed's room. I excused myself from dinner and got to work: throwing his towels out the window, upending the bed, and then—the pièce de résistance—I sprayed shaving cream on the earpiece of the telephone receiver, so that when he picked it up … Just thinking about it made me laugh.

Back upstairs, I took my position behind my own door, which was right across from Ed's, and watched through the peephole as his reactions ran the gamut from disbelief to rage. Just as I planned, he picked up the phone to dial my room and got an earful of foam. And the vulgarities that came out of his mouth! Whew! But Ed was not about to be the victim for long. He knew exactly how to get back at me: He called Father. Talk about getting into trouble. It took me hours to clean up Ed's room, but it had been worth every minute. (Now, I'll tell you a secret. I don't know if it's the fact that on tour, hotel rooms begin to feel like prison cells, but it's long been a dream of mine to check into a hotel—and I have exactly the one in mind—trash the room, throw everything from furniture to the toilet into the adjacent river, pay for the damage, and leave town. Fast.)

Even with fewer hits, we continued touring and playing two- and three-week stints in Las Vegas. In 1973 my brothers and I studied martial arts with Chuck Norris, and we incorporated a choreographed karate demonstration into our act. My part was breaking pine boards with a karate chop, which isn't as hard as it looks. What was difficult was keeping a good supply of the right type of pine boards that break easily (not that I'm suggesting I couldn't have broken any other kind of wood—yeah, right). The choreographed routine that Chuck had put together had Alan sparring with Jay, then Wayne sparring with Merrill, and me just choppin' those boards like they were graham crackers. During a tour of the South, I discovered that soft pine plus high humidity equals very, very hard boards. I'll never forget standing onstage, looking every bit a ninety-pound weakling, as the board just refused to break. *That* must have made me look real cool. Then, poor Alan. I would demonstrate my killer sidekick by shattering a board while Alan held it. I'd guess that I actually hit the board without hitting Alan maybe one in twenty times.

Probably the worst mishap we ever endured onstage happened during a karate demonstration. Chuck staged it to be safe, but it was crucial that each guy stay precisely on his mark. A mistake in timing or positioning could be dangerous, because we weren't just pretending to do the moves, we really had studied the art and were attacking with full force though not connecting. One night Alan and Jay's timing was off by a millisecond, and Alan hit Jay's nose with such force, Jay had to literally hold it onto his face. Blood was flowing everywhere, and we were all afraid Jay had been seriously injured. The show was delayed while Jay's nose was temporarily "taped on" with bandages, but the show continued. Afterward, Jay was rushed to the hospital for stitches. But Jay wasn't even the only injured Osmond. The night before, Merrill had accidentally swallowed a piece of glass that had fallen into an ice bucket, Alan's hands were bruised from me kicking those boards and cut from hitting Jay (he got stitches, too), and my hands were still swollen from trying to break boards. And poor Jimmy. He and I were jumping on our beds while he was brushing his teeth when I shoved him, he fell, and his toothbrush punctured a hole in the back of his throat.

Not to pick on Jimmy, but he was also the "star" of another memorable unrehearsed moment in Las Vegas when he was twelve. Jimmy has been an avid golfer since he was grammar-school age, so whenever we played Vegas, he'd hit the fairways. One day before a show, Jimmy got a little too sunburned and had a few too many grilled cheese sandwiches and orange freezes. Despite his feeling ill, he went on that night anyway. During "I Got a Woman," Jimmy would sing, "I want you all to know—" then pause dramatically and fix his stare on one woman in the audience. Of course, Jimmy being so young, people always laughed at this, and this evening was no different. Well, at least not until Jimmy threw up, lost his balance, and toppled off the stage, falling onto a table. A couple of us leapt down off the stage, grabbed Jimmy—whose white jumpsuit was covered in ketchup and steak sauce—and rushed him backstage. The whole time, he just kept singing. What a trouper, what a mess!

Those years were great fun for us, but after a while, the relentless routine began to wear on us all. As we approached the mid-1970s, I felt—and I believe some of my brothers did as well—that we were no longer fully in control. We would even discuss among ourselves how we felt like parts of a machine that had gathered so much momentum, there was no stopping it. Some people might have just quit, but we couldn't. We loved working with one another. The problem was that we were beginning to see ourselves as business partners. Looking back now, I wouldn't have traded our career for anything. But sometimes I have wished that we could have been only brothers and nothing more. All the time we spent together should have brought my brothers and me closer together, and in some ways it did. In other ways, though, it began to drive wedges between us that weren't obvious to me until many years later.

I guess a lot of people automatically would assume that whatever friction existed between my brothers and me grew from my success as a solo artist and later in my partnership with Marie. But that isn't what happened. At the heart of it all was the pressure to keep the machine going, to keep it running perfectly—pressure that came not only from outside, but from within. After every show, we would evaluate what had occurred, but instead of someone saying to me, "Hey, Donny, next time watch your timing on that step you missed tonight," what I got was more along the lines of, "That was terrible!" Although Father always maintained his self-control when it came to discipline, when it came to the act, his comments could take on a harsh tone, and how one person's error had let down the entire group was an oft-repeated point. These lectures never failed to make me feel very guilty. Since my brothers believed that Father's way was the right way, and, in his absence, they filled his role, their comments on my performance were often needlessly abrasive. It was one thing to hear it from Father, but another to get it from guys who were standing on the same stage as I was, making their own little gaffes no one else noticed. One of my brothers would shoot me dirty looks whenever I diverged from the well-rehearsed script. For instance, if someone in the crowd yelled out, "Donny, I love you!" and I replied, "I love you, too," this was a problem. Once, after seeing Elvis Presley leave the stage in Las

Vegas and walk among the tables, I tried it. I was thrilled when the audience loved it. But backstage, I was told, "Don't you ever do anything like that again!"

"But they loved it!" I replied.

"Well, okay, you can do it one more time, but if it doesn't work, then you better not do it again."

"Well, okay," I answered, not totally sure of what the problem was.

Some of my brothers had a habit of jabbing me in the back with a fingernail onstage, which infuriated me. I was really doing the best I could and I silently resented being reprimanded so harshly. One day recently on the set of the new show, Marie jabbed me like that and for an instant, I felt like I'd gone back in time. It was such a strong déjà vu, I surprised myself when I snapped, "Don't ever do that to me again!"

It was around this time that I first experienced what I've since learned to recognize as mild panic attacks. I rarely had a break onstage. In mid-1970s, I began singing and recording with Marie, and between singing with my brothers during the Osmonds portion of the show, singing with Marie during the duet spots, doing a dance routine with Jimmy, and then doing my own songs, it was a rare moment that I wasn't onstage. We were always under pressure, but when I was fifteen or sixteen, it seemed to increase. Sometimes just before going onstage, I'd feel almost a kind of stage fright, which I'd never experienced before. I brushed it off, told myself it was nerves, exhaustion, whatever. I would talk myself out of it and do the show.

I'm sitting in my dressing room on the set of our new show as I write this, which is a funny coincidence, since this is the part of the story where Donny-and-Marie began, professionally speaking. Through the 1960s and early 1970s, Marie had performed with us on occasion. Until "Paper Roses," there was never much discussion of Marie joining the act beyond doing an occasional solo spot or duet with me in our live shows. When we first teamed up, it was in Las Vegas, and we sang "Where Is the Love," the Roberta Flack–Donny Hathaway hit. At the time, it seemed that Marie's role would be much like Jimmy's, a special guest on the show rather than a sixth member of the group. Beginning in 1974, Marie and I began making appearances together, on *The Perry Como Show*, and, in September, *The Mike Douglas Show*, and recording duets, beginning with "I'm Leaving It (All) Up to You," number four in the fall of 1974. Performing together felt so natural to both of us, like we'd just picked up where we left off from our backyard. Except that now we had a real-life version of our old Barbie and Ken shows, *The Donny and Marie Show*.

It started innocently enough on *The Mike Douglas Show*, a ninety-minute syndicated entertainment and talk show featuring a guest cohost (or cohosts) for an entire week. Like Merv Griffin, Mike avoided the heavy issues and controversy. It was entertainment, pure and simple. From his studio in Philadelphia, he presented probably the widest range of guests of any daytime talk show, from Donny and Marie to John Lennon and Yoko Ono. It was a fun show, because you got to do everything: sing a little, help interview other guests, and talk with Mike.

The week that Marie and I cohosted Mike's show, Fred Silverman, then president of ABC, saw us. He thought we'd be naturals to host our own weekly musical variety show. I will never forget the day I was walking down the stairs in the

Here I am onstage, sometime around 1964, at six years old, with my brothers and Andy Williams, not long after I made my debut on Andy's television show. That's Andy to my right and my brother Jay to my left. *(Wolf Studios/Ottawa)*

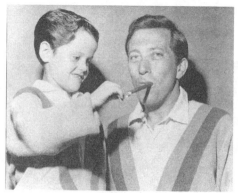

Lighting Andy's cigar wasn't one of the duties specified in our contract, but from 1963 to 1967 he was our boss, and I usually did what I was told. *(Osmond Family Archive)*

Holding the Osmond brothers' first official publicity photo. The historical significance of this is that we are not posed in age order. From left to right: Alan, Merrill, me, Jay, and Wayne. *(Santa Clara County Fairgrounds)*

That's me operating a television camera on Stage 4 in Burbank, where *The Andy Williams Show* was taped. *(Osmond Family Archive)*

In 1967 Jerry Lewis hired the Osmond Brothers to appear as regulars on his show. Over our two seasons with Jerry, I had the most fun playing his character Ralph Rotten's namesake son. Here I am in Jerry's dressing room before a taping. I remember this because that day Jerry gave me a 35-millimeter camera, because, he told me, I reminded him of one of his sons. *(Osmond Family Archive)*

When we opened the show for singer Sergio Franchi in the late 1960s at the Reno Nugget, we had our own opening act: Bertha and Tina the elephants. *(Osmond Family Archive)*

Me and my little brother, Jimmy, in the entrance to the garage in Arleta, California; we had converted it into a rehearsal hall. Here we spent hour upon hour each day, striving to remain "the one-take Osmonds." *(Osmond Family Archive)*

Jimmy and I at home. I spent so many hours singing at this piano, which I grew to hate. But I loved the harmonies my brothers and I sang standing around it. *(Osmond Family Archive)*

ABOVE: On one of the three tours of Sweden our family undertook during the mid-1960s. By then, nothing about traveling the world with seven children in tow (and sometimes eight or nine, if our older brothers Virl and Tom came along) could faze our parents. Left to right: Father, Jimmy, Wayne, Marie, Mother, me, Merrill, Jay, and Alan. *(Osmond Family Archive)*

BELOW: The owners and operators of the imaginary Donarie Hotel: Marie, seven; me, nine; and Jimmy, four. *(Osmond Family Archive)*

The performing Osmonds on tour, with our parents George and Olive Osmond, and (from back to front) Alan, Wayne, Merrill, Jay, me, Marie, and a not very happy Jimmy. *(Osmond Family Archive)*

It was 1969, and we—Jay, me, Wayne, Jimmy, and Merrill (Alan was away doing his basic training)—were performing with Nancy Sinatra at Caesars Palace in Las Vegas. That may explain the outfits. *(Osmond Family Archive)*

What a difference a few months make! This was our press photo around the time our number one hit "One Bad Apple" came out. Left to right: me, Merrill, Alan, Jay, and Wayne. *(Osmond Family Archive)*

In 1971 our recording career was going strong and we could relax a little (at least in photos). Left to right: Alan, Jay, me, Merrill, and Wayne. *(Osmond Family Archive)*

Circa 1972–74 —
the "Puppy Love"
days—we traveled
a lot and napped
when we could.
*(Osmond Family
Archive)*

I've got mail!
My biggest thrill was
receiving a letter in Utah
that a fan had sent from Europe
addressed simply: "Donny Osmond."
By the time this was taken,
around 1973, we had filled
garages with letters, cards,
and gifts from fans
around the world.
*(Osmond Family
Archive)*

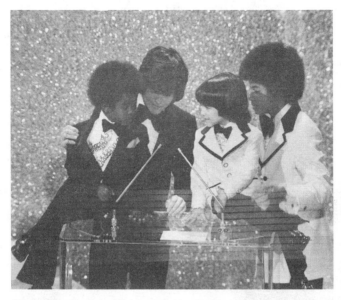

Michael Jackson and I presenting at the first annual American Music Awards show in February 1974, along with child actors Rodney Allen Rippey and Ricky Segall. After the show, Michael and I went out for pizza. *(Donny Osmond Collection)*

The Donny-and-Marie concept was born when ABC-TV president Fred Silverman happened to catch Marie, then fourteen, and me, sixteen, cohosting *The Mike Douglas Show*. Left to right: Mike Douglas, comedian George Kirby, Marie, and me. *(Osmond Family Archive)*

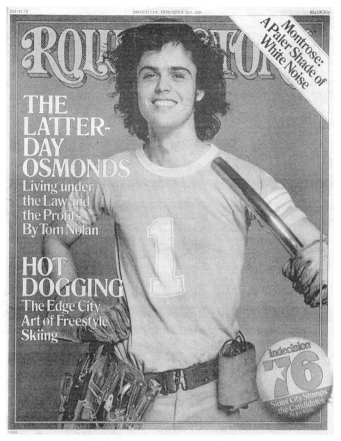

ROLLING STONE

THE LATTER-DAY OSMONDS
Living under
the Law and
the Profits
By Tom Nolan

HOT DOGGING
The Edge City
Art of Freestyle
Skiing

Indecision
'76
Sioux City Stumps
the Candidates

I appeared on the March 11, 1976, cover of *Rolling Stone* magazine wearing exactly what I had on when photographer Annie Leibovitz arrived at our home in Provo: my extremely casual work clothes and a tool belt to die for. *(Photo by Annie Leibovitz, from* Rolling Stone, *March 11, 1976. By Straight Arrow Publishers, Inc., 1976. All Rights Reserved. Reprinted by Permission.)*

Marie and I had a lot of fun doing the original *Donny and Marie Show*, and I think it showed. Clockwise from top: Marie and me as Raggedy Ann and Raggedy Andy, two of hundreds of characters we played; me "separating" Marie in one of our famous magic tricks; the amazing Captain Purple; and me, looking stupid. *(Osmond Family Archive)*

During our first season, we had many interesting guests, including these two chimpanzees. The bigger one went berserk after the first take and climbed up into the lighting grid—but not before he bit me. *(Osmond Family Archive)*

A typical *Donny and Marie Show* finale, complete with dancers and ice skaters. *(Osmond Family Archive)*

Debbie's big scene in the first—and only—Donny and Marie cinematic epic, *Goin' Coconuts*. Fortunately, she's moved on to better roles. *(Lee Sporkin)*

My parents and six of my siblings with Debbie and I at our engagement party in Hawaii. Left to right: Merrill, Jay, Jimmy, Mother, Wayne, Marie, Alan, and Father. *(Lee Sporkin)*

Debbie and I at our wedding reception. Four thousand guests celebrated with us at the Osmond Studios in Orem, Utah, June 1978. *(Photo by Merrett Smith)*

Me, my bride, my purple tuxedo, and a bow tie that could take flight with enough wind. *(Photo by Merrett Smith)*

The wedding party (left to right, back row): Alan, Debbie's brother Michael, Jay, me, Debbie, Debbie's sister Pam, Marie, Jimmy, Tom, Wayne, and Virl; (front row), Father, Mother, Debbie's mother Marge Glenn, and her father Avery Glenn (who looks like someone just handed him the bill). *(Photo by Merrett Smith)*

Professionally speaking, the early 1980s brought some wonderful moments—such as the chance to meet and perform for President Ronald Reagan and First Lady Nancy Reagan—along with a few disappointments. *(Official White House Photograph)*

With the cast of *Little Johnny Jones,* my Broadway debut, which opened and closed the same night in March 1982. *(Martha Swope/© Time, Inc.)*

In 1987—a decade after my last album— I wondered if I'd ever have a hit record again. *(Pat Dresbach)*

Shooting the video for "Sacred Emotion" with director Michael Bay, May 1989. *(Pat Dresbach)*

After "Soldier of Love" went to number two, I hit the road on what I called my "Credibility Tour." *(Terri Priest)*

Onstage during the 1989 tour with bassist Oneida James (left) and guitarist Jon Clark (right). *(Pat Dresbach)*

They all laughed when I got behind the wheel of a race car...but I won the Toyota Pro/Celebrity Grand Prix in April 1991—the first race of my life.
(Cathy Sosa)

I toyed with the idea of becoming a professional race car driver. In October 1991 I flew to England to race at Silverstone. Unfortunately, my clutch gave out and I couldn't finish the race.
(Colin Taylor Productions)

RIGHT: It was all for charity and all in good fun, but I stepped into the ring for my January 1994 three-round bout with Danny Bonaduce with every intention of winning. With my trainer Nick DiPaulo. *(Donny Osmond Collection)*

BELOW: As I like to say, I'm a dangerous kind of guy. Rehearsing for the "Glory of America" Fourth of July Show at Brigham Young University Stadium, in Provo, 1986. To the left, I'm listening to my number on a Walkman so I can practice timing the spins I'll be executing as I fly over the stadium on a cable. Not risky enough, you say? How about attaching burning Roman candles to my feet? Below, Merrill watches me just hangin' around. *(Terri Priest)*

Wearing that loincloth in *Joseph and the Amazing Technicolor Dreamcoat* gave me ample incentive to work out. *(Pat Dresbach)*

One of my favorite parts of each show was singing with the children's choirs. *(Pat Dresbach)*

With producer Garth Drabinsky (left) and composer Sir Andrew Lloyd Webber at the opening night party for *Joseph and the Amazing Technicolor Dreamcoat*, Toronto, 1992. (*©The Toronto Sun. Reprinted with Permission.*)

The reprise of "Close Every Door" during the closing night of *Joseph* in Salt Lake City, March 1998. By then I'd played the role for almost six years and nearly two thousand performances. (*Pat Dresbach*)

Performing with my brothers at the Osmond Family Theater in Branson, Missouri, 1992. Left to right: Jay, Jimmy, me, Merrill, Wayne, and Alan. *(Lori Kerwer)*

And looking back...Alan, Wayne, Merrill, Jay, and I in France, where some considered the Osmonds a heavy-metal band. *(Osmond Family Archive)*

In Branson, October 1997 (left to right): Merrill, Jimmy, me, Jay, Alan, and Wayne. *(Pat Dresbach)*

The George V. Osmond family, circa 1990 (left to right, back row): me, Merrill, Alan, Jay, Tom; (middle row) Wayne, Father, Mother, Virl; Jimmy and Marie. *(Photo by Merrett Smith)*

Debbie and me in Chicago, 1994 *(©Jorie Gracen/ Photo-One)*

Our family, around 1997 (clockwise from left): Don, Brandon, Jeremy, Debbie, Christopher, and me. *(Steve Cox)*

Not quite a year old, our son Joshua, 1998. Even at this tender age, Joshua is a discriminating television viewer. His two favorite shows: *Donny & Marie* and *Teletubbies*. *(Donny Osmond Collection)*

During the taping of my "Sacred Emotion" video, May 1989.
(Pat Dresbach)

Manning Apartments when Marie gave me the news: "They want us to team up and do a television show together!" Everyone was so happy about it. Except me. Of course, I was naturally flattered that Fred had such faith in us. But the first thought that came to my mind was, *Well, there goes my recording career.* And that's exactly what happened.

Now what's kind of ironic here is that around the time all this was happening, *Rolling Stone* magazine decided to put me on the cover and run a feature about the family. I knew that this was a big deal, but I didn't fully appreciate the significance of it until many years later. Photographer Annie Leibovitz arrived at the Riviera Apartments before we expected her, and basically took control. I'm not sure exactly what I was expecting—a makeup person, a hair stylist, some interest in what I planned to wear, a search for the perfect site to shoot. Boy, was I in for a surprise.

When I came downstairs to greet Annie, I was wearing my grubby orange T-shirt emblazoned with a "1," leather work gloves, and my cherished tool belt, which even Tim Allen would envy (and which I still have).

Before I met Annie, I'd wondered how she was able to convince her subjects to do some of the unusual, even crazy, things I'd seen in her photos. Within minutes of shaking her hand, I found out. Standing a good six inches over me, Annie eyed me up and down, then said, "Let's start."

"Well, let me go change," I replied. "I have all these great clothes picked out—"

"No, that's the way I want you, just the way you are."

My family had never met a woman quite as outspoken and confident as Annie, and everyone was wondering what kind of pictures these would be. Someone might have wanted to raise that point, but Annie got in the first word and the last: "Okay, everybody out!"

Annie and her assistant threw together a makeshift studio in a messy storage room right off the pool room that was used for the BYU students in the complex. It was just big enough for the three of us, a backdrop, and a fan, which Annie turned on me full blast. I was beginning to panic a little, because I'd been trained that everything had to be just right. Annie had other ideas. She told me not to comb my hair or change my clothes. She wanted "the real Donny Osmond," the guy who spent his spare time at home crawling through attics and getting electrocuted. Then Annie threw me the biggest curve: "Now, don't smile."

"But I have to smile."

"You're always smiling in pictures. No, Donny, you're not smiling now." Just when I was sure she would never understand me, she revealed how well she really did. "Don't smile, Donny. Just be yourself. Don't even look at the camera." Then she said something funny, I laughed, and that was the shot. My hair was tousled into a wild mane, and for once, I looked like the real Donny instead of a carefully coiffed boy. And for the first time, that smile was really mine, not the perfect, self-conscious one I put on for the cameras before.

chapter5

After a test episode of *The Donny and Marie Show* aired in November 1975, ABC gave us the go-ahead, and on January 16, 1976, our show debuted. At sixteen and eighteen, Marie and I became the youngest hosts of a variety show in prime-time history.

Although musical variety shows were among the most durable in television history, *The Donny and Marie Show* would be one of the genre's last gasps. Despite some mixed feelings I have expressed over the years, I am very proud of that show. I came to appreciate it even more around 1997, when I had to view every single episode to produce *The Best of Donny and Marie* videos. It was truly a labor of love, though I have to admit I wasn't too many hours into it before even I came up with some pretty good teeth jokes.

There wasn't much we wouldn't do to entertain our viewers. And we did it while creating a show that even the youngest child could enjoy. Even though people correctly identified *The Sonny and Cher Comedy Hour* as a stylistic predecessor, the similarities between our show and theirs were purely coincidental. The good-natured teasing that came to define Marie's and my public relationship was just an outgrowth, an exaggeration I'd say, of our real relationship. I think people could sense that we genuinely liked each other and enjoyed working together. And while I was often—a little too often—the butt of the jokes, what I remember most about the four seasons of *Donny and Marie* is how much fun we had.

It was, I admit, good, clean—some would even say corny—fun, a throwback to the kind of wholesome, family-oriented television that we grew up on. Young kids and preteens loved us, and their parents and grandparents thought we were cute. Our younger fans were split between those who wanted to marry me and those who wanted to be just like—or, in the case of boys, date—Marie. But older teenagers hated us, and the fallout from that impacted not only my solo career but the Osmonds' recording career as well. It would be a challenge to win those people over, but I don't think we ever thought we couldn't do it.

It's also safe to say, I think, that for my brothers, hit records were no longer their only priority. By then, all of my brothers except Jay and Jimmy were married, and those who were married had children. They had very sound reasons for not wanting to spend so many months each year on the road. Though we were all in it together, my situation was different from theirs in many ways. The fact was, my teen idol years had cost me my credibility as a singer and a musician. Now that I was older, I had to make a critical change in my music. At the same time, my brothers seemed more interested in pursuing new careers outside of performing. I remember hearing my brothers say that the television show would be good for all of us because we wouldn't have to tour so much or be so dependent on hit records. Well, they had wives and children, so I could understand that. That wasn't the case for me, though no one bothered to ask what I thought. At the time, I remember thinking, somewhat uncharacteristically, *Is this the best decision for me?*

As always, the decision had been made, and from that point forward, I was determined to give it my best. Once we started doing the show, even before we moved the production from Los Angeles to Orem, Utah, in late 1977, Alan, Wayne, Merrill, and Jay were involved behind the scenes. Jimmy appeared on many of the shows with dancing chickens and hippos (I'm sure he'll appreciate my reminding you of that), and our whole family participated in our annual Christmas specials. Even though Marie and I were out front, *Donny and Marie* was very much a family enterprise. In fact, Alan, Wayne, and Merrill oversaw most of the music and even wrote our closing theme, "May Tomorrow Be a Perfect Day."

Marie and I enjoyed working together. If nothing else, the show gave us both, as well as our brothers, a showcase for our talents. We sang, we danced, we joked, we acted, we got thrown into giant cream pies. If touring was the high school of my career, then the television series was where I got my Ph.D. Over the course of three years, we taped sixty-eight episodes of *The Donny and Marie Show*. Not only was *Donny and Marie* a "must-do" appearance for anyone promoting a new film, television series, or record, but we also had the great pleasure to work with some of Hollywood's biggest stars. Bob Hope, Milton Berle, George Gobel, Pearl Bailey, Kate Smith, John Wayne, Andy Griffith, Desi Arnaz, George Burns, Edgar Bergen, Roy Rogers and Dale Evans, Buddy Hackett, Redd Foxx, Lucille Ball, Danny Thomas, as well as two of our former employers—Andy Williams and Jerry Lewis—were among the guests.

One of my favorite guest stars was Groucho Marx—even though his appearance was never broadcast. Our show featured stylishly choreographed dance and ice routines. Of course, the dancers' costumes were on the skimpy side, and Groucho soon revealed himself to be quite the dirty old man. At the time, Groucho was at least eighty-six years old (though with Groucho, you never knew), and he arrived on the set with a nurse who constantly checked his blood pressure. He agreed to do the show on the condition that he could work only as long as his pressure stayed down. Everything seemed to be going smoothly—if you overlook his repeatedly asking Marie embarrassingly personal questions—and we had taped everything except the lavish finale, which was the only segment in which Groucho was to appear. We were in the middle of taping when the effects of Groucho's girl watching drove his blood pressure up into the danger zone, and he had to leave. Of course, everyone was disappointed, including Groucho. It was such an honor to meet him and talk with him, I reconciled myself with the thought that at least we had portions of the finale on tape, to treasure and, maybe, share with the world someday. When I went to get the tape, I learned that some technicians had decided that if Groucho wasn't going to be on the show, we didn't need to waste perfectly good tape that could be erased and recorded over. I couldn't believe it! The tape was gone, and not long after that, Groucho passed away.

One of my other favorite memories was working with Lucille Ball. It wasn't the first time, however. In 1972 I'd played myself—Donny cap and all—in an episode of *Here's Lucy*. I was too young then to appreciate fully what an honor it was to work with such a legend. When I recall what happened when she appeared on *Donny and Marie*, I have to cringe. Part of my job was to produce the prerecorded musical tracks we used, including the finale. Whether a guest was a singer or not, most of them did sing during the finale, and I was supposed to make everyone sound as good as possible. Now, I don't think I'm being disrespectful of Lucy or her great comedic talent when I say she wasn't the greatest singer. Picture this: Me, a teenager, sitting behind the console of our studio in the Manning Apartments basement, directing Lucy as she sang it again and again from inside the bathroom we'd converted to a recording booth. Years of heavy smoking had taken its toll on her voice, and there I was saying things like, "One more time, Lucy, come on. You can do it. That last take was pretty bad," and "Come on, Lucy, you were a little flat there." Boy, who the heck did I think I was? The whole time Lucy took my direction like the consummate pro that she was.

Every star who came on our show had his or her own way of doing things, and we had to adapt. For example, before Bob Hope arrived, our director Art Fisher told us firmly, "Bob's on his way over to the studio now. You've got five minutes to shoot the scene, then he's leaving. He won't stay to do it again. So don't blow your lines." Not too much pressure.

Sure enough, a minute into the skit, one of the straps on

Marie's overalls came unhooked from the bib. I'm sure Marie wanted to stop tape and start again, but there was no way we could. And maybe that was for the best, because it's often true that the first take has a magic you can never recapture, no matter how much you think you're "improving" on it. I know this scene certainly did.

There were so many great, truly funny moments. Milton Berle provided some good-natured ad libs, and staggered around the stage—in drag, of course—brilliantly after Marie whacked him with a giant, powder-packed makeup puff as she yelled his trademark cry from his 1950s show, "Makeup!" Now Milton knew that Marie was going to hit him, but when she actually did, he had no idea what hit him. He playfully pretended to be dazed, but I'm not so sure some of that wasn't real. Of course, having taken a few of Marie's punches myself, I knew exactly how he felt. I probably should have warned him.

Everyone who watched the show remembers Paul Lynde, the arch comedian who became a regular. Paul was a brilliant comedic foil, his urbane sarcasm in dark contrast to our sunny, sometimes not-too-bright characters. One reason Paul was so wonderful in his role was that, for the most part, he really was not acting. As he let everyone know, he hated working with kids, and he didn't care that much for us, either. And Orem, where we taped after the second season, wasn't exactly Paul's idea of a happening place. Once his scenes were in the can, he was out of there.

I have the fondest memories of comedienne Ruth Buzzi, who most of our viewers knew from *Rowan and Martin's Laugh-In*. Ruth was a wonderful person, onstage and off, and there was nothing the writers could come up with that she wouldn't try. In this business, you know that if the cameramen—who have seen everything—are laughing, it's got to be good, and Ruth could always crack them up. When I got married, even Ruth's wedding gift to Debbie and me was funny: a gin decanter marked "lemonade."

And then there was the added perk of getting to meet and work with some very beautiful and talented women, among them: Barbara Eden, Cheryl Ladd, Olivia Newton-John, Peggy Fleming, Debbie Reynolds, Cher, Farrah Fawcett, Karen Valentine, Kristy McNichol, Bernadette Peters, Lola Falana, Suzanne Somers, Rita Coolidge, Jacklyn Smith, Cheryl Tiegs, and Tina Turner.

The Donny and Marie Show was known for its broad, slapstick humor, but in our third season, we took a chance with a serious skit about a father-and-son clown team. In it, my character tries to convince his discouraged, heartbroken father, played by Andy Griffith, not to give up the work that he loves, even though jobs are rare and the clown business is dying. Since most of our creative staff came from comedy backgrounds, Andy (who, long before his weekly sitcom, made his acclaimed film debut in Elia Kazan's *A Face in the Crowd*) helped me immensely. He shared his insights into my character and gave an honest assessment of my performance. I know this skit came as a surprise to a lot of viewers, and I have to give Andy credit for it coming off as well as it did.

Of course, the critics didn't care too much for *The Donny and Marie Show*, but, in our defense, they may have taken it more seriously than we did. Oddly enough, I agreed with them on some points: It was at times too sweet, and sometimes the skits were silly. But, then again, they were supposed to be. The hopelessly clueless Captain Purple, the *American Gothic* dry- and dim-witted

Jedediah, and Zero (from a parody of Zorro in which Tom Jones played the evil, greedy governor) were but three in a never-ending parade of not-so-smart characters I portrayed each week. Even characters known for their cool and savvy became moronic once they were written for me: I played the dumb Lone Ranger (asking Buddy Hackett for his daughter's—Ruth Buzzi's—hand), the dumb Fonzie (opposite Cheryl Ladd and Karen Valentine), and, with Betty White, an Egor who made any Egor before him seem downright brilliant. I'm sure the writers would have found a way for me to make Einstein look stupid if I had the role. Now, to be fair, Marie played her share of air-headed ingenues, beauty queens, and heroines in peril—including my favorite, the recurring "The Perils of Marie." But I was the one who always held up the wrong number of fingers when I counted, the one who took the most pratfalls (despite the fact that I was the better ice skater). Why the "dumb image" stuck to me and not to my sister, I still haven't figured out. And maybe that's why the image stuck. Seriously, though, I'd like to think I'm a pretty good comedic actor. Unfortunately for me, too many people assumed I wasn't acting.

Most of our humor was so over the top that even Marie and I would often crack up. It was a rare skit we finished without one of us breaking out laughing. Sometimes that happened because we or the guests ad libbed, or one of us secretly had the writers sneak something in without telling the other. I think that was part of the show's charm. So much of what some people found corny, we approached with a nod and a wink. We never pretended to be sophisticated, and we never failed to laugh at ourselves. For example, one of my favorite bits had Marie and me pitching The Famous Donny and Marie School of Donny and Marie, a correspondence course that would turn anyone including you—yes, you—into an Osmond in the privacy of your own home. Of course, it included a set of "Osmo chops": extra-large bright and shiny false teeth. Again, I freely admit, there were times when the corn grew a little too thick. I can't count how many articles I've read through the years that allude to our "sanitization" of the Three Dog Night hit "Joy to the World." Even I had a hard time singing about how Jeremiah the bullfrog "always had some mighty fine...milk."

What I loved most about the show was the music. We also had some wonderful musical guests, including Andy Gibb, Tina Turner, Kris Kristofferson, Glen Campbell, Chuck Berry, Olivia Newton-John, K.C. and the Sunshine Band, Barry Manilow, Bo Diddley, Roy Clark, Chubby Checker, and Neil Sedaka. I especially liked doing what we referred to as the concert segment, which came right in the middle of the show. Fortunately for us, we discovered that a songwriter named Marty Cooper had already written "I'm a Little Bit Country, I'm a Little Bit Rock and Roll," but if he hadn't, someone else would have had to. It was just too perfect. For our parts of the concert segment, Marie performed mostly country songs and romantic ballads, and I chose to do the music I loved: songs by Creedence Clearwater Revival, Sly and the Family Stone, the Temptations, Billy Joel, the Edgar Winter Group, and more than any other contemporary artist, Stevie Wonder. At home and in my car, I was more than "a little bit" rock and roll. I loved soul and funk: the Ohio Players, the Average White Band, George Clinton's Parliament Funkadelic, Tower of Power, Earth, Wind, and Fire. I honestly thought that the concert segments would show that, musically speaking, there was more to Donny Osmond than "Puppy Love." If I was wrong, it wasn't for want of trying.

I believe that everything happens for a reason, when it's supposed to, and, looking back, I can see that this was the perfect time for my future wife Debbie to have come into my life. I met Debbie Glenn back in Provo, around 1975, when she was dating my brother Jay. I hadn't been dating seriously for very long, and my love life, if you could call it that, pretty much consisted of as much kissing as I could get away with without going too far. While onstage, I did a pretty good impression of a guy who'd loved and lost, in real life I was a bit of a dating dweeb. Debbie recalled that the first time she ever met me, I was decked out in a burgundy pinstriped suit and platform shoes, "charming" everyone with a series of terrible golf jokes. Smooth, huh?

Before I met Debbie (and even for a little while after, which Debbie found out about by having friends spy on me), my dating strategy involved inviting a girl who was an exceptionally good kisser to come sit with me in our garage, in the old army Jeep Wayne and I had restored. There she would marvel at the great wiring job I'd done on it. Then I'd casually put my arm around her and we'd kiss. And kiss. And kiss. I was so naive, for a while I honestly believed that for the girls, the real attraction was the Jeep!

From the minute I saw her, I thought Debbie was beautiful, with her golden blond hair and hazel eyes. Even though I knew her only casually, I first sensed she was someone I could talk to when we were on a double date—but not with each other. On our way to see an Elton John concert in Salt Lake City, Debbie and I found ourselves talking to each other more than she talked to her date, Jay, or I talked to my date, Tammy. A few weeks later, Jay and I switched; I took out Debbie, and Jay took out Tammy. I can't honestly say it was love at first sight for either Debbie or me. We dated casually for a little over two years before we both knew for sure that we'd found the one. But during that whole time, of all the girls I knew, Debbie was my favorite by far.

The Donny and Marie Show was still taping in Los Angeles, so I could date Debbie only when we happened to be back home. While I was away, Debbie and I started talking on the phone, for hours at a time. She was the first person in my life with whom I felt I could be totally honest, and over time she became my best friend. Even as a high school student, Debbie had a remarkably mature way of looking at the world. She listened to me, and even more important, understood me. It's difficult to express how deeply this affected me. It was as if someone had switched on a light and shown me a place I didn't know existed. Soon after we met, even before we began dating seriously, I began to rely on her, because when I spoke to her, she heard the real me, not that guy everybody else thought they knew.

I guess for some people, this would have been the start of a whirlwind romance. But Debbie was too level-headed and too much her own person to fall head over heels for me. The truth is, she couldn't have cared less about who I was, what I did, what I owned, or how many other girls wanted to go out with me. She was so cool about it, and that just piqued my interest even more. She was still dating another boy when we first met, and there were times I'd call to tell her to say that I was coming to town and she'd say she already had other plans. Maybe I should have taken the hint when I found out that Debbie had David Cassidy's poster pinned on her wall and mine semihidden behind the door, so that people wouldn't see it when they walked in.

But I refused to give up and found ways to endear myself to her—like showing up at her house at 5:30 in the morning, chasing her around her house, and then hitting her in the face with a cream pie. Before too long, we were officially dating. It wasn't really that simple, though. I think it was the day I came to her house and dumped pounds of confetti all over her room, taking particular care to mash it into her shag carpeting that really turned the trick. I suppose that in a way I was testing her and her parents, Avery and Marge Glenn. I knew that if Debbie and I became serious and if we got married, she'd have to have a sense of humor. (After all, I reasoned then, she might be spending the rest of her life as Mrs. Donny Osmond.) Later I learned that through all of this, her parents had become my advocates. Despite the damage I'd inflicted on their carpeting, they still liked me.

Debbie put up with a lot while dating me (and it wasn't all me, either). I learned later that some of the guys at Provo High School were teasing her because we were going out. Once she was walking through a school hallway when she heard my voice singing "Puppy Love"—it was coming from a cassette player that they had pointedly put in a garbage can. A bunch of guys stood around, smirking and laughing. Debbie coolly kept walking. Another time, when I went to visit her at school, some guys actually pelted me with dirt clods and apple cores. It was humiliating, but there was nothing I could do to avoid moments like this unless I became a total recluse. I'd learned very early on that once people form an opinion about you, it's very difficult to turn it around. I was only sorry that Debbie had to suffer because of what some people thought of me. If it bothered her too much, she never let on.

After a couple years, I found myself with an interesting problem. I could tell Debbie everything—except how much I loved her. So I came up with a plan. We had a mutual friend named Paula, who lived at the Riviera Apartments, and she agreed to help me. She invited Debbie over to her apartment, as we planned, and they were talking about me when the doorbell rang. Paula looked out the window.

Feigning surprise, she whispered to Debbie, "It's Donny! Quick! Go hide in my closet."

From inside the closet, Debbie heard me pour out my heart to Paula. "I really love Debbie, but I don't know how to tell her," and so on and so on.

Now, Debbie felt so guilty about having overheard me that during our next date a couple of days later, she confessed, "Donny, I've got to tell you something."

I interrupted her and said, "Debbie, I have something to tell you."

"No, no, I've got to tell you this first. Do you remember when you came over to Paula's place and you started talking about me?"

"Yeah?"

"Well, I was in the closet and I heard every word you said."

"You did what?" I asked indignantly. I'd worked too hard on this scheme not to play it for everything it was worth. I threw in a wide-eyed, hurt expression just for the heck of it. (And they said I couldn't act.)

"I'm so sorry," Debbie said softly, and I knew she really was.

I didn't answer right away, and I could tell she was getting a little bit nervous when I said brightly, "Well, guess what? I set the whole thing up."

Debbie gave me a quizzical look.

"You see, I knew you were in the closet. That's the best way I could figure out to tell you how I really feel about you."

For an instant Debbie looked as if she didn't know whether to slap me or hug me (a look I've come to know quite well over the years). That was the beginning of our courtship and the marriage that we share today.

It was also the beginning of a new life for me. So much happened during the years of *The Donny and Marie Show* that I felt much older than I was and more isolated than ever before. Maybe it was realizing that what would have been my high school years were now gone forever, or the fact that I'd fallen in love with Debbie, but something made me sit back and take stock. By any measure of success, I had accomplished so much, and yet I felt very much alone. I'd never have seen it then, but looking back now, I know that without Debbie, I could have easily become an emotional recluse.

I'd grown up under pressure all my life, but with the television series, it seemed there was so much more. At an age when most teenagers' worlds are expanding, mine seemed to be shrinking by the minute. Jay, Jimmy, and I shared an apartment at Manning when we were in L.A., and they both saw me become more withdrawn. I couldn't go anywhere or do anything without being stared at, and, even worse, people—even members of my extended family and people I'd known all my life—acting strangely around me. They smiled more, they talked louder, whatever I said or did was "great." I knew it wasn't real, and yet

I didn't know how to stop it. I felt like I was on a loud, whirling merry-go-round that I had to get off but couldn't.

If I'd let myself, I might have felt depressed, but I had more control than that. In those days what I felt, what I feared, what I wanted—I couldn't let them matter. I literally had no feelings. Or if I did, I saw them as threatening, something best ignored, because—as I'd learned when I wrote that letter to Mother from Sweden—feelings were dangerous and expressing them could only lead to trouble. Though my parents never consciously set out to teach me that, between Mother's eternal optimism and Father's constantly striving to please other people, I learned that cheerfully putting the needs of others ahead of my own was not only an admirable thing to do but the only thing to do. And when a dark thought crossed my mind, all I had to do was concentrate on the task ahead—the show, the song, the step, the fans, the press—and it would go away. I learned to surmount problems or go around them without ever taking the time to find out what those problems were.

Under these conditions, the average kid would have rebelled. But the average kid wasn't constantly reminded of how his selfish behavior could set off a chain of events culminating in financial ruin for himself, his siblings, his parents, and a small army of people who worked for or with them. Most of these were people I didn't know, or corporate entities for whom Donny Osmond was product. Run away? I was so emotionally crippled, that thought didn't even cross my mind. I began to feel that I had to get out from under the tremendous pressure, but I didn't even have the capacity to imagine walking away.

I had managed to smother my emotions until one day when I was about seventeen. I was in Hawaii, in our family's condo on

Oahu with Jay, when suddenly I felt myself overcome with such sadness and despair, all I could do was lie on the floor, huddled in the corner in a fetal position and cry like a baby. It seemed to come out of nowhere, and I felt a fear I'd never known. I thought I was losing my mind as my thoughts richocheted around my head like pinballs. Because I had so much in my life, I believed I didn't have the right to feel unhappy or dissatisfied. If I was unhappy, well, what was wrong with me? Millions of people would do anything to be in my shoes. Who was I to complain? Who did I think I was? It was as if someone had drawn a line separating what I was supposed to feel and what I really felt, then split me in two across it.

"I can't take it," I screamed between sobs. "I just want to be me—not all this showbiz stuff!"

Jay and I were very close then, and I'll never forget the look of concern and compassion on his face when he said, "Something's got to change."

He was right, but the question was, What? Jay and I sat and talked for a long, long time, about how we had to step outside ourselves and separate the public image from who we really were. He told me that I had the power, in my own mind, to not see myself the way other people saw me, to not let myself be turned into a commodity.

Of course, I pulled myself together, then wondered, *What is wrong with me? How could I let my emotions get so out of control?* Back in those days, the real Donny was no match for the entertainer Donny. And the entertainer in me would somehow manage to hold the lid on my fears and anxieties for many years to come.

Even then, Debbie found the real Donny and started the long, arduous task of digging him out. I realized later that one reason our relationship worked so well is that to Debbie, I was really just Donny the person. She knew of the records, and she'd probably seen me on television a few times, but she wasn't a fan in the usual sense of the word. In fact, we dated for quite a while before she ever saw me perform. The night she did, however, was one I'll never forget.

First, I have to explain a few things. It was hard for me to meet girls. No matter how confident I appeared onstage, in my real life, I was rarely any place where I could talk to a girl under "normal" circumstances. Once I became interested in girls, I used my vantage point onstage to pick out nice girls to meet. If a girl in one of the front rows caught my eye, I'd describe her to our road manager Mas or point her out from the wings, and he'd go into the audience and invite her to come backstage to meet me. I enjoyed talking to girls, and sometimes we'd exchange phone numbers and pictures, or I'd give them a special code to put on the envelope if they wrote to me. The person who handled the fan mail knew the code, so any envelope with it came directly to me. I still remember some of those letters, which I would carry around with me and reread when I was alone. I suppose they meant so much to me because in them, girls would write about the time we'd spent together, something that was real. Usually neatly written on pastel stationery, sometimes with photographs enclosed, these were different from the usual fan mail, which often arrived heavily perfumed on paper covered with exclamations of love and "x"s and "o"s. From these fans, I had amassed a collection of handmade beaded and macrame bracelets big enough to fill a garage. I carried around in my wallet dozens of photographs of girls I barely knew. These meant a lot to me then.

Once it was clear that Debbie and I were getting serious, her parents treated her to a trip to Las Vegas to see the Osmonds perform at the Hilton. I loved performing there, because whenever we did, I got to stay in Elvis Presley's suite, which was about the coolest thing you could imagine. Since 1973 or so, my family had gotten to know Elvis just a little. Not too many people realize that Elvis read everything he could find on different religions and spiritual beliefs. When he met us, he immediately sensed that Mother was someone he could talk to, and talk they did. Most people know that Elvis was very close to his mother, who died when he was a very young man, and he enjoyed talking to older women who were mothers themselves or who took care of others.

Elvis had read *The Book of Mormon: Another Testament of Jesus Christ*, and he would spend quite a bit of time asking Mother intelligent, thought-provoking questions about its teachings. Despite his fame, Elvis seemed like a lonely man. I remember all of us bunched around the extension phones, trying to hear what Elvis and Mother were talking about. A few months before he died, in fact, at about the same time Debbie came to Las Vegas to see us, Mother recalls asking Elvis, "Is it true what I've read, that if you weren't in show business, you wanted to become a minister?"

Elvis replied, "Absolutely. I wanted to be a minister, and that's where my true passion is. I'd really like to sit down and talk to you about your religion. The next time you're in Vegas, come over to the house and we'll have barbecue steaks in my backyard."

Mother accepted the invitation, but, sadly, Elvis died before we got together again. Some years later, Elvis's father

Vernon gave his son's copy of *The Book of Mormon* to my brother Alan. Throughout the book, in the margins, Elvis had written notes to himself, including in several places, "Lisa [meaning his daughter Lisa Marie] must read this." Alan kept it in his home for a while, but when so many people expressed interest in seeing it, he gave it to the Church for safekeeping.

I loved being in Elvis's suite, because it was Elvis's. I would play his gold grand piano and jump on his bed. One thing about the bed I'll never forget is how moths, drawn to the upper floors by the neon signs at the top of the hotel building, would hide in the sheets. Before you went to sleep, you'd have to wiggle your feet around to get the moths to fly out.

But I digress. Standing backstage, knowing that Debbie was out in the audience, I became so nervous, it was almost funny. I had done this a thousand times, and from the stage flirted with a million girls, but this was so different. Later, Debbie told me that when I first hit the stage, she couldn't believe that the guy up onstage was the same Donny she was falling in love with. It was a magical show, for both of us, and afterward, I invited her up to my family's—I mean, Elvis's—suite. Now, you know me well enough by now to know what wasn't going to happen, but that didn't keep it from being one of the most romantic nights of my life. Later, on Elvis's piano, I wrote two songs for Debbie, "Fly into the Wind" and "I'm Sorry" (both on *Donald Clark Osmond*, from later that year). I was always amazed at how much time Debbie and I were allowed to spend alone together. Obviously, our parents trusted us. Or didn't know we were together. I'm not sure which.

As news of our relationship got out, it was only a matter of time before Debbie found herself facing reporters and cameras.

I knew she'd lose her privacy and some of her freedom. I tried, in my way, to give her an idea of what it might be like for her, and I tried to protect her as much as I could. Still, she was regularly followed and sometimes harassed by reporters and photographers. Debbie always stayed very calm and tried hard not to let it bother her, but I know it had to be tough sometimes.

Periodically, members of the media would arrive in Provo like the advance team of an invasion. We'd hear through the grapevine that one of the tabloids or magazines was in town, tracking us down, and soon I started making a game out of eluding them. I wanted so desperately to take Debbie out on a date, but we were "under siege," so once I borrowed Mother's or Marie's curlers, set my hair in tight curls, and slept in them overnight (and you think I'm not tough). I woke the next morning with quite the impressive Afro, glued on a fake mustache, put on dark glasses and a trenchcoat, then asked Debbie to meet me at Brigham Young University. At first Debbie didn't recognize me (or so she pretended). I looked ridiculous, but we had a great date, and while people probably did notice me, they didn't recognize me. (Well, at least I hope they didn't.)

In the fall of 1977, we taped the last episode of *The Donny and Marie Show* we'd produce from Los Angeles, packed up the whole family, and moved back to Utah. For the next few years, everything we did, including the show, would literally be "home-made"—home being Orem, Utah, where the George V. Osmond Studios were dedicated on November 1, 1977. It had been only six months since a gala ground-breaking ceremony, where 1,100 guests—including local and state officials—saw, among other things, Marie driving a team of Clydesdale horses, skydivers and purple socks falling from the sky, and me digging the first hole with a Caterpillar frontloader. We had the gold records, the sold-out tours, *The Donny and Marie Show*, our family name. But the most tangible symbol of our togetherness was the multimillion-dollar, 104,000-square-foot studio complex. Everything we needed to produce the show was right there: a 24,000-square-foot sound stage, rehearsal space, editing facilities, a recording studio, and offices.

I've been asked thousands of times, "Why Orem?" If you'd asked that question of anyone in my family, we'd probably have responded, "Why not?" There's nothing a Hollywood studio could offer that we couldn't re-create in Utah, we thought. And almost every year, there were even more reasons—in the form of my nieces and nephews—for my brothers to want to go home. The cold truth of it is that for a number of reasons, many of them resulting from choices we had made, the Osmonds were considered "outsiders" in Hollywood. Our values, our religious beliefs, and our image set us apart. We weren't living the "Hollywood lifestyle," so why be there if we didn't have to? We may have had homes in L.A., but our hearts were in Utah. Especially as my brothers' children got older, Utah seemed the place to be.

More than that, though, Father had a dream. For years, we had saved and invested, foregoing most of the ostentatious trappings. Now, we believed, we would channel what we'd saved into a business venture that would support not only ourselves, but perhaps our children and their children someday. It was ambitious and, some people outside our family believed, a bit unrealistic, but that's not what any of us were thinking then. We recognized the possible disadvantages but reasoned we could overcome them. By then, we had disproved too many naysayers to start listening to them now.

In mid-November 1977, Marie and I taped the first Orem-produced episode of *The Donny and Marie Show*. Considering the importance of the move, I was surprisingly nonchalant about it all. The only part I really cared about was the audio recording studio: I had helped design it and wired the console once it was completed. I spent a lot of time in that studio, because it was where I felt most at home. It was the place where I assumed I'd record my future albums. My job, and Marie's, was to be out front, to keep the show going, and when the show was on hiatus from production, to be out performing live. Partially because of that, I suppose I didn't have quite the same emotional investment in the Osmond Studios as my older brothers, who now helped run it, in addition to producing the show. Once when I was very young, I'd casually asked my brothers, "How much do we get paid for a show?" I needed to be set straight only once; I never bothered asking again. With Father at the helm, I felt secure that everything was under control.

The Donny and Marie Show was in its third season, and we were number one in our time slot. It is amazing now to look back and see how much Marie and I had grown up in just two years. This was especially true of Marie. She was always beautiful, and her new sophisticated style made her a national trendsetter and a role model for young women everywhere. Like all brothers and sisters, Marie and I had our moments, but I loved working with her. In the best moments, I felt we were in the backyard in Arleta again, the best of pals. The big difference now, however,

was that Marie wasn't as likely simply to go along with everything I said.

I came to the first season of the show feeling very much
that I was the older brother and the boss. What I didn't learn
until right after Marie and I began working on our current
show—over twenty years after the fact—is that Marie felt that
everyone working on the show was comparing her to me. I had
no idea it was going on then, and, looking back, I have no reason to doubt her, because comparing one sibling to the other
was something that went on in our family. For instance, when I
joined the group, I was compared to Jay; when Wayne assumed
control while Alan was in basic training, we compared him to
Alan; at the start of the show, Marie was being compared to me.
(Maybe this explains why those "playful" stomach punches
packed such a wallop!)

Into the second season, Marie began to really come into
her own, and I found myself facing the fact that my little sister
was becoming a mature young woman who didn't necessarily
need to know what her big brother thought before she made up
her mind. By the third season, Marie and I were still working
together beautifully, but behind the scenes, we were each trying
to carve out and define our own positions. When I think about
it now, I can see that I was probably threatened by all the
changes then. I wanted Marie and Jimmy to look up to me and
heed what I said the way I listened to my older brothers. Unlike
me, however, Marie asked questions and spoke her mind. At the
time it confused me. I couldn't understand why we just couldn't
be the way we were before. Why couldn't Marie be a little more
like me and just go with the program? What's funny now is that

when I look back over what she and I have been through, both together and separately, I realize that maybe I should have been a little bit more like Marie.

Over four seasons of a television series, we saw about as much of each other as we cared to. And as if we didn't spend enough time together at the studio or on the road, we still lived together in the same house. The real miracle here is not that we had our run-of-the-mill disagreements but that we managed to remain close after all these years anyway. Now, before you get the wrong idea, Marie and I never really fought about anything. And maybe that was the problem. Neither of us ever felt comfortable expressing our feelings, and particularly not "negative" ones. We both held it inside and put on a happy face, as if everything were fine. That's not to say Marie hasn't done some things I felt angry about, and know I've gotten on her nerves, too. Years later, I recall once being on tour with her and getting so upset I put my fist through a wall.

I've played a lot of pranks on my siblings, but by far the worst was directed at Marie. Jimmy, Marie, and I were performing at the Hilton without the brothers. If you saw the original *Donny and Marie Show*, you saw some of the magic tricks we'd been incorporating into our act. One of my favorite illusions involved Marie standing inside a box that was divided into two sections that were hinged. Each section had a door, which I could open to show that Marie was inside, and each section could be moved, so that it would appear that Marie's upper half was to the right or left of the rest of her. Of course, it was a trick, and I'm not going to give away the trick except to say that the time Marie spent in the box was uncomfortable, to say the least.

The magic trick immediately preceded the "I'm a Little Bit

Country, I'm a Little Bit Rock and Roll" segment, and I was supposed to put Marie back together again, let her out of the box,
and go right into the song. Well, that's what was supposed to
happen. I don't know what got into me, but one night, I just did-
n't bother to "realign" Marie or let her out of the box. What a
pro, though. She did the whole number, which was not only
uncomfortable for her, but boring for the audience. Me? I stood
in the wings, laughing at the sight of my sister singing "Paper
Roses" with one part of her on one side of the stage, and the other
someplace else. When it was time for my portion, I wheeled her
offstage, and sang my numbers. When she returned to join me,
our eyes met and I knew I was a dead man. When the curtain
came down, she and Father were furious, and rightfully so.

As anyone who's seen us working together knows, however, nothing gets by Marie. Some years later, we were performing
and I guess I'd done something to upset her because when we got
to "I'm a Little Bit Country," she sang all of my parts as well as
her own. Over the years, she has duct-taped me to the luggage
rack of a bus, duct-taped my head to an airplane snack tray while
I was sleeping, and masterminded our band's rolling me up in a
carpet and stranding me in an elevator. Touché.

There were some serious moments, too. When you're that
young, you don't always appreciate how much someone means
to you. For me, that realization hit one night on a highway in
Utah. During the year *Donny and Marie* taped in Los Angeles, the
whole family would drive back to Utah on breaks in what other
drivers probably assumed was a Mercedes parade. We were all
tired and anxious to get home quickly. Father drove a van pulling
a trailer, Marie followed with Mother in her car, then Merrill,
then Alan in our mobile home, then me. Everyone was driving

too slowly for me, of course, so I passed them and stopped in the next town, Nephi, to wait.

Not long after I left, Father looked in his rearview mirror and noticed Marie swerving. Figuring she must have been falling asleep at the wheel, he slowed down, signalled, and eased the van onto the shoulder of the highway. Exhausted, Marie just followed Father, probably assuming he was on the road, and slammed her car into the back of the trailer.

After I'd waited about half an hour, I started to get nervous. It wasn't like they could have taken an alternate route; they had to come through town. I headed back and my heart stopped when, from a distance, I saw all the vehicles parked along the shoulder, except Marie's. Slowing down as I got closer, I could see that Marie's car had obviously hit something, and the windshield on the passenger side was cracked. At that moment, I saw my brothers carrying Mother into our mobile home, and I was overtaken with fear that she was dead. And then I saw Marie, crying, her face all cut up and bloodied. I stopped my car and ran to them. An ambulance arrived and took them both to the hospital, where they were treated—Mother for broken ribs and a bruised heart, Marie for cuts. To this day, I can't hear an ambulance siren without thinking back to that horrible night.

As the Osmond Studios grew, the family's business ventures seemed further and further removed from the only business we really knew, show business. We certainly had the ability and the means to turn out quality product. Take our first feature film, *The Great Brain*, a children's movie based on a popular book. Jimmy starred in the title role and was well received by critics and audiences. But it soon became clear that perhaps we weren't always the best judges of commercial potential. In terms of my solo career, I'll say just two words: *Disco Train*. This album—which I refuse to let my children see—featured a cover that now seems eerily prophetic. There I am standing on railroad tracks, decked out in a purple-sequined top hat, purple rhinestone sneakers, and white mirrored cape, happily pounding a white grand piano, oblivious of the steam locomotive bearing down on me. If only it had hit me before I recorded "I Follow the Music (Disco Donny)," "Disco Dancin'," or "Disco Train."

As for my nascent film career, here's another two words sure to strike terror in the heart of anyone who's ever witnessed it: *Goin' Coconuts*. That title says more about how the first—and last—Donny and Marie movie came to be than I care to remember. I must have been psychic, because I had a bad feeling about *Goin' Coconuts* from the start. But true love and the prospect of Debbie joining me and my family in Hawaii during the filming won me over (and later you'll see why).

The whole Osmond family continued to perform concerts when the show wasn't taping, and the audiences were as large and as warm as ever. But something had changed. Now the hits we sang weren't quite so new, and the new songs we sang weren't always hits. All of our fans had begun to grow up, and at least on the record charts, my time in the revolving door of teen idoldom was running out. The Bay City Rollers, David Cassidy's younger half-brother Shaun, and the Bee Gees's little brother Andy were the new pinup boys. After a few solo hits, Michael had returned to his place among the Jacksons—and would soon leave everyone in the dust with *Off the Wall* in 1979.

In addition to my solo recordings and those done with my brothers, I recorded many duets with Marie. Despite the massive weekly television exposure, we placed no singles on the charts in 1977, and in 1978 two just squeaked into the Top 40: a cover of the Righteous Brothers' "(You're My) Soul and Inspiration" and "On the Shelf," from *Goin' Coconuts*.

I was sorry to admit that the prediction I made on that staircase—that television would kill my recording career—proved true, and not only for me but for Marie as well. It also hurt the Osmond Brothers, though there the problem was underexposure rather than overexposure. In my short lifetime, I'd seen my family go through this cycle enough times that it gave me an almost cockeyed optimism. Sure, we weren't selling records, but there was always the next release. Something was bound to happen. I mean, I'd worked hard enough, right?

I had a great deal on my mind, so I retreated to my other at-home "hideaway," the basement recording studio in the Riviera Apartments. Unlike the makeshift one we had at Manning in L.A., this was a true state-of-the-art 16-track facility. I had a special affection for the studio, since at age fourteen, I singlehandedly wired the eight-foot-long Harrison console myself (much to the amazement of everyone). It was here I'd retire to spend hours sitting at my Arp 2600 synthesizer, or take safety copies of our master tapes and rerecord the keyboard parts, just for fun.

I had been thinking about Debbie, a lot. Debbie made me so happy, because by loving me, she gave me permission to think about what I wanted to do for myself, rather than what I should be doing for other people. I wanted to marry Debbie, but every time the thought entered my mind, I'd suddenly start playing devil's advocate, trying to see both sides of the issue—as if my private life were a career decision, like which song to record or which costume to wear. This ability to examine every aspect of a situation and respond with logic rather than emotion was one I had learned too well and leaned on too much. Whatever fears and feelings I really had couldn't last long enough for me to act on them. But now I really wanted something for myself: I wanted to marry Debbie. Would the screaming stop? Would my recording career end? How would this affect *The Donny and Marie Show*? My brothers? My parents? The people who worked for us? I couldn't say, but the track record for married teen idols was not encouraging. If I didn't love her as much as I did, and if I didn't have my emotional defenses down for once, I could have very easily talked myself out of getting the only thing I ever really wanted.

We were back home in Provo late one night when Mother came down to the studio looking for me. I was sitting at the console, staring into space, and she asked, "What's the matter, Donny?"

"Mother, I'd like to get married," I answered softly. "I really love Debbie, but I'm afraid that it would break things up, and it would ruin our show business career and everything we've worked for." Mother listened but said nothing. "I just can't ask Father. I know Father wouldn't want me to do this."

"How old are you?"

"Nineteen."

"Well, when you're old enough to ask your father, then you'll be old enough to get married," she said, with a smile.

She was right. I ran up the stairs, found Father, and nervously asked him.

"I don't know a nicer girl you could marry than Debbie," he replied.

Now, there was only one more person I had to ask: Debbie. My parents were wonderful. They convinced Debbie's parents to let her come with us to Hawaii, so that I could propose to Debbie in front of the Latter-day Saints Temple there. Everyone, including Debbie, pretty much assumed that the real reason for the trip was not Debbie's film debut (she had a cameo toward the end of *Goin' Coconuts*), but my official marriage proposal. I had the rings, and I wanted to do it the old-fashioned way. I knelt down on one knee before her, popped the question, and she said yes. It was a magical moment, despite the small group of people who watched us from inside the temple, and the fact that we had to hurry and get back to the set.

When I think about how fortunate Debbie and I have been to share the marriage and the family that we have today, I have to credit our families and our faith. It was around that time that I underwent a very personal spiritual experience that, for lack of a better term, confirmed for me that my faith is true and right. That didn't mean that living by our teachings was always easy, and my career certainly put a lot more temptation in my way than I would have faced otherwise. We believe that one important aspect of eternal marriage is the sacred nature of the relationship between husband and wife. Part of what makes that relationship unique and so special is that both partners agree that sexual relations will wait until marriage.

Now, think back to the time in which I grew up. Especially being in show business, regardless of how well sheltered we were, you couldn't escape the impression that "everybody" was doing it, and if you weren't, well, what was wrong with you anyway? But I never did. This fact recently had Howard Stern absolutely tongue-tied when I revealed on his radio show that I was a virgin when I married. "This is an incredible story....This is so unbelievable!" Howard gasped. "Steven Spielberg just said, 'I'll believe E.T., but I don't believe this!'" Poor Howard! I wonder if he ever recovered.

Howard's reaction—a mix of incredulousness and, I think, admiration—didn't surprise me, though. During the 1970s, many people felt basically the same way. I can't tell you how many people in the business told me that if I lived a promiscuous life, if the media could report that I wasn't such a good little boy now, it would really help my image. There were willing girls to be found wherever I went, and when I think back to how easily I could have strayed from what I felt was right—and, believe me, I was a very normal teenage boy—I have to hand it to my parents again. I suppose I could have done those things and no one would have been the wiser, but my parents also taught us that you can't have it both ways—you can't be a hypocrite in your heart. Even more than that, I always believed that I would find the perfect wife. I really believed that, to quote one of my hits, when I fell in love, it would be forever. And I truly believe that.

We returned from Hawaii and started planning the wedding. We'd set a date in early June, but from the moment we announced our engagement, the media simply would not leave us alone. Seeing this, Alan came up with a great idea. Why not move the wedding ahead so that Debbie and I could honeymoon at the Hilton in Las Vegas, where our family was to perform for three weeks? Of course, it would be a Temple wedding, which is a very simple and highly spiritual ceremony. A Temple marriage is distinguished from any other type, because in addition to the marriage for time in this mortal life, there is a sealing together for eternity. In order to receive this ordinance, both partners must live in accordance with the teachings of the Church. To be married and sealed in the Salt Lake City Temple held additional significance for both of us, since both Debbie's parents and my own were married there. Although I'm always happy to speak about my beliefs, there are certain ordinances that I don't speak of publicly, because I feel they are sacred. Our wedding in the Temple is one of those. Let me just say, May 8, 1978, was the most joyous day of my life.

Traditionally, the wedding is followed by a large reception for the extended family and friends, but since we were set to open at the Hilton, ours would take place when we returned three weeks later. Debbie and I went straight from our wedding to the airport, where a private jet waited to take us to Las Vegas. Up until then, we had managed to protect our privacy, but once we were married, the media's gloves came off, and so did some fans'. The shows in Las Vegas had been sold out, and we expected to play to full rooms every night. Instead, to "protest" my marriage, some fans simply didn't turn up. Some nights the room was only half-full, and that hurt. Later I heard that some fans held parties where they burned records and pictures of me. One night right before curtain, a stagehand remarked, "Yeah, well, your marriage will last about six months." Was that what the world really thought? Apparently, some did.

It wasn't too long after our wedding that Debbie saw a tabloid article that said our marriage would never last, because she'd just married me for my money, or something along those lines. Tears rolled down her cheeks as she asked me, "Honey, how can they write this sort of thing? It's not true!"

I knew something like this would happen, and I knew I

couldn't stop it. "Debbie, this is your first experience with this, but you've got to have a shell," I told her. "You know why you married me, and you know what our relationship is about. It doesn't matter what anyone else says." Of course, what I didn't say then was that it was probably still going to hurt sometimes. Since then, Debbie's endured a lot. Around 1991, tabloid reporters rang our doorbell in Utah to ask her if it was true that I was having an affair with actress Crystal Bernard, who was just a friend. Debbie simply faced them down and said, "No it's not true. And will you please leave."

Three weeks later, when the run ended, we hosted a beautiful reception. When we were planning the reception, Debbie mentioned that she had her heart set on the color blue.

"Blue?" I asked. "No, we're having a purple wedding."

"Purple?" she replied. "You've got to be kidding me!"

"But, Debbie, I've got to wear my purple tux." Yes, I'm sorry to say, there is such a thing, and I had one.

"You're not serious, are you?" Maybe Debbie didn't know me *that* well, after all. By then, my purple fixation had become a little too intense. I guess I could always blame Marie and Mother, since they were the ones who bought me dozens of pairs of purple socks (which actually saved me many hours combing through the laundry basket). Around that time, though, I began to develop an obsession with my purple socks. I know that to the world, my purple socks have become a long-running joke, but the truth is, I felt that I literally could not leave my house without them on. If I ever had to go out wearing another color, I felt weird, incomplete, as if I'd left some part of me behind. You could say that the purple socks were so much a part of my public image that in some way my feelings made sense. But that doesn't explain my irrational sense of discomfort at just the thought of wearing a different color. I couldn't imagine not being the man everyone associated with those socks, and so they became like magical talismans to me, objects with the power to ward off my own self-doubts and insecurities. On one level, I could see the toll this was taking on me, even though I hadn't yet heard the term "obsessive-compulsive disorder." But I couldn't find the strength to let it go, at least not on my own, and not yet. I had to wear my purple socks all the time. One of the few times I didn't wear them was during our Temple wedding, because traditionally you acknowledge the sacredness of the ceremony by wearing white, to symbolize purity.

Debbie understood this (maybe "tolerated" is really the word). We compromised and made our colors purple and pink, and I did wear my purple tux, although it was a very, very dark purple, so it wasn't as garish as it might sound. It was a wonderful reception—four thousand people showed up—and we received truckloads of beautiful gifts. But when we set up our new home in the Riviera Apartments, we had to go out and buy a toaster. Most newlyweds get at least two, but we got none. I guess no one imagined that Donny Osmond would want one.

For all that we had in common, Debbie and I came from very different worlds. Our first challenge was deciding which of those worlds we would live in as a couple, and which we would raise our children in. Were our children going to live as I'd seen so many children of celebrities live, far removed from normal experiences simply because they had a famous parent? Or were they going to grow up to be just like everyone else? Debbie could see that as great as my life was in many ways, there was something missing. She was also wise enough to know that our love alone wasn't going to fill that void. Something had to change, and it had to be me. She loved me enough to see that I needed to break out of my own shell, to become, as she would say, "normal." Until we were married, I never realized how much I depended on my family for everything, to a degree that was at times excessive. No matter where each of us in my family ever were, the others always knew what they were doing and where they could find them. This seemed natural to me. A few months later, when Debbie I and took a second, real honeymoon, we decided to drive up through Oregon, Idaho, and Wyoming, to visit some of Debbie's relatives. Without giving it a second thought, I phoned Father and Mother and gave them our itinerary, in case they needed me or wanted me to come back for anything, and to get their permission.

When I hung up the phone, Debbie said, "Excuse me, Donny, but we're married now. When are you going to take control of your own life?"

For a moment, I wasn't sure quite how to respond. At first, I couldn't even see the problem, but Debbie wanted me to let go, to stand on my own, and to think for myself. Boy, did she have her work cut out for her. Looking back, I can see that she came into my life at the perfect moment, because I was headed in some strange directions. For one thing, my perfectionism was edging toward the extreme. Now, some perfectionism is essential for any performer, because so much of your success depends on establishing and maintaining control, over your performance, the stage, the audience, everything. Part of learning the craft of performance is learning to fear the unexpected occurrence, the wrong note—the moment that escapes your control. Show business is full of performers known for their extreme, some might say even pathological, perfectionism, and it's no surprise, really. Watching myself in the mirror in Arleta, just barely six years old, I had already begun the process of mentally picking myself apart so I could anticipate, address, and hopefully avoid anyone else ever seeing my flaws.

By the time Debbie met me, that way of thinking had become so ingrained, I was embarking on one campaign after another to perfect myself through sheer willpower. I'd decided I'd eat only healthy food, and in my black-and-white world, there was no room for moderation. It was all or nothing. I would deprive myself of foods I loved, vowing to never again eat things like Mars candy bars, Oreo cookies, and potato chips. There's nothing wrong with wanting to maintain a better diet, but the problem was the thinking behind it and the extremes to which I'd go. It all hit me one day when, during my anti-potato-chip phase, Debbie and I were invited to dinner at a friend's home. We were served a casserole topped with crushed potato chips. As the plate was set before me, I looked up at Debbie in a near-panic. What was I going to do?

She looked me square in the eye and said quietly but firmly, "Donny, give it up and start acting like a normal person."

Shortly after Debbie and I got married, that fall *Goin' Coconuts* premiered to a less than enthusiastic reception, and *The Donny and Marie Show* began what would be its last season. Midway through, in January 1979, the show was retitled *The Osmond Family Show* and lasted only through that spring. The whole family traveled to England for what would be our last truly successful tour there. Nothing was like it used to be, it seemed. While there was no one single event that I can point to and say, "That's it: That's where it all started going bad," I had a vague sense that things weren't as they should be. Marie, Jimmy, and I were somewhat insulated from the business side of things. It wasn't that I didn't want to understand why we suddenly owned three jets and had expanded to include Osmond Films, Osmond Television, Osmond Entertainment (through which Alan and Merrill produced events at Ronald Reagan's first inauguration), even Osmond Sports Management. Sports management? Yes, sports management. And my brothers had planned to build a small community on a hill, where we would each live with our families on a street named Osmond Lane. A few of my brothers built their dream homes there, but I never did. The first home Debbie and I owned had belonged to one of the family's corporate advisers and came complete with holes in the walls and a mortgage. Until that time, I didn't even know what a mortgage was. Why I had to have a mortgage was a question I wouldn't have the answer to for another couple years.

One image always sticks in my mind, especially after the show ended, when Marie and I spent a lot of time on the road. For convenience, we had a gas pump on the studio property. There was also a beautiful speedboat we owned that I would have loved to take out more often, if I ever had the time. I remember watching as the outsiders who'd come in to run the businesses filled their gas tanks for free, and their children borrowed the speedboat whenever they felt like it. Usually I'd see this as I was on my way to the airport for another string of one-nighters, and it made me so angry. *Was this what I was working for?* I wondered.

With *The Donny and Marie Show* over, I was looking forward to taking time off and concentrating on Debbie and our family.

On July 31, 1979, our first child, Donald Clark Osmond Jr., was born. At twenty-one, I had a wonderful wife and a beautiful son. As I held him for the first time, a sense of peace that I'd never known came over me. This was a moment I'd looked forward to for so long, and it was every bit as miraculous and awe-inspiring as I'd imagined. The love I felt for him was a different love, a perfect love that made the world seem like a new and wonderful place.

It was a wonderful time for us. It felt great not to have to work as much as I had on the TV show. I didn't have a television contract or a record deal, but I still felt safe. There were always concerts, and now I had time really to explore my other options. I wouldn't say I was certain that I'd be able to do what I wanted, because I knew better than that. But I wasn't worried, either. That's how little I knew.

chapter6

Once *The Donny and Marie Show* ended, my siblings and I were pushed back out into the world, so to speak. The Osmond Studios were still up and running, turning out television series and specials for other artists, of course, but it was no longer the center of my life. I never recorded that album I thought I would there, and beyond several family television specials we would produce in the coming years, I rarely had occasion to set foot inside.

The popularity of the show had created a demand for Osmonds in every possible configuration: the Osmond family; Donny and Marie; Donny alone; Marie alone; Donny, Marie, and Jimmy; and Jimmy alone. I get dizzy just thinking about it. Although we'd never really stopped touring, even when we were producing the series, live concerts were again the main income source, so we all hit the road. A couple of times a year, Jimmy, Marie, and I did our three-week engagement at the Las Vegas Hilton. And when our brothers joined us, we were billed as the Osmond Family. It was an odd time, in a way, because it seemed as if every one of my performing siblings had something happening but me. Jimmy was building a remarkable career as a singer and a television star in Japan. Beginning in the mid-1980s with Michael Jackson's *Thriller* tour, Jimmy became a top concert promoter in Japan. My brothers worked on my sister's short-lived 1981 musical variety show and continued to work at the Osmond Studios, on various projects and producing events.

Nineteen eighty proved a turning point for all of us in ways we couldn't possibly appreciate then. Though *The Donny and Marie Show* had been canceled, we were still extremely positive about our prospects. Perhaps because I'd spent so many years out in front, it was painful for me at times to realize that many people in our organization believed that they'd gotten all the mileage out of my solo career there was to get. Marie's career, everyone said—behind my back and to my face—was the one to invest in now. It didn't bother me that Marie's career was taking precedence over everyone else's. From a business point of view, there's no denying that she had emerged as a solo artist and, more important, a performer the public really loved. I don't want to sound envious, because I wasn't. I didn't want what Marie had. I only wanted what I'd had before: the confidence of the people who ran my career. How would I ever turn my image around, advance my own career, if even the people who sat in the offices we had worked so hard to pay for didn't believe in me?

That spring, the entire family left for a world tour that took us to England, Asia, and Australia. It was an ambitious tour, produced on a scale that dwarfed even the biggest tours of our mid-1970s heyday. In those days, I stayed out of the loop in the planning stages, but the first time I heard about it, I remember wondering, *Why are we taking out such a big production? Why don't we scale back, so we could realize a bigger profit for our efforts? After all, I'm not doing this for my health.* None of us had placed a single on the British charts since 1976, when my sister and I released "Deep Purple" and the Osmonds had "I Can't Live a Dream," neither of them major, Top 10 singles. When we'd gone to England for an abbreviated tour just the year before, we'd found it a different place, at least musically speaking, somewhere between the last gasps of disco and the first ripples of new wave. A promoter convinced my family he could make it happen for us again. He assured them that all the girls who'd screamed for us in 1972 and 1973 would come out again, even if just for old times' sake. But when we got to England in 1980, most of them were gone.

Between not having hit records there (usually the only reason to tour) and working with a promoter who turned out to be less than effective, we found ourselves onstage, staring out at half-empty theaters. Not long into the tour, we were forced to scale down our accommodations. We discovered that the promoter had closed his business and disappeared. At a family meeting, Father asked us to vote on whether we should stay or go home. We voted to stay, assuming the duties the promoter should have assumed. Once we did, we were playing to full houses again. Then only a week and a half after we'd arrived, Merrill fell ill and had to fly back home to the States. On the last night of a five-night run at the Royal Theatre, in London, all of us—including our wives and children—said good-bye to Merrill onstage and sang "He Ain't Heavy, He's My Brother." From then, until the end of the tour—which took us to Newcastle, Glasgow and Edinburgh, Scotland, then Coventry and Leicester—I took over the lead. Even though the later shows, which we promoted ourselves, drew capacity crowds, it was a disappointing, dispiriting time for all of us. Although no one actually said it, I think we could all see that just being the Osmonds wasn't enough anymore.

Two days after we got home, we were on the road again, with a tour of the Midwest before boarding a plane for Bangkok, Thailand, in late August. If I remember correctly, there were ninety-two of us traveling for this tour, which took us to Malaysia, the Philippines, Australia, and Hong Kong. Besides ourselves and our families and musicians, we brought along magic tricks, lasers, dancers, our stage crew, and an incredibly extravagant show that included indoor fireworks.

The tour ended with two shows in Hong Kong, which immediately sold out. By that point, everyone was anxious to get back home and so tired we were all getting a little punchy. During what was supposed to have been our last show, the crew showered us with Styrofoam packing peanuts during "Singing in the Rain." Midway through, we learned there were thousands of people outside the theater, all elegantly dressed, demanding to see the show. It was quickly decided that after a brief rest, we would do a third and final show.

Throughout the tour, the man in charge of the indoor fireworks had done a wonderful job. Not only was it an exciting addition to the show, but—most important—no one had gotten hurt. The trick was the addition of an oxidizer, which made the fireworks burn faster, so that by the time they began to fall from the air, there were no flames and no danger.

As we sang the closing medley "Are You Up There" and "I Believe," fireworks exploded over the audience, as usual. But something was wrong, and from the stage, we could see people slapping themselves, screaming, and jumping up out of their seats. We quickly realized that the technician had forgotten to add the oxidizer, so that burning fireworks were showering down on the audience. It was the most appalling, frightening thing I'd ever witnessed from the stage, and as the curtain came down, we all ran to the wings, worried. Thinking quickly, someone on our staff went out into the auditorium, found everyone whose clothes had been singed, and told them, "The Osmond Family would really like to meet you." We spent the next several hours greeting and talking with these "lucky" fans.

In many ways, it was the trip of a lifetime. We were received by presidents and heads of state. But, financially, it was a disaster. We drew huge crowds everywhere in Asia and Australia, but the enormous expense of traveling with such a huge entourage, not to mention carting along the more spectacular components of our stage show, like the dancing waters, ate up our earnings. And yet, we just kept going, like someone had wound up the machine again and forgotten how to turn it off.

Back at home, we resumed touring amid rumors that we planned to each go our separate ways. Marie was set to do her variety show, the newspapers reported that I had a movie contract (to be honest, I don't recall), Jimmy would continue his solo career, and Alan, Wayne, Merrill, and Jay would each be performing individually as well. As it turned out, reports of the

Osmonds' demise were premature. My brothers would continue to sing together as a quartet for several years to come, but nothing would ever be like it was.

As I looked over my itineraries from these years, it struck me that in some ways, we were right back where we started, performing at the bigger hotels, Vegas, and the occasional television program. It was a good living, and in a way, less demanding than doing a weekly series, but I couldn't help feeling that I'd taken a step backward when I should be moving ahead. I didn't mind singing the old hits. I just wished there were some new ones to go along with them. As time went on, and the set list grew to contain more covers of other artists' current hits, I have to admit, I hated it.

On the bright side, I suppose, I'd crossed a crucial career threshold. For all that *The Donny and Marie Show* cost my recording career in credibility, I was generally regarded as a permanent show business fixture, an all-around entertainer who could still draw crowds and who could still make news. These are great assets, believe me. Now I had to figure out what to do with them.

There were some interesting times then, to be sure. I was touring with my band when a friend asked if I'd perform at a rally for Governor Ronald Reagan, who was then running for president. We did a couple of numbers, then Debbie, Don Jr., and I got into one of the waiting limousines to take us to the airport. About ten minutes later, after he'd given a brief speech, Governor Reagan, who was going to the airport, too, just happened to get into the same car. For the next half hour, we had a great conversation. I was surprised that he was so warm and relaxed, and that he knew so much about our church, which he admired. After Reagan won the presidency a short time later, Marie and I performed at one of the inaugural celebrations Merrill and Alan produced in Washington, D.C.

Whenever we played Las Vegas, I sang "Johnny B. Goode." Marie would take one side of the room and I'd take the other, and we'd get the audience to shout "Go—go, Johnny, go!" People loved it, and so we thought we could do the same thing at the arena in Washington, and have the president's supporters sing out, "Go—go, Ronnie, go!" When we did it, the crowd went crazy, which was really something, considering this was not your run-of-the-mill rock concert audience. A spotlight was shining on the president and the first lady, and I could see they were loving every minute of it. When I said, "Come on, Ronnie! Go!", President Reagan rose from his seat, smiling broadly, and shouted, "Go!" The next day, however, I read that some journalists felt that I had been "disrespectful" of the president.

On June 8, 1981, our beautiful little baby son Jeremy James was born. Every child's birth is special, and Jeremy's arrival reminded Debbie and me again how blessed we were.

Later that year, the family embarked on our last major international tour. Shortly before that, I traveled with Father to mainland China, where I was honored to host the first live cultural exchange satellite program to emanate from there. Unfortunately, the trip was cut short when we learned that Debbie's brother-in-law Dave Clyde had been killed in a truck accident.

That fall, Marie's show ended, and later we taped two television specials, "Backstage with the Osmonds" and "The

Osmond Family Holiday Special." It was interesting to see these specials again after all these years, because you could see that the family dynamics were changing, at least onstage. Alan, Wayne, Merrill, and Jay were relegated to the background, while Marie, Jimmy, and I took center stage, each with our own solo spots.

One special contained footage of me at home with Debbie, Don, and baby Jeremy. As fate would have it, this segment was taped the day I told Debbie we were packing up and moving. I'd just gotten the lead role in a revival of George M. Cohan's 1904 classic all-American musical *Little Johnny Jones*.

Landing the title role was a major coup for me, but on a personal level, it meant so much more. It was my first opportunity to define myself as an individual and as an adult. Though I'd never done musical theater before, I had spent enough time on the stage that I and the producers thought I knew my way around. Now, you may know already how this part of the story ends: *Little Johnny Jones* officially opened and closed on Broadway in a single night. But this isn't so much about exactly what happened with my Broadway debut, but how it happened and why.

When first approached about doing the show, I had some reservations. This production had been touring the country with plans of moving to Broadway in early 1982, but for some reason the current star, David Cassidy, was not going to be with the show much longer. Thinking back now, it's kind of funny that here I was being offered the chance to take over David's role, especially considering the totally fictitious "rivalry" supposedly brewing between us since the teen idol days. On one hand, it was ironically amusing. On the other, though, I gave a lot of thought to whether taking this role would remind people of the teen idol business at a time I was desperate to escape it. And I say this with no disrespect to David, of course. More than any-one else in the world, he probably understands the professional dilemma I faced.

In nearly three years since *The Donny and Marie Show* ended, not much had happened for me professionally. I hadn't recorded an album since legendary ex-Motown producers Brian and Eddie Holland attempted to give me a new adult image with *Donald Clark Osmond*, in 1977. I remember thinking at the time that these were the first producers who encouraged me to sing the way I wanted to sing. I've always been a fan of soul and R&B music, and so working with the team responsible for hundreds of classic hits by groups such as the Supremes and the Four Tops was an added bonus. But, looking back, I guess you could say I tried too hard. Record buyers were familiar with Donny, but they didn't want Donald Clark Osmond. And there were a few times between then and *Little Johnny Jones* when I wasn't so sure they were that interested in Donny, either.

From that night onstage in Chicago, when I was just six, the audience had always been there for me. Now, I wondered, where had everyone gone? I didn't like what I felt, so I devel-oped what you could call a defensive posture that probably came across to those who didn't know me well as a bit on the egotis-tical side. I didn't mean it that way, and I certainly didn't have the self-confidence to really be egotistical. But the barriers I faced seemed so enormous, the only way I could face them was to find a way to make them smaller in my mind. That's why after watch-ing David portray the spunky, all-American hero, I convinced myself the show—despite a punishing amount of dancing, high-energy production numbers, and a score that included "(I'm a) Yankee Doodle Dandy" and "Give My Regards to

Broadway"—would be a piece of cake. Hey, I reasoned, I've had hits, I've sung on stage, I've danced, I've acted—I've done it all. What could possibly go wrong?

I was so afraid, yet in an odd way, so confident, too. I put everything I had into this show. Debbie and I sold our home and rented a house in Englewood Cliffs, New Jersey. It was the first time we lived so far away from our families, and with me spending nine hours a day in rehearsals, Debbie was pretty much left to care for Don and Jeremy. Me? There were evenings I'd come home so exhausted from tap dancing that I literally could not lift my feet to walk up my front steps. But I never stopped. Ever.

In January 1982, before we were scheduled to open in New York, we took the show on the road, with a month-long run at Washington, D.C.'s Kennedy Center for the Performing Arts, followed by two weeks at Boston's Metropolitan Theater. The reviews were very good in Washington, slightly less enthusiastic in Boston, but the demand was strong enough that it seemed a small step to Broadway. We began three weeks of previews in New York, and the audience response was fantastic. Several times each night, we stopped the show because of standing ovations. As opening night approached, I began to regain my confidence. For the first time in a long time, I could look at a brandnew venture and tell myself, This time it's going to work.

I was sleeping at home in New Jersey, right before opening night, when I had the most bizarre dream. Now, I'm not a person who analyzes or even pays much attention to every dream. But, like many people, I've experienced a few dreams that are so distinct and vivid that I did wake up wondering what they meant. In this one, I was at the theater, in my costume, singing and dancing when suddenly the music went silent and I looked out into the audience and saw no one. Everything stopped. There was nothing but me in the darkness. I was jolted awake. *That was strange*, I thought. A few minutes later I managed to fall asleep.

Opening night was everything a performer could ask for. My dressing room at the Alvin Theater was brimming with cards, flowers, and balloons from well-wishers. Father and Mother, Jay, Marie, Jimmy, and Debbie were in the audience, rooting for me. The music came up, the curtain rose, and I stepped out and gave what I still feel was one of my best performances. And that wasn't just my imagination: Standing ovations again brought the show to a halt several times, and there were many curtain calls at the end. I remember thinking to myself, *This is great! This is going to work!*

I rushed back to my dressing room, changed, and with Debbie, my parents, Jay, Marie, and Jimmy got into a limousine to go to the big celebratory party. I felt so high. I couldn't wait to see the reviews. In New York City, you can pick up the early edition of the next day's paper mere hours after a show ends. Even before we left the theater, I noticed a strange look on Jimmy's face, as if he had something to tell me. I didn't ask him what, because my mind was someplace else. As we approached a corner, I saw a newsstand.

"Stop, please," I told the driver. "Let's get the papers."

I riffled the pages until I saw my picture. As I scanned the reviews, my heart sank like a stone. While none of the critics raved about the show, those from the *Daily News* and the *New York Times* at least attempted to balance criticism with praise. The *New York Post*, on the other hand, was relentlessly vicious and personal:

"...*I would say*," Clive Barnes wrote, "*that [Donny Osmond] is modestly talented (for example, he doesn't fall down or anything) but positively obnoxious.... Looking aggressively lost, like a failed candidate from a Dale Carnegie course, he tries to use charm as if it were a paper mask. His singing is conventional, his acting a thing of the past, and as for his tap dancing, he is like a toothpaste advertisement with terpsichorean delusions.*"

A tense silence filled the limo, and I could see the hurt on everyone's faces. I wanted to crawl under a rock, but I was expected at the party, if that's what you could still call it.

"Donny, the producers are going to close the show," Jimmy said gently. "I heard that unless the reviews were great, they were going to close it anyway."

I didn't understand. I knew what he was saying, but it wasn't making any sense to me. Amid all the backslapping and hand-shaking before opening night, they'd given me the impression that they were committed to the show, that they believed in me. Now this. Jimmy then said, "But, you know, I think it's all for the best. You needed to get out of here."

"What?"

"Well, I had a dream the other night that's made me feel that something really bad was going to happen to you here." Jimmy went on to explain his dream, which was exactly like mine in every detail.

Debbie, who knew about my dream, looked at me. My face went white. "I had the same dream," I said. "Let's get the heck out of here."

But there was still the party. The limo stopped outside the restaurant, and I knew there was no turning back. I had to face everyone. I took a deep breath, then said, "Okay, let's go." As long as I live, I will never forget walking in and the silence that fell as every conversation stopped and all eyes turned toward me. In place of the hero's welcome the scene had been written for, all I got were tense, fake smiles and halfhearted consolation. People met my eyes for a second, then they looked away. As I sat in the booth, feigning interest in my food and trying to make small talk with anybody who had the compassion or the nerve to approach me, I felt like I was being buried alive. I had to get out of there, away from everything.

The next morning, I rented a U-Haul trailer, packed up the house, and started growing my beard. I was leaving everything—Broadway, New York, the critics, my dreams—behind, gathering up Debbie and the boys, and we were going back to where it was safe, back home to Utah. But even then, my escape was only temporary. I knew I had to come back to the theater someday and prove to myself that I could do it. Just not now.

We spent the next few weeks driving home to Utah via the scenic route: to Hershey, Pennsylvania, Disneyworld in Orlando, Florida, through the South, up into Oklahoma across to New Mexico—wherever. I didn't care. I just sat behind the wheel and drove. I couldn't think about the show; I couldn't think about anything. I hoped no one recognized me (although being Donny Osmond did get me out of a couple of speeding tickets on that trip). I wished everybody could just forget who I was. I wished I could. Beyond that, there isn't much else I can recall about that trip.

Upon returning to Utah, Debbie and I rented a small house

and spent some time just being a family. A few weeks after the show closed, Father and Mother accepted a mission call to Hawaii for the Church. On December 9, 1982, my twenty-fifth birthday, I went there to see them, because I was at a crossroads and needed Father's advice. There were so many different ways I could go, but I couldn't decide alone. Should I join my brothers again and go country? Hit the road again with Marie, perhaps? Or even, as some people suggested, go for a glamorous, grown-up, Las Vegas audience? Try musical theater again? Chase that elusive recording contract? Just give it up? I turned to Father, because I knew he would be honest, and I respected his opinion immensely. During a lengthy, emotional talk, he let me know that I shouldn't give up, that I had the ability to succeed, and that it was time for me to make my own way in the world.

Father was right. All I had to do was look around. Things were changing. Marie was planning her June wedding to Steve Craig. *Side by Side*, the made-for-television film account of my family's early years (starring Marie as Mother) had recently aired. Alan, Wayne, Merrill, and Jay returned to the charts with their first country single as the Osmond Brothers, "I Think About Your Lovin'." I knew I couldn't hide out forever, and I got back to work. Later that year I made my second appearance on *Love Boat* and costarred in a made-for-television Western, *The Wild Women of Chastity Gulch*. It wasn't exactly where I wanted to be, but it was something.

At least I'd never have to be concerned about money. The studio was always abuzz with activity, and when I went out on the road, I assumed that the portion of my earnings that went back into the partnership was really working for me. But then that all changed too. One day in 1982, there was a meeting with three of our most trusted advisers, our attorney, Rich Hill, Bill Waite, and our in-house accountant Steve Hortin. By then, several other executives and consultants had come and gone. None of them could find new, reliable sources of income to keep the ventures afloat. However, that didn't prevent any of them from continuing to take a salary. We learned the hard way that, given the choice, most people would not come to Utah to do what they could do just as easily in Hollywood. It was just a ninety-minute flight from L.A. to Salt Lake City, but it might as well have been a trip to the moon. After *The Donny and Marie Show* was canceled, not enough business came to Orem—or "Oremwood," as one of my brothers called it in a wildly optimistic moment —to cover the immense cost of keeping over two hundred people on salary, not to mention meet all the financial obligations the family had incurred to build the studio, plus support approximately ten other commercial ventures.

I'll never forget the meeting at the studio where we got the bad news. After reviewing everything, Rich estimated we were less than two weeks from having to file a Chapter 11 bankruptcy.

"What is Chapter 11?" I asked, then trying to make a joke, I added, "I didn't read that chapter."

The look on Rich's face told me this was no laughing matter. I didn't learn exactly what Chapter 11 entailed, but I did know what it meant on a very practical level: We were going to have to sell off everything we could, because beyond the risk incurred by the Osmond Brothers Partnership—the corporate entity everything grew out of—we were each individually liable for the businesses' debts.

Hearing the news, I felt like I'd been hit by lightning. How was it possible? I knew the studio wasn't doing as well as we'd hoped it would. But, surely, I thought, somebody had to be minding the store. Surely, if we really couldn't afford these things—like the private jets, the sports facility complete with indoor and outdoor racquetball and tennis courts, our own gas station—the people at the top would have said something. You would think.

While we certainly made ill-advised choices in some people we put in positions of power, the truth of the matter is, the seeds for this debacle had been sown years before. We were too trusting, too willing to always see the good in people, and too quick to overlook their shortcomings. And I'm not saying this to make us all look good, because in a business like this, that's not being a good person, it's being a good victim. Growing up, we were taught that it wasn't the dollar signs we should have our eyes on, but the musical notes. Maybe that was naive, but you have to consider how Father and Mother saw it then. Would you tell your fourteen-year-old kid that he was worth one-ninth of $60 million? On the other hand, maybe if we'd had some idea of what we were making, we might have been a little more cautious.

Of course, hindsight is always twenty-twenty. We could have built the studio in Salt Lake City rather than Orem. We could have converted an existing warehouse as opposed to building from the ground up. We could have concentrated on making the studio profitable before we turned our corporate hand to other things. I could have made sure I took more of an interest in how the business was being run. But would that have made a difference? No one can really say. And you can run the scenario in other ways, too. We could have stayed in Los Angeles, and each of us spent our share on big mansions and fancy cars. Then where would we have been? Years later, I had a dream that everything in Orem had succeeded beyond our wildest expectations. Everyone in my family was a multimillionaire, obsessed with material things and far removed from the values we grew up with. All these years later, I can honestly say, that would have been worse.

Every one of us was devastated by this turn of events, but no one as much as Father. After all, it had all begun as his dream, and in my opinion, everything would have worked out well had he not been asked to relinquish control. I think it was the first time in Father's life that he really allowed someone else to make the important decisions about his family. So although what occurred was not his fault, he was very upset with himself for letting the control slip from his hands. Contrary to what most people think, it's as hard to hold on to wealth as it is to earn it. Whatever we had was ours because Father had overseen our finances with an eye to establishing our future security. The importance of money was always what you could build with it, not what you could buy. To most of our paid advisers, this low-risk, long-term strategy was too conservative, too old-fashioned.

Another outgrowth of our family's philosophy was reflected in how the partnership was structured. Everyone's earnings went into a common pool from which we were each paid an equal salary. At the time, I couldn't imagine it being any other way, but having a family changed the way I saw it. When I was single, it was one thing to be out doing a series of one-nighters, living in hotel rooms, and eating every meal off a room service tray. But when that lifestyle became my own family's—and Don and Jeremy were still just toddlers—I wasn't so accepting anymore. What bothered me almost as much was knowing that I wasn't out there working to support my immediate or my extended family as much I was shoring up this "empire" and fattening our advisers' wallets.

When it came time to build the studio and expand into other areas, I think Father felt a little out of his depth, and so he agreed when my older brothers pushed to bring in the outside advisers. While what happened was never Father's fault—in fact, it would be the conservative investments he'd made over the years that saved us in the end—to this day he finds the subject nearly impossible to talk about. I have tried in so many ways to tell him that I never blamed him for what happened, that I've seen similar misfortunes befall other performers for much the same reasons, that I believe he did the best he could. Of any of us, Father should shoulder the least blame of all.

There was a big meeting at which Bill, Rich, and a couple of other people we could truly trust outlined our options. One was straight bankruptcy—in other words, just walk away from the debt and let our creditors scramble. The other was a plan to restructure the debt and pay everyone off. Bill and Rich wanted to be sure that everyone understood the full implications of each course, and so they flew in a high-powered attorney from a major San Francisco bankruptcy firm. That attorney concluded his presentation with a very strongly worded recommendation that we file for bankruptcy and leave our creditors to sort through the spoils. By any business textbook, that would have been the way to go. But it would have been wrong.

Father listened, and then he reclaimed his position as the boss. He stood up and said firmly, "There is no way this family will declare bankruptcy. That is not an acceptable solution.

Work this out. We live in this community, and I will not stand by and let our name be dragged through the dirt."

The funny thing about this time was that although we had lost well over $30 million, it didn't change the way Debbie and I lived except that I found myself out on the road more. Looking back at how I lived then and do now, I have to say a lot of Father's attitude rubbed off on me. While I've always had a nice, comfortable home, I never lived ostentatiously. In fact, I felt guilty about spending money on anything. At the time the business collapsed, I was driving around one of two Chevettes Marie and I had received for doing a commercial, and still storing a few years' supply of Hawaiian Punch I'd received from doing the commercials with Marie in the late 1970s. I never spent a lot of money on clothes, because, for one thing, I had no fashion sense (if you don't believe me, turn to the photo section). Debbie and I had agreed from the start that we'd always have a home our children would feel comfortable in. This explains a leather couch we have had for years with duct tape covering the tears and decorative pillows strategically placed to cover it.

Now, I don't want to give the impression that I accepted all this bad news with a smile on my face. I didn't. I was furious. And my not saying anything about the inequity of that isn't an indication of what a good person I was but the result of being someone who still didn't feel entitled to his own feelings. Personally, I didn't immediately miss a lot of what we lost because it wasn't all real to me in the first place. And losing the Riviera and the Manning apartment complexes where I'd grown up did hurt. What was painfully real was knowing how much of our work, our energy, and our money were lost with the studio. For me, the most painful part was Father losing his beloved ranch a few years later. I know that it broke his heart, and at the time it hurt me to know that after all the millions I'd helped earn, I was powerless to help him save it.

Each of us emerged from the financial ruin a somewhat different person, more cautious, a little less confident. The ship was down in the water, and we were each in our own lifeboat, paddling with whatever we could find. For me, that meant spending most of 1983 and 1984 touring with Marie, and occasionally Marie and I with our brothers. In the mid-1980s we performed wherever we were wanted: from the White House, for President Reagan's second inaugural, to state fairs.

The ship had been slow in sinking. As early as 1981, there were signs that all was not well, and employees were laid off and buyers dismantled pieces of the empire. I know there were people, both in and beyond Utah, who weren't entirely sympathetic to the downturn in the Osmond fortunes. To some people in Hollywood, it was simply, "We told you so." We tried to buck the system, and we'd failed. To some in Utah, the collapse was viewed as a comeuppance. I suppose it's just part of human nature to take a little pleasure in seeing people who seem to have everything go through hard times. It was a humbling experience for all of us. And at times, an embarrassing one.

I'll never forget going down to a car dealership in Provo to buy a little "repli-car," a Volkswagen with an MG body that cost about $13,000. "I'd like to buy this car," I said, approaching a salesman.

"Oh, Donny Osmond!" he replied, smiling. Then his tone changed to one of mock suspicion. "Well, I don't know. Can you afford it?"

I stood there embarrassed beyond words, as the guy turned

to his partner, and practically smirking, said, "Hey, don't you think we'd better check this guy's credit? You never know."

Furious, I left the showroom, drove straight to the bank, wrote myself a check for $13,000, handed it to a teller, and said, "I'd like that in singles, please." I packed them in my briefcase, drove back to the car dealership, and silently dumped the cash on that salesman's desk.

I was lost and desperate to make something happen that would get me back in the game. But it had to be something I was proud of and something that was my own. I wanted to break away from my family professionally and start all over again. I started affecting a hipper, new-wave style, in bright pastel jackets and skinny ties. When I look back now at some photographs of myself then, especially posing with my siblings, I cringe with embarrassment. And I know I embarrassed them. I just wanted to start finding the new me, whoever that was going to be. Instead, I found myself touring with Marie, and the stress took a toll on our relationship then. To be honest, part of it was the fact that Marie's solo career was moving ahead while I couldn't even scare up a contract. For reasons different from mine, I'm sure she wasn't any happier with the situation than I was. Now Marie and I were partners in a venture we didn't choose, for reasons not of our own making. To make matters even more difficult, in late 1984, news of problems in Marie's marriage began to hit the press. Marie and her husband separated, and they later divorced. I know how much her marriage meant to her, and the public humiliation she suffered at the hands of the tabloid press made us all wish we could protect her, and her son, Stephen. But Marie is very strong. Even amid all that personal disappointment, beginning in 1985 she solidified her place as a top country artist with three Number One hits in a single calendar year—"Meet Me in Montana," with Dan Seals; "There's No Stopping Your Heart"; and "You're Still New to Me," with Paul Davis—and "Read My Lips," number four.

Nineteen eighty-five started happily for us, though, with the birth of our third son, Brandon Michael. After talking it over with Debbie, I decided that the only way I could ever rebuild my career was to move to Los Angeles. The real estate market in Utah had gone soft and we couldn't sell our home, so we spent some time living with Jimmy at his place in Toluca Lake, close to Hollywood. Like me, Jimmy felt adrift then, but unlike me, he had never really depended on the Osmond family fortunes. An entrepreneur since childhood, Jimmy had managed to create his own empire built on his early 1980s success as a top recording artist and television star in Japan. Jimmy had a level of independence I've always admired. Here I was, in my late twenties and I could barely read much less understand my own tax returns. Jimmy, on the other hand, had been preparing his own corporate returns for his many businesses since he was thirteen.

Jimmy and I were always close. When we were younger, he would tag along with me, and I would teach him how to assemble his own Heath kits. Being younger and having had his own solo career, Jimmy, I think, understood what I was trying to do better than anyone else except Debbie. In a way, my older brothers came up in a show business environment that was entirely different from what I now faced. The old steam shovel approach, as I like to call it, of just getting out there and working and working until you succeeded wasn't the way to go anymore. The whole music industry had changed overnight with the advent of MTV.

I wanted my recording career back again, but I was realistic, too. Before *Little Johnny Jones*, I cut some demos with producer David Foster and guitarist Jay Graydon for their L.A.-based studio band project called Airplay. Previous to recording with me, the group had released one critically acclaimed album, and we had recorded about eight tracks for a possible second. I felt that we had the right chemistry, but before we got anything off the ground, both David and Jay were drawn away to other projects, and it all fell apart. With Jay, however, I did record one track called "Chain Reaction" (not to be confused with the Diana Ross hit written by the Bee Gees), which had a sharper edge than anything I'd recorded before.

In 1984 I traveled to London twice at the invitation of Princess Anne to participate in a show to benefit the Children's Royal Charity Fund. During one of these trips, I got the chance to perform on a popular British television series called *Live at the Palladium*. Ten years had passed since my last charting single there, so I decided to sing "Chain Reaction," hopeful that someone might see me and offer me a record deal. Granted, the odds were long, but it never hurt to try, right?

I'd sent a tape of the song over to England, and the television producers put together a production number, with about a dozen dancers. When I arrived, we ran through it, and I was very pleased with how it turned out. The show was live, and I remember standing backstage in position, waiting to go on, really psyching myself up thinking about how many people would see me and how this was my shot. I was set to go on immediately after beloved veteran British comedian Tommy Cooper finished his act.

Standing behind the curtain, we couldn't see Tommy, but we could hear his routine. The audience roared with laughter as he imitated an old man having a heart attack at the sight of a beautiful model who walked across the stage. On cue, he clutched his chest and fell to the floor. The crowd applauded and laughed even louder. Less than a minute later, the applause had begun to wind down, but Tommy was still lying on the floor, maybe trying to milk it, we all presumed. Within seconds, the host walked briskly to Tommy, knelt down, and said, "Okay, Tommy, come on. The joke is over." Then, "Oh my God, he's dead! Somebody call an ambulance."

They cut to commercial and hurriedly drew down the curtain, from which Tommy's feet stuck out for the audience to see. (For legal and medical reasons, Tommy could not be moved by anyone but paramedics or the police.) Obviously, another man's death is nothing to joke about, and I didn't take it lightly. But as the staff scurried around getting things ready so the show could resume, I couldn't help but think, *I can't follow that.* The ambulance arrived, and they moved Tommy's body. The show did go on, but the audience was understandably subdued.

Knowing how unpredictable this business can be, I formed the Donny Osmond Entertainment Corporation, through which I developed and produced many different programs. I'd gotten some experience directing (my first project was a television special of a concert by jazz saxophonist Grover Washington Jr. for another production company), and I purchased the rights to the original *Donny and Marie Show* with an eye to repackaging them for syndication. In late 1984, I'd taken the company public, making me the first pop star you could actually own shares in. Still, I would be lying if I said that sitting behind a desk or behind a camera was all I ever wanted to do.

While I would never describe our relationship as "close," Michael Jackson and I both recognized that we were bonded simply by having lived through childhoods few other people could imagine much less understand. Once, when I was about fourteen or fifteen, I was over at his house in Encino, and we stayed up until about two o'clock in the morning talking about what it had been like growing up. It seemed like there wasn't anything one of us could say about how our lives had been that the other did not understand. And, in fact, I know I feel that in terms of my childhood as a performer, no one could have the same insights into my experience as Michael does. It was clear then, however, that I had been protected from some of the hardships and situations Michael experienced.

Around 1983, Michael and I started talking on the phone. He invited Debbie, Don, Jeremy, and me to his home to spend an afternoon. Michael seemed to enjoy showing off his menagerie—the llamas, monkeys, and snakes—and we had a wonderful time. It was during this visit that for the first time I noticed the signs of vitiligo, the skin condition he would later speak of publicly. Not long after that, he invited me to go with him to see a Jim Henson fantasy film called *The Dark Crystal*. Michael drove us in his Rolls-Royce, and I remember he was not the most conscientious driver. Once around this time, we were leaving Toto keyboardist Steve Porcaro's house, and Michael had such a hard time backing out of the driveway, I finally had to get out and direct him.

Back at his house, he showed me his shrine of gold records,

trophies, and awards. Every time I'd ever spoken with Michael, he was always very interested in my family and how we were raised, and particularly curious about Father and how he treated us. Though both of our fathers were very strict, Father was not as harsh a disciplinarian as Joseph Jackson. I think Michael sensed that my siblings and I shared a closeness with our father that he did not have with his own.

Michael knew I was trying to revive my recording career, so when he offered advice, such as, "We've got to dress you differently, man," I tried to take it in the spirit it was intended, though I felt a little self-conscious. Michael knew I was making the rounds, meeting with record company executives and producers. Time and again, I heard the same story: We love the way you sing, and we'd love to sign you, Donny, but we can't break that image. I appreciated their honesty, but that never made it any easier to hear. However, it was Michael who I guess you could say put it all into sharp focus for me. I was with him at a recording studio, where he was working on a project with Quincy Jones. They needed a ride back to Quincy's office. The three of us were in my car when I said, "What do you think I should do to get my recording career off the ground again?"

Without missing a beat, and without a trace of humor, Michael replied, "Change your name. Your name is poison." I think I waited a millisecond for a laugh or some sign that he was just kidding, but he wasn't. Quincy, who in the next year or so would consider signing me, concurred. I was hurt and stunned, but said nothing. I fixed my eyes on the road ahead and just kept driving.

Time was of the essence, so I turned to professionals with proven records to help me. I signed up Norman Winter, a well-known and flamboyant press agent whose most famous client happened to be Michael Jackson, and I began renewing contacts in the business. I knew that I'd never be able to sell the public a new Donny Osmond unless I could get the industry behind me first. That might sound cold and calculating, but believe me, behind every wonderful, heartfelt record, there's an army of people whose business it is to calculate the odds on every decision, from the songs you record to the colors you wear. It's a business where, despite the fairy tales some artists like to spin for the press, there is no such thing as pure luck, and hard work can end up amounting to nothing. You always hear artists attributing their success to the fact that they believed in their dream, but that's only the beginning of it. I knew then that if I didn't get the right people to believe in my dream first, nothing I did would matter.

At this stage of my life, everything I did professionally was geared toward putting the old Donny Osmond as far behind me as I could. And sometimes, at least in my family's opinion, I ran too far in the other direction. Norman lived by the credo that any publicity was good publicity. I agreed with him that I had to change my image, but we didn't always see eye to eye on exactly how. David Crosby's name was all over the media, because he had turned himself in to the FBI and was facing a prison sentence for drug possession (which he began serving the following spring).

"Donny, that would be a great thing for you to do," Norman's associate said. "That'll put you right in the news, and that's what we need to do. We need to create a reason for the press to talk about you."

Sounds crazy, right? But I'm almost embarrassed to admit

that for a few minutes, it made sense. It was one thing to be photographed hanging out with Billy Idol, Joan Jett, Eddie Murphy, and Boy George. But this idea, like Norman's brainstorm that I should pose for *Playgirl* magazine, went way too far. Back home in Utah, some members of my family were alarmed at what they were seeing and hearing about me.

That's not to say some good things didn't come out of my association with Norman. Ironically, the things he put into motion that were most helpful for me were not publicity stunts. Through Norman, I became involved in Frank Zappa's anticensorship campaign to stop the Parents' Music Resource Center (PMRC) from labeling recordings according to their lyrical content. I dressed up as a high-ranking Nazi officer for an MTV commercial to dramatize the dangers of censorship, and that fall I appeared as a guest on *Nightline* expressing an opinion many people were surprised to hear coming from me. That doesn't mean I think all music is appropriate for all listeners. There is music that's definitely inappropriate for kids, and there always has been. But I believe that the power to restrict what children listen to lies in the hands of parents, not the government and not record companies. Besides, human nature being what it is, there's no better way to ensure that children will want to hear something than to tell them that they can't.

Through this, I met Frank Zappa and his family, including his son Dweezil, on whose 1991 album I sang "Stayin' Alive." I'd never met anyone quite like Frank, and we had a very provocative and interesting conversation on many topics. I remember in particular him asking me about my religion. Frank was perhaps the most intellectual person to ever pick up a guitar, and curious about everything. After I explained some of our beliefs, he asked, "But how do you know? How do you know that it's real?"

"I know by faith and prayer," I told him. And while Frank didn't share in my beliefs, he was open-minded and respectful.

The second thing Norman helped facilitate proved crucial to my "comeback." British guitar legend Jeff Beck was making a video for a song called "Ambitious" from his *Flash* album. The title refers to his reputation as one of rock and roll's most dazzling guitarists. Jeff first made his mark in early 1965, when he replaced Eric Clapton in the Yardbirds and briefly shared lead guitar duties with future Led Zeppelin founder Jimmy Page. Later, as the leader of the Jeff Beck Group (which in its earliest version included Rod Stewart and Ron Wood) and through his hit jazz-rock instrumental albums of the 1970s, he solidified his stature as one of the most important guitarists in rock. "Ambitious" was his first track since 1973 to include vocals, so it was an honor to be asked to participate, although I was not alone; Jimmy Hall of Wet Willie and Marilyn McCoo also sang, and Parker Stevenson and *Fantasy Island*'s Herve Villechaize made cameo appearances in the video under the premise that we were all auditioning for the part. The video opens with us signing in. When asked about my prior experience, I reply, "I used to sing with this chick named Marie." "Ambitious" didn't become a hit single, but my presence in the video and my hard-rock performance sent the message throughout the industry that I wasn't the same cutesy Donny everyone remembered and that even I could poke a little fun at myself.

One thing led to another, and I did a few talk shows, a cameo with James Brown on the television series *Throb*, all while continuing to go out on limited tours with Marie. I'd just about exhausted all of my options in Los Angeles, and the cost of maintaining all the accouterments of celebrity was beginning to wear me down. But it seemed like every time it began to look hopeless, a little something would happen to make me believe that maybe things were about to turn around.

That image. I couldn't go back in time and change it, so, I reasoned, maybe if I could tarnish it a little, show myself to be a real person....A press person working for me convinced me that I should cooperate with a story being written about me and my family. Whether it was someone working for Norman or the journalist himself, I don't recall, but I was told specifically by this person that the story would concentrate on my attempts to make a comeback and that it would be published in *Rolling Stone* magazine and be tied in with the tenth anniversary of my cover appearance. (Many years later, I learned that *Rolling Stone* knew nothing about this, even though both magazines were owned by the same publisher.) So I surmise that this was a ruse not only to get me to cooperate but to encourage other family members to talk. Regrettably, I fell for it.

The writer spent several days with me in Los Angeles and seemed sympathetic when I spoke of how hard it was to live in the gleamingly wholesome shadow of my family and how that was working against me now. It would be easy to say that he tricked me or that he took things I said out of context. The truth is, I would have done well to choose some of my words more carefully than I did. Reading it today, I come across as critical of my brothers' handling of our business affairs, envious of Marie's success in country music, and overly confident about my own, then slim, prospects. The worst part of all, though, was that I had trusted the writer so much, I'd called up members of my family, including Mother, and encouraged them to speak with him.

When the article appeared, it was published in *US* magazine, not *Rolling Stone*, under the title "The Fall of the Osmonds." The reading line—"How bad planning, a bad image, and a little bit of greed sank the careers of America's most clean-cut family"—pretty well summed it up. I'll never forget being with Rob Dias, my best buddy from childhood. After skimming the piece, he asked me, with a hurt look on his face, "Donny, how could you do this to your family?" As you can imagine, my family was thinking the same thing.

Occasionally, though, something happened to give me hope. Around this time, after listening to some demos I'd made with David Foster and Jay Graydon, Ed Eckstein, the president of Quincy Jones's label Qwest, contacted me. Quincy was interested in signing me, and with uncanny prescience (despite his having once agreed with Michael that my name was poison), he had it all figured out.

"Now, this could be interesting," Quincy said. "We could come out with some really good music, but under a different name initially. The music would be established, and that would give you a start, then we would reveal who you really are."

Unlike some discussions I'd had with other record company executives, this one actually led to something concrete: a deal memo, which spelled out the basics of my future contract terms. With a deal memo in hand, I assumed that when Quincy called and asked me to meet him in his office, we were going to sign the deal.

Quincy was cordial and very kind, but the mood in the room wasn't what I expected. "Donny," he began, in a measured, sympathetic tone, "I have to trust my promotion people out across the country."

At first I wasn't sure where Quincy was going, and I felt my heart picking up some extra beats.

"I proposed the idea of signing you to all the promotion people," he continued. "And they all came back with the same answer: It's going to be too hard to change the image. I'm sorry, Donny, but we're not going to be able to sign you."

What did I say? I honestly don't know. In fact, I don't remember leaving the office or driving home. All I remember after that is thinking, *Not again!* Maybe I was fighting a losing battle. Debbie, Jimmy, and a few other people believed in me, but when I look back now, objectively speaking, I can see why someone might not. After my meeting with Quincy, I turned to Norman and said, "Now what?"

"We're not having any luck here in L.A., so let's try New York," he replied. So we did, and there I got the break of my life, from the most unlikely place. I was performing at an all-star benefit at the United Nations in New York City for UNICEF, when my manager Steven Machat introduced me to Peter Gabriel. Now, when you go to events like these, you say hello to everyone and mostly make small talk. At that time Peter Gabriel had merged his roots in early Genesis's progressive rock with a sharper, more political vision that reached millions through hits such as "Biko," "Shock the Monkey," and "Sledgehammer," from *So*—one of my favorite albums. An artist in rock's avant-garde and a critics' favorite, Peter Gabriel was the last person I expected to hear asking me, "So, Donny, what's going on with your recording career?"

I was a little taken aback by his interest. Nevertheless, I

could see it was genuine, and in a lapse of cool, I poured my heart out and gave him an earful. "We're trying to create press, but it doesn't make any sense to me," I told him. "I don't want that kind of press. All I want to do is make good music."

Peter said, "You're absolutely right. You know, if the music is right, everything else will follow suit. I've got an idea: Why don't you come over to my studio in England and let's get to work."

I was stunned. As anyone who knows his music can tell, Peter is definitely someone comfortable with taking chances. But on me? It was hard to believe. Around this time, Steven Machat had helped orchestrate a deal with an Epic Records A&R representative named Frank Rand, and I'd done some demos. We eventually signed a recording contract, and that financed my trip to England and the production costs I'd incur working at Peter's. My producer there would be a Senegalese guitarist and songwriter named George Acogny, who coproduced some of Peter's solo work.

This wasn't an easy decision, because while on one hand, it was the professional break I'd been hoping for, we simply couldn't afford for Debbie, Don, Jeremy, and Brandon to accompany me. Though I planned to alternate a few weeks in England and a few weeks back home, Debbie and I realized the separation would be difficult on everyone, especially the boys. I always knew that the material things didn't matter to Debbie, that she loved me for who I really was. Still, I wanted things to be better for her and our children. It was now over nine years since my last record, and the writing was on the wall. I didn't know what I would do if this didn't work. I went to England believing this may be my last chance. More than anyone else in the world,

Debbie understood this and knew what it meant to me. I couldn't have left without her support and her blessings.

I arrived in England in the fall of 1986, and found a hotel room in Bath, near Peter's studio. I flew home as often as I could, but it never seemed to be enough. Every night, back in my hotel room, I would write in the journal I kept on a yellow legal pad, and listen to the same CDs over and over again: Tears for Fears' *Songs from the Big Chair*, Steve Winwood's *Back in the High Life*, and Peter's *So*, which included my theme song for this phase of my life, Peter and Kate Bush's duet "Don't Give Up."

Things happened very quickly after Peter introduced me to George Acogny. Frank Rand came over to visit, and we started pulling together songs for the album. I showed them a song I had written called "Only Heaven Knows," which is about my own "lost" childhood and how my sons helped me recapture some of what I'd missed. George had some very interesting, progressive ideas. He also brought in some great musicians, including bassist Darryl Jones, keyboardist Peter Vetesse, and drummer Manu Katché, and we started recording at Ashcombe House. When I arrived at the studio the first time, on a freezing winter day, I was a little surprised to see that the place where Peter had recorded most of his greatest hits was literally a barn smack in the middle of farm country. But there was something in the atmosphere, something mysterious and almost primitive, that made it easy to create, to try new ideas.

George, who had produced such world music stars as Manu Dibango and Youssou N'Dour, set up everything perfectly for me to record one of my favorite tracks. It was a ballad called "What Am I Here For," and he set the mood perfectly: candlelight and a picture of Debbie. Working with George, we cut ten or eleven tracks, including three that appeared on my album: "Groove," "Only Heaven Knows," and "My Secret Touch," which George and I cowrote. A few times while we were recording, Peter Gabriel dropped by. Nothing I was doing was in his style, yet he offered some very odd yet insightful suggestions about the instrumental tracks. We also recorded some songs that were very different, at least for me. One entitled "Fire It Up" had a heavy Afro-pop influence, and generally all the other tracks were more complex with a stronger emphasis on rhythm than anything that was released. But these never saw the light of day, and as of this writing are still sitting in Virgin's vaults in England.

What happened? Maybe a better question would be, What didn't. I hadn't even completed recording with George when out of the blue, I was informed that Epic had dropped my contract. Frank Rand was no longer working there, and no one at the label could get behind the project. All the months of work were on the verge of going down the drain when Peter Gabriel stepped in again and encouraged his label, Virgin, to sign me. Virgin had an extremely eclectic roster that included Genesis, Culture Club, Human League, and numerous punk, reggae, ska, and world music acts. Now, to be honest, the label's chief, Simon Draper, was not jumping up and down to have me on board. I know that Peter called in some favors to make this work for me, and I'll always be grateful to him for saving work that otherwise might have been lost forever.

I continued recording with George and was very happy with what we'd done. It was a brand-new sound for me; it didn't sound anything like the Donny of the past, and for the first time I could carve out my own niche. When we submitted it to Virgin, however, Simon Draper did not share my enthusiasm.

"We don't have a hit here," he said. "We can't put out an album without a hit." I knew he was right; an album without at least one hit single is the proverbial tree that falls in the woods: Nobody ever hears it.

With my new album on the verge of being released in England, I agreed to sit for an interview with Harry Reasoner for 60 Minutes. Everyone around me warned me not to do it. Bill Waite told me that when it came to 60 Minutes, there was no such thing as a positive piece. I must have been so high on what I'd recorded, in a burst of confidence, I felt that I could be the exception to that rule. Everything was riding on this, and I was determined to do anything to make it happen. I took the 60 Minutes people at their word, and believing them to be fair and sympathetic, I opened my heart. In fact, I was so honest and open that after the piece aired, a member of the group Air Supply phoned Bill Waite and expressed concern for my well-being; he thought I looked suicidal!

Well, if I wasn't that way when I taped it, I sure was by the time it aired. I knew it was over the minute Ed Bradley introduced the piece with "It's not a question that will keep many of you awake nights. Some are saying, 'Donny and Marie who?' A lot more know and don't care whatever became of them." There were the dramatic shots of the abandoned studio in Orem, a transparent attempt to surprise Marie with some awkward questions, and then there was me. None of the questions was easy to answer, and I lost my footing a little when Harry asked, "What if your album goes out there and dies? What do you do then?"

After a long pause, I said, "I don't know. It's possible. It's really possible. It won't be the first time something has gone south for me. I'd try again."

Inside, I was a nervous wreck, but I managed to give the impression I was cool, in fact too cool. Here and in other interviews over the next few years, I could see myself falling into a defensive demeanor that bordered on arrogance. I was trying to convince the world of something I wasn't so sure I believed myself anymore, and the stress of it was taking a toll. I didn't know then that the work had only just begun.

Virgin was anxious to start recouping its investment, so without a complete album ready to release, the label put out "I'm in It for Love" in mid-1987. It was written by Andy Goldmark and Patrick Henderson, and I recorded the demo in the broom closet of Andy's New York apartment. I knew this would be what we call in the business a "loss leader," sort of a sacrifice fly you hit in the hopes of doing better with the next single. That bothered me a little, because it's always been one of my favorite tracks. After a single week at number seventy on the British charts, "I'm in It" was off the charts, though not for want of our trying. The promotion people at Virgin and I worked that record every way we could imagine. I did television appearances, record store signings, radio interviews—you name it. Maybe there'd be better luck next time, with "Groove"—a hard-edged, funk track we'd recorded with club play in mind. My new manager, Ged Doherty, and his partner Martin Serene convinced me to try a new look, cut my long hair short and drop the tailored suits for denim and black leather. I hit the promotion circuit again, but "Groove" did even more poorly than "I'm in It for Love" and didn't even chart.

People at Virgin introduced the prospect of working with me to a New York–based team of songwriter-producers named Carl Sturken and Evan Rogers. They had strong R&B credentials, including hit projects with Stephanie Mills, Karyn White, and Cheryl Lynn. They've since been responsible for many major hits, both in the U.K. and here, including most recently the Brand New Heavies, Boyzone, Eternal, and 'N Sync's 1999 smash "(God Must Have Spent) A Little More Time on You." When I heard their demo for "If It's Love That You Want," I fell in love with it. And a week or so later, when I received a demo for "Soldier of Love," I knew I'd found my producers.

Carl, who is a singer, and Evan, who plays guitar, were great to work with. They loved the challenge of "remaking" Donny Osmond, and we all shared the same dry, off-the-wall sense of humor. Their studio, on the quaint main street of the otherwise posh and quiet Bronxville, New York, was comfortable. Together we wrote "Hold On" and "Faces in the Mirror," and I recorded their "If It's Love That You Want," "Sacred Emotion," and "Soldier," a track I have to say I wasn't all that crazy about after I'd finished it. I liked it well enough, but I'd never have picked it as the hit.

It was now about a year and a half of traveling back and forth to England, with nothing really to show for it. I'd done everything Virgin had asked of me, including making countless appearances anyplace the promotion staff deemed it was good to be seen. I was around so much that one magazine ridiculed me by interspersing real photographs of me at different events with pictures it had doctored to give the impression that I was literally everywhere—including on ex-Eurythmic Dave Stewart's honeymoon. I was embarrassed beyond words, and hearing "Puppy Love" every time I walked into a radio station didn't exactly help. But I stuck it out.

The key was radio play, and with only two radio stations in

England, the handful of people who programmed them were incredibly important. Unlike here in the States, it's nearly impossible for a single to slowly take hold in one market, then another, until it breaks nationally. In England, there's only one market, and it's sown up tight, unless you have an "in." I was almost ready to pack it in for good when in the summer of 1988 Virgin decided to give me one last chance and released "Soldier of Love." I made the same rounds in the media I had before, and by then I guess everyone got to know me well enough. Things started turning around in May, when I performed live at the Montreaux Festival, right after U2 and before Public Enemy (talk about an eclectic bill). The show was broadcast live to England and fifty other countries, and the next day, people were talking about what a great job I'd done, especially since I was among only a few performers to sing live.

Slowly but surely, "Soldier" began creeping up the chart. From eighty-three, to sixty-nine, to forty-six, to forty-two. Of course, Top 40 is where you want to be, and during the Sunday countdown show that would reveal whether I officially had a hit or not, I was scheduled to play in a celebrity cricket match. Some fans were there to cheer me on—and keep track of the countdown. When it got into the mid-thirties, I began to worry that it had started dropping back down. I was at bat when suddenly one section of the crowd started screaming. I looked over and it was the fan club. But what did it mean? Then I saw a big card with the number "33" written, and over the PA the announcer told everyone the great news. I'd made the Top 40. I had a hit. Though I missed the next pitch and my team lost, everyone crowded around me, shaking my hand, and offering congratulations. I couldn't believe it, and when I was alone there on the field, I cried. A few weeks later, it peaked at number twenty-nine.

Within a few months, Virgin released my last single there, the upbeat "If It's Love That You Want," but it never stood a chance. I made dozens of appearances; I even made a last desperate attempt to try to personally meet with some influential Radio 1 disc jockeys, who singlehandedly determined what records got played. They wouldn't even see me. It seemed like "Soldier of Love" should have cleared the way, but the old barriers flew back up in my face. It seemed that for every new song I sang live, for every interview I gave, my past had to have "equal time." Though I'd been around in England over two years by then, I was always competing against the boy who'd posed the national security threat fifteen years before. I took the hint. In November, I packed up and went home for good. That month Virgin released the CD entitled *Donny Osmond*, but it was more a business formality than anything else. The push was over. The CD didn't have a prayer, and as Christmas approached, neither did my career. On the flight home, I stared out the window and wondered what line of work I'd be in that time next year.

chapter 7

I was so happy and relieved to be back home in Utah, with Debbie and the boys. An optimist by nature, I tried to make sense of the past two years. I wanted to salvage something from all the work and disappointment, something that might redeem it for me and my family. But it was very hard. I couldn't bear the prospect of ever putting myself or my wife and children through such an ordeal again. In my darker moments, I even downplayed the positive things that had come out of that time. The price seemed too steep, or maybe I was just tired of fighting.

Shortly after I got back home, I invited my manager Ged and another of his clients, singer Paul Young and his wife, to join Debbie and me for dinner. I chose a chic, exclusive restaurant, because this was going to be my last big blowout. I even offered to pick up the tab for everyone, but when the bill came, I wished

I hadn't. We really couldn't afford expensive dinners like this anymore.

Virgin had dropped me from its roster, and I had no record deal in the United States. Around this time, Ged came to my house and said, sadly, "I wish you all the luck in the world, but there's just nothing more I can do for you." I went ahead with plans to start a home security business. Of course, everyone I spoke to about it was surprised, but I was careful to make it sound like I was investigating this option as a "sideline," another business besides my singing career. What I didn't say was that I didn't think I had a singing career anymore.

For a long time now, some members of my extended family had expressed their concern about how I was going about things professionally. As time wore on, their impatience with my dogged determination about my career began to show. Everyone else, except Marie, whose career was as strong as ever, had put performing on the back burner. My brothers had gone country because, as Alan observed, "We couldn't compete with guys who bite the heads off bats." Jay had gone to college in 1985 and was working at BYU as an admissions counselor, and Jimmy was now more entrepreneur than entertainer.

Through it all, I could always turn for support to my brother-in-law Brian Blosil, whom Marie married in 1986. A record producer, Brian saw the business a little differently than some in my family. He seemed to understand what I was trying to achieve, but right after Ged quit, even Brian seemed exasperated with me. "Get rid of the leather jacket and the jeans; shave your face," he said. "Quit trying to be like George Michael." I quickly excused myself, then sped off in my car.

Now what? I turned to Bill Waite, whom I'd known since he

began working with my family in the mid-1970s. "Bill, you've watched all these other guys try to manage my career. Maybe you have some ideas," I said. Bill agreed to give it a try and immediately sent out copies of *Donny Osmond* to every record company executive in the country. We hadn't heard anything by mid-December, so I decided to take a trip to Utah to spend Christmas with my parents. By then I'd resolved that I may have to put show business behind me, and I'd reached the point where that was actually okay. In fact, having some sort of plan to look forward to felt a lot better than looking back, licking my wounds, and trying to figure out what had gone wrong.

Out of the blue, Bill called and said, "You'll never guess what happened! They're playing 'Soldier of Love' on WPLJ in New York!"

"Come on, Bill," I said. "I'm not in the mood for a joke right now."

"No, Donny, it's true. They're playing it, and getting requests for it. It's the number-one requested song on the play list."

"Are you kidding me?" I exclaimed.

"No, Donny, but there's one catch: They're not saying who you are. You're a 'mystery artist.' They want you to fly to New York and be on the air live when they reveal your identity."

"Get me a ticket!" I said. "I'm there!"

I hung up the phone and called out to Debbie: "They're playing my record in New York! I can't believe they're playing my record in New York!"

Which was great, except for a couple minor details. One: Nobody could buy the record because I had no label deal in the United States. In fact, every company that had received a copy of the Virgin Records release of *Donny Osmond* turned it down flat. Two: Even if there had been a CD waiting in the bins, how would listeners find it, since they didn't know who recorded it? It was an interesting predicament to be in, but I was so excited, I didn't care. And in an odd way, I was glad it happened like this, because it only proved what I had always believed: If people could just listen…(I would like to say, "without prejudice," but that phrase has already been spoken for).

Fortunately for me, that's exactly what happened, and I never can tell this story without reminding myself how easily none of this could have happened at all. I later learned that a fan had passed an import copy of my CD on to Jessica Ettinger. Jessica was the interim program director of WPLJ-FM in New York City, one of the country's top, most influential stations. She liked the record but knew she couldn't just put a Donny Osmond record on the play list, so she added "Soldier of Love" to the rotation and the disc jockeys credited it to "the Mystery Artist." Suddenly I had a hit. Now, I could have been insulted by the whole mystery artist business, but a hit record is a hit record. Given how well it was going, I almost wondered if maybe I'd be better off never revealing my identity. I couldn't miss the irony in Jessica having stumbled upon the exact strategy Quincy and Michael had suggested a few years before.

I flew out to New York and was live on the air when WPLJ announced my identity, after weeks of promotional buildup. The best part was seeing the station's phone lines light up after I said, "I'm Donny Osmond," and hearing callers say how much they loved the record and how glad they were that I had released some new music. For the next couple months, radio stations from coast to coast picked up the song, most of the time with the mystery artist gimmick, other times without. And then there were a few instances where getting "Soldier of Love" took a little elbow grease. Literally.

The comeback story behind "Soldier of Love" got a lot of press, and record companies were soon knocking at my door, for a change. Bill Waite and I spoke with several, but I decided to go with Capitol, because its head of promotion, John Fagot, impressed me as someone who would get behind my record and make things happen. Of course, it couldn't possibly be this easy to get the record out here in the States, and it wasn't. Before I signed my deal, an executive from a label I hadn't recorded for in more than a decade attempted to block the deal with Capitol. It was a nuisance more than anything else, and it failed. But there were a few moments when I wondered if this record wasn't cursed.

Capitol released the album in May (with "I'll Be Good to You" replacing "Grand Illusion" from the Virgin Records version). I found myself doing countless live radio interviews with stations across the country. By then, I knew the drill: The disc jockey would play a bit of "Puppy Love," there would be a couple of jokes about my teeth and my goody-goody image, and eventually we'd all settle down and the disc jockey would play "Soldier of Love." Then one day, John Fagot called me and said, "Donny, I've got some bad news. They won't add your song in Tampa, Florida."

"Well, tell me: What do I have to do to change that?" I asked.

"It's not that simple, Donny. There's a disc jockey down there named Cleveland Wheeler, and he just hates the record and he hates you."

"Give me his number. Let me see if I could change his mind," I replied.

"Don't do it, Donny. We don't really need Tampa anyway; just forget it."

"No, John, just give me the number." A day or two later, I called Cleveland's show live during morning drive time.

"Hi, Cleveland, this is Donny Osmond." After we exchanged a few on-air pleasantries, I said, "So I hear you aren't playing 'Soldier of Love.' Can you tell me why?"

"Well, Donny," he replied, "I think your record stinks. I don't like you. And, as a matter of fact, nobody in Tampa likes you."

Okay, I thought. Before I could answer, Cleveland's sidekick, a young woman, came on the line. "Hi, Donny," she said.

She sounded like she was about my age, so I figured, maybe she'd liked "Puppy Love" or maybe *The Donny and Marie Show*, or maybe she had had a poster on her wall, or something. So I turned on the charm. "Hi. It's nice talking to you—"

Before I could finish my sentence, she said, "You know, I really don't like you, either, and I agree with Cleveland about your record. It really does stink. You're trying to copy George Michael or something."

"Well, you guys, I'm really sorry to hear that." I had to think fast. "What can I do to make you change your minds?"

"Okay, Donny, let's have some kind of a contest," Cleveland said.

"Okay."

"How about an arm-wrestling contest?"

"You're on!"

"You win, we add the record to our play list. I win, you go home with your tail between your legs."

When I called John Fagot with the news, he said, "I told you, you're digging a hole for yourself. That guy's gonna eat you up alive."

"Oh, John," I assured him, "I live for these moments."

A couple of weeks later, the big day arrived. Amid a cheering crowd and news cameras, I faced my opponent. In the station's parking lot there was a flatbed pickup truck, on the back of which sat the table where we'd determine the fate of my record. The station had shrewdly scheduled the match for lunchtime, so the place was packed. On one side of the parking lot were Cleveland's fans, and on the other, mine. Camera crews from news programs, including *Entertainment Tonight*, were out, and there was a buzz of anticipation in the air. Cleveland was a pretty big guy, and I got the impression he thought this would be a cinch. We would see.

We'd agreed that the winner would be decided from the best of three matches. The adrenaline was really pumping, so by the time we got through the introductions and preliminaries, I was more than ready. I quickly beat Cleveland the first match.

"Yay, Donny! Yay!" the crowd roared as I pinned his arm to the table.

Cleveland wasn't about to be shown up in his own town. Maybe I underestimated him a little, because he won the second match a little too easily.

"Yay, Cleveland! Yay!" his followers shouted.

I took a deep breath, we locked hands, and the referee counted off, "Three! Two! One!" For a few seconds, it looked like

I had him, but then he came back surprisingly strong, and as I watched my arm slowly being forced down, I said to myself, *You cannot let this happen.* Something surged through me, and— bam!—Cleveland was down! I won.

"Yay! Yay, Donny! Way to go, man!" the crowd screamed, as Cleveland and I shook hands. True to his word, Cleveland did play "Soldier of Love," and so Tampa was not lost. The record became a hit there, too.

By March, "Soldier of Love" was on the national charts, and that June it peaked at number two. *Donny Osmond* eventually went to fifty-four. In May we filmed the video for the next single, "Sacred Emotion," which got extensive play throughout the summer and into the fall, and got as high as number two on VH1's countdown. The video for "Sacred Emotion"—and also two from my next album, "Sure Lookin'" and "My Love Is a Fire"— were directed by a young man fresh out of film school named Michael Bay, who would later go on to direct such hit movies as *The Rock* and *Armageddon*.

It was a busy, exciting time. And the irony of how it all unfolded wasn't lost on me or my brothers, who often felt they were working against their name, too. I'll never forget the emotion in my brother Jay's voice when he said, "You've finally done it, Donny. You've broken through." I later learned that once Richard Branson, the owner of Virgin Records, heard that "Soldier of Love" had hit in the United States, he wanted to rerelease it in England too. I guess he didn't know that his company had already dropped me.

It was time to go on the road. With a thirty-four-city tour in the works, we held auditions for a band. I'd never actually handpicked my own band before, but I was determined to go out with a group of musicians who not only could play my music but give it the depth—the soul—that I'd always wanted to put across. Some rock stars consider the planning and preparation that go into a tour tedious and boring, but I loved every minute of it. Choosing the musicians, staging the show, fine-tuning the lights and the sound and the choreography—every detail had my full attention. When the auditions were over and the dust settled, I had my dream band: keyboardist and musical director Rory Kaplan, and guitarist Jon Clark (both alums of Michael Jackson's band), backup singer Jenny Douglas (who'd worked with Mick Jagger, among others), drummer Jeffrey Suttles (who'd played with Paula Abdul), bassist Oneida James, and keyboardist Ron Reinhardt. Neither Oneida nor Ron had a lot of experience touring. But they were all amazing players, and we blended as if we'd been working together for years. Critics in every city we played lavished high praise on the band, and I was very proud of them and grateful to them for helping me fulfill a creative dream I'd had for so long. Choreographer Vince Paterson staged the show, and the lighting was designed by Phay McMahon, who usually worked much bigger shows, for acts including U2, Metallica, and Def Leppard. I thought everything came together beautifully, and it was especially heartening to read reviews where critics noted the staging and the lights. It was a great team.

There wasn't a lot of money, so the tour—which I called my "credibility tour"—was an interesting journey back to the old days. Being together on the same not-so-fancy tour bus, driving from show to show, and hauling our own lights and sound equipment might be viewed as hardships. For me, it was just part of the adventure. Some of the band mates and support staff were accustomed to the first-class accommodations they'd enjoyed while touring with other, bigger artists. Yet no one complained when dinner was pizza reheated in the bus's microwave or the closest truck stop's special of the day. I'm pretty sure that when some of my musicians ordered meals on tour with Michael or Mick Jagger, no one asked them if they wanted to "super size" it. The hotel and motel rooms we stayed in lacked certain niceties. The fine Belgian chocolate on the pillow and the little basket of French hand-milled soaps were conspicuously absent. (Oh, the hardships!) Traveling to a date, we often had to stop at a pay phone along the way, so I could do a live phone interview with a disc jockey in the next town. We truly were all in it together, and on those nights when we arrived backstage to find a half-empty house, the band would rally around me and cheer me up: "You can do it, Donny! It's gonna be great!" I don't know if I could ever thank them all enough.

The tour kicked off in Phoenix—one of the first markets to add "Soldier"—in late October, and we made our way up the West Coast, across the Midwest, moving to the East Coast, with dates in New York City, Washington, D.C., Nashville, Salt Lake City, Las Vegas, and finally, L.A., in mid-December. Ticket sales were not always as strong as we would have liked, but the people who turned out were all warm and enthusiastic—from teenagers who knew me only through my new videos to older fans who, like me, had survived "Puppy Love" and everything else. As much as I'd tried to distance myself from the past, I knew that some people coming to see me now had been with me since those old hits. Rather than insert a quick, perfunctory medley, once in a while the band would leave the stage, and I sat at the piano to sing "Go Away Little Girl" alone. Oh, and I did a little of "One Bad Apple"—nicely reggae-fied—but after a few bars, I cut it off with a good-natured "That's enough of that!"

To be honest, though, I was most encouraged by the reviews. Of course, the critics had to refer to my past—which in a strange way, didn't bother me anymore—and make note of my new, "hot," "sexy" look in tight (not really) jeans and leather. But they really listened to the music, too. I loved reading headlines such as "Successful Escape from Bubblegum Past," "Funky Donny Osmond Pops the Nostalgia Bubble," even "Donnymania: The Sequel." That last headline might have bothered me were it not for the review itself: "Osmond has pulled off an Elvis-style comeback that will likely secure his place in the entertainment industry for a number of years to come." And no one missed the message behind my encore: Sly Stone's "Thank You (Falettinme Be Mice Elf Again)." I meant it.

Just a few months after the tour ended, it was time to start thinking about the follow-up album. I approached it with enthusiasm tempered by a heavy dose of reality. Nineteen eighty-nine had been a dream ride for me, and I'd have loved to have seen it go on forever. But I'd been around too long not to know better. Despite all the great reviews, despite the fact that people were taking me seriously, I never let myself forget that "Soldier" started up the charts with a big boost from great timing, pure luck, and—let's be honest—a good gimmick. I had to wonder, *Would I always need a gimmick to be heard?*

With *Eyes Don't Lie*, I wanted to go for the funkier, harder, more guitar-driven sound the first album teased at but didn't always quite deliver. As executive producer, I chose three different writing-production teams, joining forces again with Carl Sturken and Evan Rogers, Ric Wake (then best known for his work with singer Taylor Dayne), and David Gamson (whose work with Scritti Politti I admired). I worked on it intensely for five months, and the result was, I felt, stronger—musically and sonically—than *Donny Osmond*. The album led off with Carl and Evan's "My Love Is a Fire," an unbridled funk track that includes a sample/tribute to the Ohio Players' "Fire." I cowrote "Just Between You and Me," which featured a guitar solo by Def Leppard's Phil Collen. (Unfortunately, after the session, Phil decided he'd rather not have his name on a Donny Osmond album and instead we credit one "Rory James Collen," his son.) The strings were arranged by Jeremy Lubbock, who worked on albums by Chicago and Al Jarreau.

In the fall of 1990, we did a brief tour of major cities that coincided with the release of "My Love Is a Fire" and the album. I finished that tour in October, and Debbie and I were home in Los Angeles awaiting the birth of our fourth son, Christopher Glenn. His birth, on December 12, 1990, made the holidays so much more special for us. This, I would always remind myself, was what mattered most.

I had very high hopes for this album, especially "My Love Is a Fire," a number-twenty-one hit that I'm still convinced would have made the Top 10 with the right promotion. Michael Bay directed a very provocative video for it, as well as a funny one for "Sure Lookin'," that featured a cameo appearance by Dweezil Zappa. Unfortunately, the album's release coincided with a change in leadership at Capitol, and the new powers that be didn't get behind it. By early 1991, the commercial fate of *Eyes Don't Lie* was all but sealed. You didn't need a crystal ball to know that all signs were pointing toward the cut out bin. By spring of

1991, when "Love Will Survive" failed to enter the Hot 100, I was disappointed but not entirely surprised. I wasn't touring enough to support my band, and each musician was so talented, it was only a matter of time before other artists made them better offers. I was sad to see the band break up, but I couldn't promise them steady work. They all deserved whatever came their way.

I was resigned to my fate. In a strange way, I sort of half-expected it. I'd had my moment—and it was a great, once-in-a-lifetime moment—then it was gone. Again. The difference between this time and all the disappointments I'd had in the past was that for the first time, I didn't feel the need to fight it. I'd proved my point to the industry and to myself. For my music, I'd come full circle.

I was still doing some concerts, and I never missed a chance to turn people's preconceptions inside out. I'd guested on my friend Dweezil Zappa's 1991 album *Confessions* with a very undiscolike "Stayin' Alive," and when he did a show at the Roxy, on Hollywood's Sunset Strip, he invited me to be his guest onstage. Now, the Roxy is intimate by rock club standards and a cool place to be seen. On the night of the show, I arrived early and laid low out in the audience, which, looking back was probably unnecessary. Who seeing me there would ever guess I'd be singing that night? No one, I'd bet.

About fifteen minutes into his set, Dweezil announced, "We've got a special guest star singer that came in and guested on the album. And we'd like to bring him onstage right now. Please welcome Donny Osmond!"

I stepped onstage, to the silence of a few hundred jaws

dropping. Now, I have to say, no one booed, but the reception was so chilly, you could have hung meat. Standing behind the mike, I looked over at Dweezil and said, "You ready?"

"Yeah, you ready?"

Then we plunged into a hard-core, heavy-metal, pile-driving version of "Stayin' Alive" that brought down the house. I guess they discovered that, among other things, I'm also a little bit heavy metal. At least when I need to be. I was once doing a daytime show at the Oregon State Fairgrounds, in Salem, for about two thousand people. Everyone was loving it, except three fat, burly bikers down in front. Every time I looked over at them, it was like a bad déjà vu of that night in Paris, when the Osmonds inadvertently freaked out those Hell's Angels with our white suits and banjos.

I was singing when suddenly I heard a high-pitched, sing-songy, "Don-nee! Don-nee! Please sing 'Puppy Love.'" I looked across the crowd and realized it was the three bikers, laughing and mocking me. Through the next couple of numbers, they kept calling out to me in these girly voices, and I think they were disappointed that I was ignoring them, though it was getting harder to do. Finally, I'd had it. I spun away from the audience and stopped the band midsong. Walking slowly to the front of the stage, I stared right at the hecklers.

"Hey, you three down there!" I said, pointing to them. "You want 'Puppy Love'? You got 'Puppy Love!'" Rory kicked it off, and Jon came in with crunching metal chords that just about blew everyone out of their seats.

"AND THEY CALLED IT PUPPY LOVE!" I sang as if I'd just bitten off a puppy's head and spit it into the crowd. Not that I would ever do that, really.

"OH I GUESS THEY'LL NEVER KNOW! HOW A

YOUNG HEART REALLY FEELS!" I have to say, I almost scared myself. It was fun singing "AND WHY I LOVE YOU SO" with every ounce of hate and rage I could summon. The crowd was screaming, like I'd unleashed some monster, but they were lovin' it. When I was done, I walked over to the three now surprisingly subdued guys and said, "Is that enough?" They cheered, and the whole crowd joined in.

I could have kept making records forever, but I had a family to support and my pride to maintain. I knew I'd be happier being a success at my second career choice than being a failure at my first. The funny thing is, that in the wake of "Soldier of Love," my manager fielded dozens of offers, but the one that kept coming across—and for the most money—was a Donny and Marie reunion to perform in places like Las Vegas and Atlantic City. It was tempting, and we were flattered to be asked, but it wasn't something we were interested in doing then. I also sat through a few preliminary discussions about possible television vehicles, but I just couldn't see that working for me, either. I started looking seriously at other options.

While I was in Los Angeles, Bill Waite introduced me to an actress named Crystal Bernard. We became friends, and she helped me get into an acting class at the Beverly Hills Playhouse. I'd been thinking about taking acting ever since *Little Johnny Jones*. Although I couldn't articulate it then, I sensed that my job onstage as a singer and my job onstage as an actor were different. I realized that one miscalculation I'd made with *Little Johnny Jones* was not developing my character sufficiently that the audience would look at me and see Johnny Jones before they saw Donny Osmond. I was fortunate to work with some wonderful teachers, including Milton Katselas and Jocelyn Jones.

Jocelyn asked us to do a "picture exercise," which entails finding a photograph of anyone and then creating a ten-minute piece about that person as you imagine him. You can sing a song, recite a poem, or perform a play that you've written yourself or another work that you have adapted from another source. The point is that you present it in your character. You can choose anyone but a famous person or a celebrity.

In a copy of *National Geographic* I found a photograph of a weathered, black welder who worked on the docks. He looked to be about fifty-five years old, but you could see in his face that life had aged him at least a decade beyond that. Rather than create his character from scratch, I discovered one named Troy Maxson from August Wilson's Pulitzer Prize–winning play *Fences*. In the play, Maxson is a phenomenal Negro League baseball player denied the chance to reach his potential simply because he is black. His bitter rage and haunted resignation lie at the heart of the play. Rather than simply recite the lines as written, I condensed the gist of the play into a ten-minute monologue I wrote myself.

I spent weeks pulling my character together: I searched secondhand stores until I found the exact outfit, down to the same welder's goggles and even the ring he wore in the picture. I practiced Troy's slightly stiff, beaten-down gait and his rural Southern dialect until I felt I was him.

The way I'd written the scene, Troy starts out speaking softly. Life had worn Troy down, and I wanted everyone to understand his defeat and his sadness. But I did it for another reason. I wanted everyone in the audience to stop and listen intently. As Troy tells his story, the humor and optimism that sustained him shine through, but ultimately the rage he's repressed for so many years rises up in him until he can no longer control himself. Close to the end of the piece, Troy is screaming at the top of his lungs, but he finishes his soliloquy on a note of stoic resignation, quietly saying, "And that's my life."

Playing my part, I felt as angry as I'd ever been—or allowed myself to be—in real life. My classmates gave me a standing ovation. Jocelyn rose and gestured for everyone to sit down. I couldn't believe it when I heard her say, "I've been judging these picture exercises for about twenty years, and this is one of the best I've ever seen—not because of his acting, because..." and then she proceeded to give me detailed constructive criticism. "But," she added, "look at the research this guy has done," and she pointed out the fact that I'd found exactly the same ring.

After I took my place back in the class, Jocelyn's comments took a more personal turn. She said, "I see a lot of inhibition in you, Donny, because of your past." There in front of my classmates, Jocelyn encouraged me talk about why that was so. I surprised myself, describing how trapped I felt in the Manning Apartments as a teenager, the breakdown in Hawaii, and some of the hard times I'd gone through. It had taken me a long time to feel the level of trust you need to get anything out of a class like this. By the time I was done, I couldn't hold it back; I was crying again, but not as Troy Maxson, as me.

"Now, you're a writer, correct?" Jocelyn asked.

I said yes.

"You write music?"

"Yes, I do."

"Good. Then write me a song about breaking those walls down. And I want you to sing it for the class in three weeks."

A couple weeks passed, and while I had been jotting down

ideas in the third person, something kept me from completing it. I'd write lyrics, then look at them and decide they were too personal or too revealing, and set them aside. (When I'm writing something, I never throw out any early notes or drafts, because I like to go back and trace how ideas evolve.) Anyway, here I was, just two days before I had to give Jocelyn my song, and I had next to nothing. The obvious idea would have been to write about breaking down those walls and how happy I was to escape them. But the more I thought about it, the more I realized that I didn't really want to break down all the walls around me as much as I just wanted to create a door in one, so I could venture outside. I really wanted—I needed—always to come back. By then, I'd made my peace with being Donny Osmond. I'd stopped running away. I didn't need to destroy my past to live fully in the present. I still needed to know that shelter was there when I needed it. I went back to my old notes and realized that what I wanted to say lay in the lines I'd crossed out before, among them:

> *And, oh, you don't know how it feels*
> *To be the perfect boy in town.*
> *To do as you're told, to love inside a shell*
> *That's been created*
> *By so many people who have shaped*
> *The way they think that I should always be.*

A few days later in class, as I sang the last verses of the song, I could see from my classmates' and Jocelyn's expressions that this wasn't exactly what they expected.

You see, with these walls I've devised a clever plan
That turns this boy into a man...
And now these walls I keep
Are not the barriers I once thought,
Nor the roadblocks that would stop me exploring.
No, you see, these walls, they do have doors,
So I can go outside once more,
And know who I am, from where I come
Where I feel good, when I'm myself,
Behind these loving walls of mine.

Writing that song helped me see that I didn't need to break down all the barriers to find myself, that all I needed was the freedom to choose when and how I went outside them. I accepted that there were some walls, some kinds of emotional protection, that I would always need around me.

Over the summer of 1991, I entered—and won—two celebrity car races: the Toyota Pro/Celebrity Grand Prix, in Long Beach, California, and the Texaco/Havalon Grand Prix, in Denver. I always liked to drive fast, but I wasn't "into" cars as I was growing up. I never owned fancy cars, and my real joy was taking even the most mundane models—like my beloved Chevette from the late 1970s—and customizing it with every conceivable electronic gadget I could build. I also used my car as a rolling office/rehearsal studio. Whatever music I was working on, I brought along my tapes and played them over and over and over, refining my singing or the arrangements.

When the invitation to race came, I figured at the very least I could have some fun, and—more important—I was determined to win. About a week before the race, I met a professional driver who put me in a car and showed me the basics as well as a few tricks. While a race like this isn't the Indy 500, it's still a race, and you have to be quick, decisive, and cautious. Driving at speeds of up to 150 miles per hour, anything can happen. Of course, you take every possible safety precaution—crash helmet, fireproof suit and gloves, a full-body harness to hold you inside—but accidents do happen. During a practice run in Long Beach, I came up behind a car and was doing about 90 miles per hour mere inches from its rear when in the middle of a long turn, I passed it. Just seconds later, that car caught fire, the cab filled with smoke, and the driver slammed on his brakes. Had I still been right behind him, we surely would have crashed.

The day of the Toyota race, we took off from a running start, and actor Craig T. Nelson, from the sitcom *Coach*, had the coveted lead position. He was an amazing driver, and I couldn't beat his qualifying time, so I knew I had a tough race ahead. We were neck and neck for a while, then I took a chance. As we headed into a turn, I deliberately bumped him just enough to get him to back off. Obviously, this has to be done with great care, and I know Craig wasn't too happy with me after that. But he did fall back, and I took and held the lead until I crossed the finish line. I loved winning, and hearing guys, for a change, shouting, "Donny Osmond rocks!" That was the icing on the cake.

That was exciting, but it was winning my second race, in Denver, that made me seriously consider going pro. Racing appealed to me on several levels: It had all the thrills and glamour of show business, plus I could really speed without having to talk my way out of traffic tickets.

The Denver race was different, because included in the field were semiprofessional drivers. During the qualifications, I just couldn't go fast enough to earn that pole position, no matter what I did. So I found a couple of professional drivers and walked the course with them. They showed me the places where I could shave off a few milliseconds, which doesn't sound like much but can actually spell the difference between victory and defeat. Going into the race, one thing was certain, once the green flag dropped after a two-lap warmup, I had to pass the two drivers ahead of me or I could kiss it all good-bye. I knew what to do. The question was whether I had the nerve to do it.

The race was on, and I floored it on the straightaway before the first turn. Now, on the left-hand wall that runs alongside the track, there are decreasing numbers as you approach each turn—usually 4, 3, 2, 1. You pass by them in less than a second, but they're very important, because they tell you approximately how much distance left to brake before you come into the actual turn. As you may recall from driver's ed, you slow into a turn and accelerate coming out. You never brake in mid-turn if you can help it. As we approached the end of the straightaway, there were three of us running neck and neck going into the turn. Someone would have to fall back. The question was who.

One important rule of racing is that you never look at the other cars. You drive your own race. I was approaching that first, right-hand turn with my front left bumper just inches from one guy's right door. To his left, he had the third guy running right alongside him. Now picture all of this happening in not much more than two seconds: The 4 goes by—no one gives. At 3, I know I have to slow for the turn, but the other two cars are still beside me. At 2, the driver on the far left falls back, and, using a controlled bumping technique, I hit the guy beside me, which enabled me to maintain my speed without going off the track. I took the lead going into the turn. It was an aggressive, potentially dangerous, and barely legal maneuver, but I made it and was leading the race.

Now, the two guys I'd beaten into the turn came after me with a vengeance, trying to reclaim the lead coming out of the turn. I misjudged my position and glanced the left wall, losing my left sideview mirror. In a race, you're blind without your sideview mirrors, because you can't see in your rearview who's coming up alongside you. For the rest of the race, the two drivers were doing everything they could to catch me, especially on the left side, where they knew I wouldn't see them until it was too late. I had to drive looking over my shoulder, which is extremely dangerous, but I badly wanted that race. I wouldn't let it go. Going into the final turn, I still had the lead, and when the checkered flag dropped, I'd won by two or three seconds. Later the two drivers who'd given me such a run told me that they were surprised at how aggressively I'd driven. Even I was surprised not to get a black-flag warning. After that, professional race car driving became less a dream and more a viable option, though Debbie was not totally pleased.

In early 1992, if I'd been asked to list my possible future career options in order of probability, returning to musical theater would have been somewhere pretty far down the list. I've never walked away from a challenge, but my experience with *Little Johnny Jones* left me with an almost reflexive fear of returning to anything like that. I couldn't bear the thought of failing that publicly again. So when Bill called me to say that my agent had booked me for an audition in New York City, I replied, "Are you kidding? I don't even want to think about it."

When I learned that the play was a revival of the Andrew

Lloyd Webber–Tim Rice musical *Joseph and the Amazing Technicolor Dreamcoat*, I wasn't very excited. I was already familiar with the role of Joseph, loosely based on the biblical figure whose brothers sell him into slavery because they envy his father's favoritism, his glorious multicolored coat, and his prophetic dreams. And I also knew Webber and Rice's multigenre, pop-style score, because I had seen Jimmy perform the title role in regional productions during the early 1980s. For some reason, Joseph has always been an ideal vehicle for pop singers, and—dare I say—teen idols. I remember thinking about who'd played him before: David Cassidy and my brother Jimmy. I didn't mean any disrespect toward them, but the role seemed to have taken on a life of its own, and I worried it would be hard for me to play it without people thinking I was going back to being the old Donny Osmond.

Bill understood what I was saying on one level, but on another, I think he had a better sense than I did about what a great opportunity this was. There were so many things I'd been offered over the years that I couldn't or wouldn't do, for various reasons. I avoided anything that would remind people of the old Donny image, so that eliminated a lot of television appearances. I wouldn't be part of anything that ran counter to my religious beliefs. So, for example, when it seemed you couldn't have a rock video without models in suggestive poses and revealing costumes, I'd insisted on a reedit of my video for "My Love Is a Fire" to tone it down. Clearly, I was swimming against a heavy tide, and I know this didn't endear me to the people at my record label. But I couldn't compromise, and I was willing to live with the consequences. Bill, who belongs to the same church that I do, understood me better than most managers would have.

Despite my reservations, this was still a great opportunity, if only because I would be auditioning for Canadian producer Garth Drabinksy, the man whose productions then accounted for over a quarter of all receipts from live theater on the North American continent. It would have been shortsighted of me not to at least have taken the audition simply to meet him. Garth, then in his early forties, was already well known in show business circles as a tenacious, single-minded producer who knew exactly what he wanted and usually got it.

Since I had a full calendar of commitments in Los Angeles, the only way I could audition was to take the overnight "red eye" flight to New York, audition, then fly home to Los Angeles by the same evening. On the way to the airport, I stopped at Tower Records on Sunset and picked up the soundtrack CD from an earlier production, just to familiarize myself with Joseph's two key numbers that the audition called for: "Any Dream Will Do" and "Close Every Door." I figured I'd listen to them on the flight to New York, so when I got there for the audition, they would be fresh in my mind.

I settled down in my seat and popped the CD into my portable player, slipped the headphones on, and…The next thing I knew, we were making the final approach to land in New York and I was still holding the CD player in my hand. *Oh, no,* I thought. *This can't be happening.* I'd fallen asleep right after takeoff and slept through the entire flight. I looked at my watch. I'd have just enough time to get to my hotel, freshen up, and get to the theater for my audition. I was furious with myself. How did I let this happen? I began to panic; then I realized that I probably wasn't going to get the role anyway. Maybe instead of getting all worked up over it, I should just accept it and do the best

I could. It didn't take much time to learn the songs. But to create the character, and to act the part—which is what distinguishes musical theater from any other kind of singing—I needed time I didn't have. For the next few hours, between listening to the CD and getting to the theater on time, I kept repeating to myself, *I'm not nervous at all. I'm not nervous at all.*

Of course, anyone who saw me backstage waiting to go on could probably see I was about to jump out of my skin. I was yawning a lot, from both nerves and exhaustion, but I put up a good front, attributing it all to being up all night on the red eye (though I'd slept the whole way). Inside, though, the legacy and burden of having been one of the "one-take Osmonds" was weighing on me. I felt like an amateur. I was thirty-four. How could I be so stupid?

Someone called my name, and as I walked on to the stage, I decided to apply a little reverse psychology: *I don't want this role,* I kept telling myself. *I don't care.*

I spotted Garth sitting in the audience with four or five other people. He wasn't that much older than me, but when he spoke, his voice had the rough, no-nonsense tone of someone who'd been in the business for decades more. I walked to the front of the stage and staring out into the near-empty house, said, "Mr. Drabinsky, I'm sorry, but I'm not completely prepared for this audition." These are words usually uttered by actors who have no desire to ever work again, but I knew I couldn't fake my way through this. I wasn't asking for special consideration, and I didn't deserve any, either.

"Well, do something, kid," Garth replied in his gruff voice.

I took off my leather jacket, and said, "I'll sing 'Close Every Door' "—the more vocally challenging of the two songs—"but

I'll be reading the lyrics, since I haven't committed them to memory."

"Okay, that's fine," Garth with a discernible trace of annoyance.

Clearly, I wasn't going to score any points here being an unprepared Donny Osmond, so instead I chose to be Joseph, lyric booklet in hand and all. I recalled the moments I'd spent at the Playhouse being Troy Maxson, and how I'd mentally willed Donny Osmond to disappear. I drew a deep breath and started singing. I couldn't "think" about my expressions or my gestures or any other aspect of my "performance," because I came to the stage with nothing. It came straight from the heart, because that's all I had to offer. Strangely enough, after a few notes, my fear slipped away, and I found myself actually feeling more confident artistically, not in spite of it being out of my control, but because of it.

Toward the end of the song, in the line, "For I know I shall find my own peace of mind," there's a very high note on the second "shall." I knew that if I missed it, I didn't stand a chance. But I nailed it.

I finished and waited for some response from the five people in the audience. The five seconds of silence that followed my last note seemed to last forever. Then I heard Garth say, "Come here, kid." I walked down into the audience, and he committed to me right then and there. "I think you're the right person for this and you've got the role if you want it."

"I'll think about it," I said, still not sure if this was for me.

Back home, Debbie and I talked this over for days. It wasn't an easy decision. Financially, it was a great offer. Still, I knew that if I took it, my recording career and anything else I might wish to pursue would have to take a backseat for at least six months, maybe a few years. But the biggest concern was having to move the boys to Toronto. Rehearsals were set to begin in Canada in May for a late-June opening in Toronto. A live theater schedule—usually performances every day but Monday, two shows on Sunday and Wednesday—made weekly commuting an exhausting and expensive option. We decided that we would all move to Toronto.

During rehearsals, I worked with and got to know the show's director, Steven Pimlott. He was the person who helped me most in refining my approach to the role. As we reviewed the story, we were both amazed at the parallels between my life and Joseph's. Like me, Joseph had been a sort of golden child who at seventeen fell out of favor and was sold into slavery by his brothers. Now, I don't mean to equate my career with the life of a biblical character, and doing the original *Donny and Marie Show* wasn't exactly like doing hard time in ancient Egypt. But at approximately the same age, Joseph and I had endured about a decade of being lost, of struggling to find our purpose. Steven showed me how to draw on the emotions of these experiences and incorporate them into Joseph's character.

More important, though, Steven turned around my attitude about performing. He taught me the lesson I would have done well to heed before the curtain rose on *Little Johnny Jones*, and it was exactly what I needed to learn. He pointed out to me that the approach that had worked for the kind of performing I'd done before—basically going onstage, turning on the engines, and letting the audience know I was there to do anything to please them—wouldn't work in musical theater.

"You have to unlearn all that," Steven told me one day early on. "Erase it from your memory, because now you have to create a world onstage that is your own. You have to make the audience feel like they're being allowed the chance to peek into your world."

At first, it was hard to understand exactly what he meant—it completely contradicted everything I'd ever learned before. I had to learn to ignore my instinct to play to the crowd, to seek openly that connection I thrived on. The "Soldier of Love" tour had reminded me of how an audience's acceptance and applause was my drug. Instead of reaching out to them, I had to create something in my performance that would make them come to me. Learning to seem oblivious to everything outside the stage—especially the audience—was one of the most difficult things for me to change.

I'd learned my part and rehearsed the songs until I could sing them in my sleep. Still, as we got ready for the previews, there were a few surprises. For me, the biggest one was the little—emphasis on little—white loincloth I wore pretty much throughout the show.

Going into my first costume fitting, I knew I'd be bare-chested during most of the show, and I'd already endured the torture of waxing for that clean, smooth look. When the wardrobe person handed me what looked like a few strips of white cloth, I asked, "Where's the rest of it?"

Everyone looked at me, and the women working on the costumes almost started laughing: "Donny, that *is* it."

I put it on, looked in the mirror, and thought, *No way.* One piece wrapped around my seat and a second piece, about ten inches wide hung straight down from my waist to about mid-thigh. It wasn't really that daring, but it was a lot less costume than I'd ever worn onstage before. I emerged from the dressing room about to die of embarrassment. True, I would be wearing white Speedo swim trunks underneath it, but still…All that held it all together and on me were a few snaps, and during the "Potiphar" number—where the evil Mrs. Potiphar attempts to seduce Joseph—she would give the front piece a tug. There were times when I was amazed (not to mention relieved) that the whole thing didn't just come off.

I tried hard to be professional about it, but one night about two weeks after opening night, the realization of how undressed I was hit me, and I started turning red from embarrassment. Everyone onstage could see it. Janet Metz, the actress who played the narrator, whispered to me, "What's the matter?"

Out of the side of my mouth, I whispered back, "I just realized I'm almost completely naked out here!" Everyone in the cast knew how I felt, so over the six years I played the role, it got to be a little game to see if anyone could get Donny to lose his loincloth. A couple times, they almost succeeded, and two of the three crucial snaps popped open, but thank goodness, they didn't. I managed to protect my loincloth and my honor almost to the end. And then, wouldn't you know it, of all the cities for the thing finally to come off, it happened in Salt Lake City in early 1998. The actress playing Mrs. Potiphar gave it a yank, and that was it. The show stopped as the audience, the cast, everyone—including me—broke out laughing.

We had our first previews in Toronto, at the Elgin Theater in mid-June, then we opened to wonderful reviews on June 24, 1992. Sir Andrew Lloyd Webber was in the audience for the premiere, and I called him up onstage to take the final curtain call with us. The audience went berserk, and I was so proud to stand beside him. As we stood there, he turned and gave me a compliment I will never forget: "That was fabulous. And, by the way, where have you been keeping that voice all these years?"

The reviews were wonderful. I was thrilled, of course, but I kept trying to rationalize my good luck. Well, I would tell myself, this is not Broadway, and audiences and critics are more forgiving. Or maybe it was just a great cast in a spectacular production—which it was—and I was just lucky. But as we moved from Toronto to Minneapolis that fall, then to Vancouver, British Columbia, to Edmonton, Alberta, Canada, and, in September 1993, Chicago—the country's second-biggest theater city outside New York—I knew it wasn't a fluke. In the weeks leading up to our Chicago opening, I was particularly nervous. Everyone at Live Entertainment (the show's production company) kept talking about how the show's future depended on what happened in Chicago. If we could sell a three-month run, that would be great. But if we could go beyond that, I was told that this could last "a while." I would never have dreamed then that "a while" in Chicago would be over a year, or that I would play *Joseph* for almost six years and nearly two thousand shows.

I enjoyed the sense of family and camaraderie everyone working on the show shared. To keep things interesting, the cast and crew developed silly games we'd play onstage. One involved trying to pass a small rubber Gumby and Pokey from one cast member to the other onstage without anyone in the audience seeing it happen. You never wanted to get stuck with Gumby or Pokey unless you were in a position immediately to hand them off unobtrusively. One night I ended up with both Gumby and Pokey at the start of the dramatic "Close Every Door." What could I do? I sang, clutching the prison cell bars, as Gumby and Pokey smiled beside me.

Everyone in the show was wonderful to work with, but I had a special rapport with my good friend Johnny Seaton, the actor who played the Pharaoh as Elvis. Johnny was a fantastic Elvis impersonator, and his Pharaoh was truly the King, from his slick blue-black pompadour to his blue suede shoes. Johnny and I loved to banter back and forth onstage, and there were times when our ad-libbing got us both in trouble with our resident director, Madeline Paul.

Of course, you always have to be prepared onstage, but some of my most memorable moments occurred when things went awry. The show's finale was the "Megamix," a 1990s, hip-hop medley of the entire score during which I flew out over the audience on a cable attached to a harness. No matter how many times I had to fly over the audience, I never got tired of it. One night a friend came to see me before the show and gave me a box of creamy chocolate eclairs. Of course, I left them on my dressing room table. I had already warmed up and cleared my voice, and the last thing a singer should do is eat or drink anything rich and thick before a performance, since it can affect your singing. I had several costume changes during the show, and every time I came back to my dressing room, the eclairs looked more delicious. But I resisted almost until the end.

As we neared the end of the show, I ran back to the dressing room while everyone onstage performed the "Megamix." I got into the flying harness, and put on the Technicolor dreamcoat. And since I only had to sing a couple of lines while flying over the audience at the end, I figured one eclair couldn't do that much damage. I grabbed an eclair and took a big bite as I walked to stage left, where I made my entrance. Surely, I'd have it down before my cue came to run out, take my bow, fly, and sing.

I miscalculated, in a big way. I ran out onstage, still chewing and chewing as fast as I could, trying to be inconspicuous. I executed a twirl with my cape, and the audience is shouting and clapping—and I was *still* chewing. I walked to the front of the stage, a couple of the dancers hooked the cable to my flying harness, and I started flying over the audience. Here comes my vocal cue—and I was still chewing. Oh, well, nothing I could do about it, I had to sing. Let's just say that there were a few people in the audience who got a little bit more than just a show about Joseph and his Amazing Technicolor Dreamcoat.

After so many shows, there are those moments when actors do go on automatic pilot. I was in Minneapolis, and we were in the middle of my big, dramatic number, "Close Every Door." At the time, Debbie and I were designing the house we planned to build in Utah, and during a few bars' interlude, where the children's chorus sang, "la, la, la..." my mind wandered to how I wanted my future home office arranged. I was posed dramatically in my prison cell, a look of longing and sadness on my face. All the while I'm thinking, *A window behind my desk, then a door into the studio right over there...*when suddenly it was my cue to resume singing and I drew a total blank. *The words! The words!* I had to sing something. Since I couldn't recall Tim Rice's lyrics, I supplied some of my own, something about the horizon, I think. Now, if you didn't know the score, you might assume that Tim Rice had written something so profound, so oblique, it was just over your head. If you did know the song, though, you knew I was in major trouble up there and sweatin' bullets.

In the six years I played Joseph, I spent the most time in Chicago, which became sort of a second home to me. A lot of interesting things happened there. I found a new manager, Jill Willis, who had worked with The Artist (Formerly Known as Prince). She was the first person I ever interviewed who came to the table without a lot of preconceptions about what I could and could not do in the future. I got my first taste of cohosting a talk show when I sat in for Regis Philbin on *Live! With Regis & Kathie Lee* for a day in January 1994. I also gave Regis a loincloth like the one I wore in the show. (I wonder why he never wore it on air.) In less than a week, I was privileged to sing the national anthem at both a White Sox and a Chicago Bulls game. Sure, some of the guys booed me before I started, but after I hit the high note on "free," no one was booing when I was done. And it was in Chicago that I first stepped into the boxing ring.

This bizarre episode began back at the East Bank health club where I trained every day. As luck would have it, Danny Bonaduce—whom you may recall as adorable, precocious little redheaded Danny Partridge from *The Partridge Family*—was working as a disc jockey in Chicago at WLUP, a classic-rock station known as the Loop. Danny also trained at the same club, and I'd seen him around a few times. One day, I was doing a phone interview with a good friend of mine, another Loop air personality named Jonathon Brandmeier. I really liked Johnny B, because even when I had nothing going on, he sort of put his wing around me and would have me on the show now and then.

As we were talking, Danny's name came up and I made the sort of off-the-cuff, smart-alecky comment that's gotten me in hot water before (and would again in the future), something like, "Yeah, Danny, he thinks he's so buff. He walks around the gym looking at himself in the mirror," and so on. How could I know that at that moment Danny was in his car, listening to every word, and not liking it too much. I think Danny would be the first to admit that he can be pretty aggressive, so I probably shouldn't have been surprised when he called Johnny B from his cell phone and I found myself immersed in a heated, three-way conversation dominated by Danny's fun-hearted insults.

"You think you're so tough, Donny," Danny sneered. "I could beat you to a pulp."

"I don't think so, Danny," I replied.

"Well, it sounds like we've got a fight on our hands," Johnny B observed. "Are you guys willing to duke it out?"

Now, I knew Danny had done some fighting over in Japan, but I wasn't afraid. It was a challenge, and that was enough for me. Besides, with so many people listening, what could I say without sounding like a total wimp. I'd never boxed before in my life, and I wasn't much of a fighter either. In fact, back in Provo when the high school guys would come after me, it was usually Jay who saved me. The whole truth is…I'd never been in a fight in my life. (Surprised?) However, Bill Waite and I had promoted about a dozen lightweight bouts, and I had spent some time ringside, so I knew a little about the sport.

Emboldened by my awesome arm-wrestling victory over Cleveland Wheeler in Tampa, I told Danny: "Hey, I'm game."

"Absolutely," Danny replied. "I'm in it, too."

So we were on, but not because we had any real animosity toward each other. From the beginning, we both saw the fight as a fun way to raise some money for charity. We agreed to meet in the ring at the China Club about two months later, and go three three-minute rounds. It was heavily promoted by the radio station, so we knew there would be a big turnout; the tickets sold out in ten minutes. And we later heard that traders were betting the fight on the floor of the Chicago stock exchange.

Although this wasn't a "serious" fight, I still was determined to win. For the next two months, I trained with three boxing trainers, including one who had worked with heavyweight champ George Foreman. The training was excellent in terms of teaching me the basics and getting me psyched up. The only oversight—which I didn't realize until it was too late—was that no one really hit me. I guess either they didn't think the fight would be serious, or they didn't want to hurt me.

It seemed like everyone in Chicago was waiting for this fight. The station kept counting down the days. Television crews from all the networks and ESPN as well as a boxing expert from *Sports Illustrated* were going to cover the big event. Everyone in the cast and crew of *Joseph* got into it, encouraging me and constructing an Egyptian-style sedan chair on which I would make my grand entrance. Finally the day arrived.

Of course, Chicago being Danny's adopted hometown, he had a little bit of an advantage, cheering-wise. I had Debbie, my boys, practically everyone from the show, and my own contingent of fans. Some stagehands from *Joseph* carried me to the ring in my sedan chair, and the crowd went crazy. It was so great. My first impulse was to smile, because I was enjoying every bit of this moment, but I stopped myself.

Then Danny strode out, and the place went even crazier. Johnny B, who was emceeing the match, gave a spirited running commentary that kept the audience's excitement at a fever pitch. We stood in our respective corners, got our face masks on, the gloves, the Vaseline (so that a punch slides off your skin instead of ripping it off), and the last instructions from our trainers. It was just like a big fight scene from the movies, with the tension so thick in the air, you could cut it. I'm sure that for some people, just the image of "Danny Partridge" and me slugging it out was bizarre enough. For me, though, it all seemed so surreal, from the card girl who was actually a transvestite to seeing former heavyweight champ Leon Spinks in the crowd. Then we heard the bell.

We both came out of our corners and started throwing punches. We both resorted to some tactics more appropriate to a schoolyard than a boxing ring: backhands, elbows, rabbit punches. I was holding my own well enough until—*wham!*—Danny punched me right in the face so hard, I saw stars. I could feel my eye swelling up and taste the blood gushing out of my nose. That was it! I don't think I'd ever been this angry in my life. I went after Danny and knocked off his headgear, so they stopped the fight. He and I were yelling at each other so much, they couldn't resume for a couple of minutes. Part of it was theatrics, but I was also pumped. As *Sports Illustrated* later said in its coverage of the bout, I was no Ali—but for a few moments there, I understood how Ali felt in the ring.

In the second round, I made sure Danny lost his headgear on three separate occasions. I know I landed more punches than Danny did, and so when the fight was over, and they announced him the winner, I wasn't pleased, but I was a good sport.

"You won it fair and square," I told him, and we removed our gloves and the tape off our knuckles. Danny was standing in the winner's circle, about twenty feet from the ring, delivering his victory speech when suddenly he started spouting these extremely crude, vulgar remarks about Marie. I saw Debbie sitting ringside with my children, and then I saw Danny make an obscene gesture with his fist and arm. I lost it. Before I thought, I jumped out of the ring and started making my way through the crowd separating the ring from the winner's circle.

Danny screamed something insulting back, and I shouted, "You want to go bare knuckles? Come on! I'll take you bare knuckles!"

The next thing I knew, all three of my trainers had jumped on me, and a group of guys were trying to contain Danny. I was so furious, I managed to throw off all my trainers, and I was pursuing Danny through the crowd, which was parting like the Red Sea. Everyone sensed that this wasn't just a show anymore, and if Danny and I weren't each being held by policemen, someone definitely would have gotten hurt.

Now, a couple of interesting things happened. One was that most people assumed that I was angry because I'd lost the fight. Not true. While I wanted very much to win, I took the fight for what it was. I'd have quietly left the ring had Danny not started talking about Marie the way he did. And I also think it was somewhat contrived on his part, because he had to know what would happen if he used that kind of language and made those kinds of suggestions about Marie.

The other development didn't come to light for a few days. I thought I'd acquitted myself well enough in the ring, and I began hearing that some people felt I'd been robbed, as they say. Leon Spinks stated to *Sports Illustrated* that "They shouldn't have given it to the guy who kept losing his headgear," and even the magazine wrote, "At least the proceedings resembled real boxing in one respect: The judges screwed up. They gave a split decision to...Bonaduce, who, when not doing an imitation of the

Australian crawl, set a world record for losing his headgear....
For his part, Osmond...did land more scoring blows than Danny
Bonaduce." ESPN concurred.

In the midst of the postbout melee, my assistant happened
to walk by the judges' table and see the actual scorecards they'd
kept. Thinking these would make great souvenirs, she took
them. A couple of days later, when she really looked at them, she
brought them into my dressing room and said, "I want you to see
something." The judges had given me more points; I'd won.
Looking at the scorecards, I had to laugh. For a fight that really
wasn't, this was the perfect outcome. And I really doubt that the
sports world is clamoring for a rematch.

chapter8

In late January 1995, *Joseph* ended its record-breaking sixteen-month run in Chicago and moved to the State Theater in Minneapolis for a return engagement. The biggest change for me occurred in my personal life, when Debbie and I agreed that she and the boys would move back to Utah so that they could lead a more "normal" life. Whenever I mentioned her and the boys leaving Chicago, I know that some people assumed it was because we were having problems, but that's not so. After a lot of discussion and consideration, Debbie and I agreed that the boys needed to have a home, a school, and a network of friends that would not be subject to change every time *Joseph* moved on to another city. Especially with Don in high school, we noticed vast differences in curriculum from schools in one city to another, which complicated the adjustment process.

Our decision that I would commute was difficult for all of us. And from the first day they left, we all missed one another so much. But in the end, we knew it was the best decision for the boys. I was acutely aware of what I'd missed by not attending public school or having many friends outside my family. We wanted it to be different for Don, Jeremy, Brandon, and Christopher. We wanted them to grow up in one place that they could call home, where they belonged, a hometown. I don't think my children should be deprived of a normal childhood just because their father has an unusual job. Besides, it wasn't fair to ask Debbie to move so often and be cut off from her family and friends, either.

Like everything, the decision for my family to move back to Utah came with a price. I kept in constant touch with Debbie and the boys, sometimes calling and talking to them several times a day (eventually I got a video phone). The truth is, though, I was not being the father I'd always envisioned I would be. Like all parents, I suppose, I grew along with my sons. When I look back at my early fathering skills, they were not the greatest. As much as I love my children, and as hard as I struggled to establish my own individuality, it was difficult for me always to grant them the same freedom to be who they were. When Don and Jeremy were little, I'd get upset if they didn't look right at the camera when we took family pictures. I hadn't yet come to terms with how destructive my own perfectionism was, so I tried to force it on my children. In those early years, my parenting style was based more on mimicking what I'd seen growing up than doing what I really felt in my heart. I tried to assert my authority. I could be short with the boys, and for a while, I did spank them. It wasn't until Brandon was born that I began to relax a bit, to trust in the values Debbie and I had instilled, and to trust our sons to find their way. It wasn't always easy for me to resist the need to control everything, but I did eventually learn, as Debbie so eloquently put it, "to be a dad, not a dictator."

My living away from Debbie and the boys was something, she and I agreed, that couldn't be helped. Financially and career-wise, we knew too well that what goes up inevitably comes down. Besides being a wonderful creative experience for me, *Joseph* was the most secure job I'd had in nearly two decades. And around this time, my producer started talking about taking the show to Hawaii and then Broadway—an offer that was hard to refuse. With my professional future outside the show uncertain, Debbie and I agreed that I should stay with it.

Now, I could rationalize that I was providing for my fami-ly, that this was what happens when a parent is in the business, that my boys knew that I loved them, and all that. At the end of most days, though, the bulk of the burden of raising them fell on Debbie's shoulders. And there were times when it wasn't easy. Sometimes we argued, taking positions that boiled down to my implying—wrongly, I must add—that she bore responsibility for our sons' behaviors and run-of-the-mill problems by being there, and her letting me know—correctly—that I bore it by not.

While I spent every moment I could with my boys, and usually had one of them with me for a week at a time wherever I was, I did miss a lot. For the first couple of years with the show, I had only Mondays off, so I would fly out after the Sunday night performance and return in time to perform on Tuesday night. Quality time is a fine concept, as far as it goes. But I'm not kidding myself: The hard work of parenting is in the mundane, everyday exchanges we overlook, like helping with homework or running an errand together.

As my two older sons entered their teens, they let me know in no uncertain terms how they felt about my absences over the years. Had I been the same parent I was fifteen years before, I would have sternly reminded them that I was their father and sent them to their rooms, end of discussion. But how would they ever learn to stand up for themselves, to fight for what they needed to be emotionally whole, if they couldn't open their hearts to their own father? It hurt to hear my two older sons tell me that they couldn't talk to me. But I know that if they didn't really feel it, they wouldn't say it. And if they feel that way, it's my responsibility as their father to understand why. Interestingly, this philosophy runs counter to much of what my father practiced while raising my siblings and me. Years ago, I was a bit taken aback when Father told me how much he admired me for not reprimanding or embarrassing my sons in front of others. I can't tell you how much that meant to me.

By early 1995, I had been with *Joseph* more than two and a half years. Although playing the role was essentially doing the same thing every show, no performance was ever exactly like any other. Unlike singing in concert, where there is always room for improvisation and small errors, acting, singing, and dancing with a large cast is an exercise in precision and timing. Not to say we each didn't slip up occasionally; we did. And with live performances, there's a healthy amount of nervousness all performers experience.

Sometime around 1994, I began feeling a kind of anxious-ness that was unlike anything I'd ever felt before. I'd been a little nervous about every one of my performances all my life, but there were ways I could circumvent the anxiety. For as long as I can remember—whether I was onstage or in a business meeting—I knew that if I just got that applause at the end of the first song, a laugh when I made a joke, my nervousness would diminish, though never go away. I'd been through the wringer so many times, before and after "Soldier of Love," that I didn't feel like the same person anymore. It was a feeling I couldn't quite pinpoint or articulate. No matter where I was, I felt subordinate to other people and uncertain, especially in business situations.

The only time I ever felt really confident was in the recording studio. Each time I put on the headphones, I'd go into another world, a state of flow, so to speak. As I'd listen to the playback, I knew I could sing. That wasn't the problem. But sometimes I felt that was the only thing about my career that I really did know. Everything else was a mystery, and by the time *Joseph* came to me, I was more emotionally battered and scarred than I realized. Ironically, it was during *Joseph*—when, professionally, things looked like they couldn't have possibly gone better—that the nervousness began taking a new form. Opening night in Chicago, during "Any Dream Will Do"—the second number in the show and the first in which I appear—I stopped singing, hoping the children's chorus would be loud enough to carry the note I couldn't sing. I didn't know what was happening to me, but I couldn't control my voice. So I stopped singing altogether and just mouthed the words.

By far the worst episode occurred while I was onstage in Chicago, in 1994. One of the show-stopping numbers was "Song of the King," which featured Johnny Seaton portraying the King of Egypt as the King of Rock and Roll. Pharoah begged Joseph to interpret his troubled dreams. I was kneeling before Johnny with my back to the audience, getting ready to sing "Pharaoh's Dream Explained," when the room started spinning around me and I was sure I would black out. The night before, I had blown the lyrics to the song that was coming up, and the fear that it might happen again loomed larger and larger as the music played and my cue got closer.

Unless you've experienced a panic attack yourself, you might find it hard to understand what it feels like, but bear with me as I try to explain. Once the fear of embarrassing myself grabbed me, I couldn't get loose. It was as if a bizarre and terrifying unreality had replaced everything that was familiar and safe. I felt powerless to think or reason my way out of the panic. It had a whole strange, hallucinatory quality to it; for example, I could see myself down on the stage as if I were flying above it all, but I couldn't get back "inside" myself and take control. In the grip of my wildest fears, I was paralyzed, certain that if I made one wrong move, I would literally die. Even more terrifying, I'd have felt relieved to die.

Kneeling before Johnny, I kept trying to remember the words, but they slipped through my fingers like mercury, defying me to try again. The harder I tried, the more elusive they became. The best I could do was to not black out, and I got through the show, barely, by telling myself repeatedly, *Stay conscious, stay conscious.* Another time, the only way I got through the ballad "Close Every Door" was by envisioning my late Grandma Davis's face and imagining having a conversation with her as I went through the motions of the song. And these attacks of nerves weren't just about performing onstage. I remember being so wound up at the prospect of cohosting *Live! With Regis & Kathie Lee* that I didn't sleep at all the night before and got nauseous right before I went on. Later, when I learned to "rank" my panic attacks on a scale of 1 to 10, these would all qualify as 10s. Another time, my anxiety was so overwhelming during my audition to play the voice of Hercules in the Disney animated feature, my performance was embarrassing. It was one of those moments when I started to wonder if I could continue a singing career at all.

Something was definitely wrong, and at first I clung to a "reasonable explanation": the schedule, the commuting back and forth, the fact that I was living so much of my life away from Debbie and the boys, my responsibility to a successful show. But deep inside, I knew that none of it made sense. I'd performed under every adverse condition imaginable. I'd carried a good deal of responsibility since I was a child. Why couldn't I do it now? I wasn't on tour. I knew the show backwards and forwards. The audience was back, and they accepted me just fine. So why was everything suddenly going so terribly wrong?

By the time we reached Minneapolis in early 1995, I was pretty certain that the stress of being away from my family and the weekly round-trip flights were wearing me down. Either that, or I was just losing my mind. Everything was beginning to annoy me. I would be short-tempered with people and sometimes even suspicious of them, which is not my style. What did they want from me? Why couldn't they leave me alone?

I was in my dressing room, sitting at my makeup table when I heard our stage manager Dianne Woodrow announce, "Fifteen minutes to curtain." By then, my routine was down pat—the makeup, the wig, the costume. Every night it went off without a hitch. This night, though, I sat at my makeup table paralyzed. I just couldn't bring myself to do anything. I felt sick and clammy with sweat. I looked down at my hands, they were shaking. When Giovanna, the woman who did my hair, came in to put on my wig, the glue wouldn't even stick to my forehead, I was sweating so much.

"Are you sick?" she asked.

I couldn't answer.

When I heard "Five minutes to curtain," the panic rose until I didn't know what I was doing. In a fit of rage, I picked up every jar, bottle, can, brush, mirror—whatever I found on my dressing table—and threw it all at the wall, screaming. I caught my reflection in the mirror and thought, *Who is that man?* Then I dropped back into my seat, put my head down on the table, and started bawling. My friend and dresser Stephen McMulkin found Dianne and told her, "Something's wrong with Donny."

Dianne rushed in, took one look at the room, and knew something was terribly wrong. "What do you want to do, Donny?" Suddenly, I felt like I was back in Hawaii, in a ball on the floor, crying to Jay. My mind raced back and forth: *Yes, I can do this. No, I can't. I can pull myself together. No, I'm falling apart. I can go on. No, I can't.* I just couldn't get a grip, and even as I said, "No, I'll be okay. I'm going on," I knew I wouldn't. I was relieved to hear Dianne say, "No, you're not going on." It was like someone was giving me permission not to have to live through the panic.

They announced that I would be unable to perform that night, and just five minutes after the regular curtain time, my understudy, Vance Avery, went on. The funny thing about it was, once I knew I didn't have to go onstage, the panic evaporated. I felt fine, like I could do anything in the world—except, of course, walk on that stage.

The anxiety waxed and waned. Some nights I went on and everything was fine. I confided in Debbie, of course, over the phone, and in Jill Willis, who was there in Minneapolis. They could see that I needed help, but what? I couldn't even articulate what I was feeling. I was nervous, but after thirty years of going onstage, how could that be possible? And, besides, this was something way beyond anything you could call stage fright. There was more than that. I couldn't stop agonizing over the craziest things. I'd lie in bed at night wondering, *What if...?* and then imagine a series of possible events that might unfold, all of them culminating in my being humiliated. I kept myself awake for hours mentally plotting elaborate, labyrinthine strategies, plans, and contingencies so that no matter what happened, I would be in control. What made it even more maddening is that there wasn't a shred of logic behind my thinking. No one was asking me to defend myself now. I was exactly where I always wanted to be. And there were moments when, intellectually, I knew that. Emotionally, though, it was a completely different story. Once my mind took off on something, it was as if I'd been kidnapped and tied to a roller coaster. I couldn't stop it. Naturally, the sleep deprivation only made everything else worse. I had to do something.

One morning, I phoned Jill at six o'clock, crying so hard I could barely speak. "I don't know what's wrong with me," I whispered. "But I have to go home. I have to go home." After a few days' rest, home in Utah, I felt ready to go back to work, but something still was not right. I tried acupuncture, which helped a little. I even managed to fall into a dead sleep during treatments, but I was feeling more jittery. It was a vicious cycle, because as my emotions and my behavior became more threatening to me, I tried even harder to suppress them. Next we tried homeopathy, and Jill found a reputable practitioner who prescribed an herbal concoction diluted in a few teaspoons of vodka. I don't know how much it helped, but it was weird to think that I was drinking "legally." Like the acupuncture, we reasoned that this was noninvasive and safe. The worst that could happen is it wouldn't work and I'd be back where I started. But that didn't help much either.

My state of mind was deteriorating so rapidly, I seriously started to consider drinking alcohol for real. I was that desperate. I know for most people, this would be no big deal, but, in light of my beliefs, it was. I didn't even know what it felt like to drink, but in my worst moments, I'd recall people saying how it relaxed them and made them forget their problems. That was all I needed to hear.

Then I lost it.

My "weekends" home had been expanded to include Mondays and Tuesdays. I usually left Utah early Wednesday morning to fly back to Minneapolis for that night's show. Of course, I never looked forward to saying good-bye to my family, but suddenly I was beginning to dread it. At first, a general uneasiness would settle over me like a fog, beginning a few hours before my flight. Then it would begin the night before, then it would keep me awake nights until most of the time at home I was completely focused on—obsessed with—leaving and so afraid to go.

One Tuesday night, I was lying in bed awake, shivering, in

a cold sweat. I scared Debbie to death, because neither of us knew what was going on. Debbie's father, with whom I'm very close, came over and talked to me to see if he could help. I calmed down a little, but Debbie insisted we go to the emergency room anyway. Something was seriously wrong. I was deathly afraid of something but I didn't know what. And the more I tried to tell myself there was nothing to be afraid of, the more afraid I became.

By the time we got to the hospital, I was damp with sweat and shaking uncontrollably, so hard that I almost couldn't walk. Some unnamed, unknown fear had my heart racing. The closer it got to daybreak and my flight back to Minneapolis, the more violent the shaking became and the colder I felt. I was taken to a private examination room, where they hooked me up to an EKG to be sure I wasn't having a heart attack and drew blood for tests. Lying on the table, I remember waiting for the doctor to give me the results. Secretly, I was hoping that he would tell me that I had a disease that meant I could never go onstage again. I was ready to hear anything.

"Mr. Osmond, I have some good news," the doctor said a couple of hours later. "There's nothing wrong with you." Instead of breathing a sigh of relief, I was thrown into another panic, because if there was nothing physically wrong with me, then my worst fear had been confirmed: I was going crazy.

"All you need to do is take a break"—which was impossible, because of my schedule—"maybe you need to go on a long vacation and go fishing." I hate fishing. The doctor gave me some pills, some kind of sedative, and sent me on my way.

I got dressed, and as I walked out of the hospital, Debbie remembers that I was smiling and cracking jokes to make everyone laugh. "It was like Donny still had to be onstage," she recalled. I'd always found it easier to relax if I did something to make people like me, and this was no different. Slowly it began to dawn on me that I'd been doing this my whole life. What was I doing? What was I so afraid of?

We got home, both shaken and scared. "I've got to get to Minneapolis and do the show," I told Debbie.

"You can't do the show," she said. "You are not doing the show."

"I have to, Debbie, I have to go. You know what kind of complaints I'm going to get from people if I'm not on that stage. What will people think of me if I miss a show? And you know the kind of pressure I get from the producer when I'm not there."

"Well, if you're going, I'm going with you."

A few hours later, Debbie and I were en route to Minneapolis, not that I had any idea where we were. The pills had taken effect, and I was so out of it, Debbie practically had to carry me through the Denver airport, where we caught a connecting flight. I slept the entire trip. Once we got to my apartment and the medication wore off enough, I started making plans to go on that night. "I've got to do it," I told Debbie.

She disagreed with me, but I insisted and I did go on that night. It was one of the most difficult challenges I have ever faced. But for the next three days, I sat with Debbie and cried, asking her probably a hundred times, "How am I going to get through this?" and begging her not to tell anyone. I would have done anything to make the pain go away.

"Donny, why do you feel that you have to be perfect onstage?" Debbie asked.

I looked at her. It seemed like such a crazy question. I had to be perfect because I had to be perfect. Wasn't it obvious? It was expected of me.

"Donny, you don't have to be perfect. The people in the audience don't know how you think the performance is supposed to be. If you mess up a line or make a little mistake, who knows? Who cares? And do you really believe that people will think less of you because you're not perfect?"

I thought, and I hate to admit it, but the answer was, Yes, I did think people would stop liking me if I wasn't trying to be perfect. It was ridiculous and irrational, of course, but it was real to me. Debbie had watched this whole process evolve over the years, and she knew me so well, that years after that night in the emergency room, she could say that she wasn't surprised at what happened to me. I would later discover that most people who knew me well weren't surprised, either. That's when Debbie said the words I needed to hear: "Just go out there and be average." I would never want to be just average, but at least now I had permission not to be perfect.

Though I hadn't missed that many performances, everyone at Live Entertainment, the company that produced *Joseph*, was concerned. As fate would have it, there had been an actor in another of the company's productions, *The Phantom of the Opera*, who suffered similar symptoms to mine. Dan Brambilla, an executive who worked for Live Entertainment, had the name and phone number of a psychotherapist, Dr. Jerilyn Ross, who specialized in treating what most of us would call stage fright. For the past several months, I'd tried everything I could to avoid seeing a psychologist. I needed help, but in the back of my mind, I worried that my problem would end up in the press and everything I'd worked so hard to build back up would crumble to dust.

After I learned that there were many other performers Dr. Ross had treated, I relaxed a little. Besides, I'd reached a dead end. If I didn't stop this madness, it was all going to be over for me, anyway.

We had just closed in Minneapolis and moved on to Toronto, for our third run there. Dr. Ross flew to Toronto before opening night to work with me. The most amazing thing about meeting her was that I finally found someone who understood exactly what I was going through. No fear or belief I told her about struck her as unusual or bizarre. Not only had she been treating people like me for years, but she herself had once suffered from severe anxiety attacks. When I discovered that I was not the only person in the world like this, it was like someone had given me a second chance at life. There was a name for what was happening to me—social phobia—and a course of treatment. I can't even imagine what my life would have been like had I not found Dr. Ross.

She explained to me that social phobia is one of several common anxiety disorders. Some experts believe that as many as one in eight Americans have experienced a social anxiety disorder at some time in their lives; it may in fact be the third most-commonly diagnosed psychiatric condition. Social phobia can take a range of forms, from a common fear of speaking before strangers to a debilitating, irrational fear of leaving one's house that can persist for decades. As I read through the case histories in Dr. Ross's book, *Triumph Over Fear*, I found myself relating to their irrational behavior, because it made perfect sense to me. When Dr. Ross wrote of her own struggle with anxiety, which could cause her to feel like she wanted to jump out of a high window, I knew exactly how she felt.

People who suffer from social phobia are afraid to do anything in public—including walking down a street, eating in a restaurant, asking someone for directions—because they fear they will be ridiculed. It's not unusual for someone with social phobia to believe that people are watching them wherever they go, whatever they do, and that they are laughing at them as well. For most people, this is an irrational fear. No one is looking at them or laughing at them. In my case, however, there was an element of reality to my otherwise irrational fears that had to be considered as well. From an early age, I was being looked at wherever I went. And I was laughed at as well. But, as Dr. Ross demonstrated to me, my mind took things that were real and exaggerated and distorted them. In the grip of panic, I experienced an internally generated fantasy, not reality.

Treatment for social phobia involves learning to identify the conditions that result in an attack and then discovering the techniques you can use to bring that anxiety to a manageable level. Therapists who treat this use talk therapy in conjunction with cognitive behavioral therapy, because the goal of this treatment is not so much tracing how the phobia began or why you suffer from it, but teaching you practical ways of dealing with it. Sometimes this involves facing your fears under controlled circumstances, or teaching yourself to stop your irrational thoughts before they take hold. Social phobia is not a condition that can be "cured" the same way you cure a disease. It's always there. Just by teaching me that I wasn't alone and that there was a way out for me, Dr. Ross changed—maybe even saved—my life.

The first step was learning to identify a panic attack as it came on. Next I had to "rate" it on a scale from 1 (minor) to 10 (full-blown) and then find ways to bring the anxiety down. I assumed I could handle my problems alone, but Jerilyn explained to me that I would need to find a "safe" person, someone who would be aware of my problem and on whom I could depend to help me bring an attack under control. I'd become friends with J.C. Montgomery, a cast member and my workout buddy at the gym. I asked him to join me for dinner after the show one evening and I explained everything I was going through. J.C. kindly agreed to become my "safe" person. So, for instance, if I started to feel an attack while onstage, I could look at him, or if he happened to be near enough, I could lightly touch his arm, and it would help bring me back to "reality."

You learn to manage anxiety by facing it head-on, which is exactly the last thing you believe you ever could do. One of the first things Dr. Ross and I did was walk on the stage during the preshow setup opening night, before the audience was admitted. I was having an anxiety attack that I described to her as a 6. The theater was empty, except for about twenty ushers who were grouped together getting instructions from the head usher. I stood with my back to the seats for about ten minutes. I was frightened because, I told Dr. Ross, I just knew the ushers were looking at me and laughing or criticizing me.

After about ten minutes of talking to me, she said, "Donny, turn around."

"I can't turn around," I said softly. "I'm now at an eight."

"Force yourself. Look at them."

I did. I turned around. No one was there. The ushers had all left while we were talking. I was nearly paralyzed with fear over something that wasn't even happening, which aptly describes all social phobia. The fear was in my mind.

The next day, I mentioned to Dr. Ross that whenever I buy

something, it's impossible for me to return it, no matter what's wrong with it. "I know it sounds really stupid," I said. "But I go into a complete panic." So Dr. Ross presented me with a plan. That day, we were going to the Eaton Center, a shopping center across the street from the theater, where I would buy a shirt. The next day, I would return the shirt to the store and get a refund.

Sounds simple enough, right? The mere thought of it had me terrified beyond words. Public places like malls always frightened me because so many people were there. I'd made it a habit many years before to walk from point A to point B as quickly as possible. When I was a teenager, if I ever stopped walking, there was always the chance that a crowd would gather. My fear wasn't about people or crowds per se, but the fact that I could never predict or control what they would think or say about me. Just anticipating that kind of situation sent my mind racing: *What if they looked at me? What if someone stopped me? What if someone spoke to me? What if someone started ridiculing me? What if...* This kind of irrational thinking was like a perpetual motion machine: The more I thought about it, the faster the thoughts came. The faster those thoughts came, the more outlandish and frightening they were. All of it stemmed from my need to control everything that happened to me and my absolute terror at finding myself unprepared or unable to cope with anything unexpected. *What will I do? What will people think? Will I look stupid?*

Dr. Ross and I walked across the street, and as I entered the mall and saw people, I felt my face start to flush. I wanted to jog to the store where I was going to buy that shirt, but Dr. Ross set the pace, walking normally.

"Okay, Donny, give me a number," she said softly as we walked.

"I'm up to about an eight."

"Why?"

"Everybody's looking at me."

"Okay, so just look at the floor and count the tiles."

I looked down and started to do it, but I couldn't even concentrate on that simple task. "It's not going away," I said.

"Okay, Donny, walk over here and grab the corner of this table," she answered. I did, and the minute my hand touched it, the panic subsided to a 3. Dr. Ross gave me other exercises I could use to help control the panic: For example, I could picture butterflies flying randomly and then try to visualize them beginning to fly in a circle. Or try to count in a way that required some concentration—backward by threes from two hundred, for example. The goal was simply to focus on something other than the fear, because your concentrating on the anxiety is exactly what feeds it.

A few minutes later, inside the store, I felt my panic rising again. Dr. Ross told me to pick up a piece of merchandise on display. When I did, it went back down again. Now, the entire time I was in the mall, my panic never went down to 0, but anything under 5 or so, I could cope with.

We went into a shop. When I bought the shirt, I thought I was going to die because I knew what Dr. Ross expected me to do the next day.

The following day, Dr. Ross accompanied me back to the mall. Again, the panic struck, but I started to find the skills to render it manageable. And this time, I realized that though people were looking at me, no one was stopping me or saying anything. They recognized me, and they smiled or waved, but that was all.

During the two days Dr. Ross spent with me, I felt like a child again holding my mother's hand. On the third day, she had to leave, and I walked to her hotel, where we met in the lobby to say good-bye. I knew this was going to be hard, because even in this short time, I'd come to depend on her. Intellectually, I understood my problem, and I knew I had the tools to help me deal with it. But, typically, I also worried about what would happen if the exercises failed, if I found myself in my dressing room crying again, unable to go on. Complicating matters, I also felt myself become anxious at the prospect of becoming anxious; in other words, I was developing a fear of being afraid.

When she said, "I have to say good-bye now," it was the last thing I wanted to hear. In fact, I had to move to a corner of the lobby so that no one could see me cry. She explained that what I was feeling was normal, almost like the separation anxiety young children feel when they're away from their parents. At that time I felt that not even Debbie understood me as well as Dr. Ross did. I watched her walk out the lobby door, and I knew I was on my own.

I had to perform that night, which I dreaded. But I kept reminding myself of what Dr. Ross told me: "When you're thinking that you're actually going to die, allow yourself to have an out in any situation. Even onstage. What's the worst thing that could happen? You could run offstage, and people will accept that. You're not going to die up there." Knowing that I wasn't trapped, that I wasn't going to die, diminished the anxiety. I had to consciously remind myself that, as Debbie said, I didn't have to be perfect.

Later, I did the show in a complete state of panic. I felt like every note I sang, every move I made was wrong, and it was only a matter of time before everyone stood up and walked out. But I didn't run off the stage, though I knew I could. And I didn't die. The minute I got backstage, I phoned Dr. Ross.

"I did it! I got through it!" I exclaimed like a little kid. I was elated.

Over the next couple of weeks, the panic came on a few times, but I found that the more I practiced managing it, the easier it became. More important, though, I stopped becoming anxious before the fact. The minute my mind would start to race with possibilities, I'd tell myself, *If I lose control, I know what to do.*

No one knows exactly why people develop social phobia. There may be a biological predisposition, or you might have certain experiences that make you vulnerable to it. In my case, it may be a combination of the two. Armchair psychologists could theorize that it was my childhood that "caused" my social phobia, but that would be wrong, because there are millions of people with social phobia who never even played a tree in their kindergarten play. Was there something about the way I was raised? Perhaps if I'd grown up like most people and hadn't been so isolated, it might have been different for me. But then again, maybe not. People who suffer from social phobia come from all walks of life, all types of experience and background. What made me "susceptible" was not how I was brought up so much as how I thought about myself. In Dr. Ross's book, she describes someone like me, who thinks, "'By taking care of everyone around me, I'll be liked. If I let my own feelings show, I may not be liked, so I'll try even harder to please (I'll ignore my own feelings) and thus be more well liked.'" Reading that, I realized that Dr. Ross knew me before she even met me.

I couldn't go back and change my past, so I had to begin

looking at it differently. I couldn't simply let go of the hurt and disappointment I'd endured. But I could remind myself that I wasn't crazy, that my reaction was normal although exaggerated, and that I would get through an attack. Obviously, the problem had been developing slowly for years, and I saw the irony of it manifesting so intensely during *Joseph*. It was clear that I'd invested *Joseph* with a lot more meaning than first meets the eye. Much of it concerned my devastation over the failure of *Little Johnny Jones*. In my mind, I'd drawn fine distinctions between success in other areas, like recording, and success in live theater. No matter what else I accomplished, I knew deep inside, I could never repair the damage or have closure about *Little Johnny Jones* until I proved myself in the same circumstances.

So you might think that if I'd never gone onstage again, I'd have been safe. Ironically, had I not been performing when my social phobia struck, I'd probably have been even worse off. Rather than wanting to run off the stage, I might have become someone who never left his house—or even his bedroom— again. Social phobia is a condition of paradoxes, and it was really a blessing that I was in a show then. Not only did it force me to face my fears, but I had the opportunity to prove to myself how much of what I feared was exaggerated and unrealistic. Equally important, at a time when my self-esteem was in the gutter, the audience each night reminded me that the stage was the place I had always wanted to be.

Before this happened, I would never imagine that Debbie and I could possibly be closer. But facing this together only increased our appreciation and respect for each other. That journey toward emotional independence to which Debbie had been edging me along ever since we met was now complete. I realized

I could love people without having constantly to prove myself exceptional or special or—here's that word again—perfect. I could stop trying to convince other people about who I really was when I learned to stop trying to convince myself.

That year brought many good things, too. I recorded my CD entitled *Four* in Minneapolis with Ricky and Paul Peterson. And while in Chicago, before going to Minneapolis and Toronto, I got a call from Ruth Lambert, who does casting for Disney. At the time I knew nothing about the company's upcoming animated feature *Mulan*, but you can imagine how I felt when she said, "We've listened to your audition tapes from *Hercules*. B. D. Wong is going to be doing the speaking voice of Captain Li Shang. You sound so similar to him that we'd like you to do Shang's singing voice. You have it if you want it."

"You mean, I don't even have to audition for it?" I asked.

"No, it's yours, if you want it." As I mentioned in the introduction, Shang is Mulan's teacher, who by the end also becomes a love interest.

"I'm there!" I was so excited. I flew out to Los Angeles and recorded "I'll Make a Man Out of You." It wasn't my first experience voicing animation. I'd played myself in *The Osmonds* cartoon series, a role I reprised recently for the Cartoon Network's misguided Romeo *Johnny Bravo*. And I guest starred on *Space Ghost Coast to Coast*, but this *Mulan* was in an entirely different realm. As I was recording my song for *Mulan*, I couldn't help but think that this was something my grandchildren would see one day.

That summer I was really looking forward to performing in Brigham Young University's annual Fourth of July Stadium of Fire show. Alan was producing it, as he had several times before, and every year he tried to top himself. It wasn't enough for Alan to have made the *Guinness Book of World Records* for igniting over a million firecrackers simultaneously so that they produced a *boom!* heard for miles and created a big, dark mushroom cloud on the football field. There was also something bigger, better, and more outrageous he could try—usually using me in some death-defying stunt.

Of course, I loved every one of them, some more than others. In 1981, I performed in the show, and made my grand entrance standing on the skids of a helicopter. That meant I was *outside* the helicopter, securely strapped on to be sure, but still... As planned, the helicopter flew into the stadium then rotated, so the crowd could see me. The crowd loved it! And when we did the stunt at BYU, it went beautifully. The next day, Alan produced virtually the same show at the Arizona State University. We were using a different helicopter and a different pilot, but no one was unduly worried. During the rehearsal, as we were approaching the stadium, Alan radioed the pilot, "We're having some technical problems. We're going to be about fifteen minutes. We'll get right back to you."

Fifteen minutes wasn't enough time to get anyplace where we could land and take off again safely, so the pilot said to me through my headphones, "We've got fifteen minutes. Let me show you Phoenix." What could I say? I was scared to death, but it wasn't as if I had any choice. I got a truly memorable bird's-eye tour, then we returned to the stadium on cue, completed the rehearsal, and were ready for the show.

No matter how carefully you plan anything, the devil is always in the details. And in this case, two: One was forgetting to tell the pilot that he would be landing amid a fireworks display in progress, and the second was not knowing that he had been a pilot in Vietnam. With the first explosion, he began diving into the stadium and showing off by spinning doughnuts. *We didn't rehearse this,* I was thinking, and though I kept singing, inside I was screaming, *Get me off this thing!* When we were about two feet above the ground, I made a big mistake: I jumped off. Since the pilot didn't anticipate that, he didn't compensate for the drop in weight, which caused the copter to jerk upward suddenly. He reacted by landing abruptly, and I watched in horror as one of the two skids missed me by mere inches.

But I didn't have a second to comprehend how narrowly I'd cheated death before I was running through a tunnel of fire formed by the synchronized firing of Roman candles. It was spectacular. Alan figured that if people got a thrill seeing me run through Roman candles, they'd probably really like seeing me flying through the air with a couple of them tied to my feet. Another year, Alan had me flying on a wire, from one end of the stadium to the other. A control button I held in my hand ignited the Roman candles on my feet. As if that wasn't exciting enough, I was also spinning around, head over heels, in midair, with sparks and flames shooting from my heels.

We were always extremely safety conscious, but somehow we failed to factor how the flames from the Roman candles strapped to my shoes would be affected by my spinning motion. I'd only spun around a couple times before I realized the back of my neck was burning. When they lowered me to the stage, guys rushed out and disconnected the fireworks as quickly as possible. The whole time, I just kept singing like I didn't have a care in the world. Ah, show business! Back home Debbie had made me promise I'd never do anything like that again.

By 1996, we were all older and wiser. My entrance for that year's show was supposed to have me hanging on a rope ladder from a helicopter that would lower me onto the stage. I was so excited about my upcoming stunt that I mentioned it on Rosie O'Donnell's show. What happened after that made running through a tunnel of fire look pretty tame. If you missed it, let me give you a brief history of how, for the first time in my life, not only did someone call me "mean," but one woman actually convinced a nation that I was a bad guy. It was the image switch my former publicists and managers from the 1980s could only dream of. And to think, it was so easy: Open mouth, insert foot.

As anyone who watches her show knows, Rosie O'Donnell has an encyclopedic knowledge and great affection for every facet of pop culture, from Broadway musicals to old TV sitcoms. I had no idea that Rosie was a Donny and Marie fan from way back, and so I was thrilled to be invited to appear on her fourth show. I flew to New York from Boston, where *Joseph* was playing, for the Friday, June 4, 1996 taping. Rosie introduced me, and I walked onstage to enthusiastic applause. When Rosie offered me the de rigueur hello hug, I dipped her, and she stood up in a mock swoon. We had a lot of fun, as she held up my old albums, showed me where her brother Timmy had melted the nose on her original Donny Osmond doll, and explained how she and Timmy played Donny and Marie in their backyard.

Rosie was so great to me, but I didn't fully appreciate how sincere she was. I was so used to being teased about my teen idol past, I misinterpreted her interest in it as having a mocking edge that it really didn't. When the conversation turned to what I was doing now, I mentioned the upcoming Fourth of July show.

"I'm doing this great big spectacular show at BYU Stadium,"

I said. "I'm hanging from a helicopter. That's how I make my entrance."

"That's a little dangerous, Donny," Rosie replied with concern.

"Of course. But that's what I love. I'm a dangerous kind of guy, you know."

"Well, that's usually what I think of: Donny—dangerous," Rosie said with a touch of good-natured sarcasm. "I'm willing to go be your stunt double for that, 'cos I don't want you to get hurt."

"Oh, I won't," I assured her. "It's gonna be fun. It's gonna be great." And then I said it: "And, plus the helicopter can't handle that much weight, so…"

"I think Donny Osmond just insulted me," Rosie announced to the audience. And with that, they turned on me. "In that case, I'm gonna hold up another album cover." When Rosie held up one that included "I'm a Little Bit Country, I'm a Little Bit Rock and Roll," she asked me to sing it with her. When I demurred, she grabbed it and ran: "You just told me that I was chubby on national TV," Rosie said. "You basically called me a big old pig, Don…You hurt my feelings a little bit. I think maybe I'd feel a little better if I sang 'A Little Bit Country, A Little Bit Rock and Roll.'"

The way the audience was cheering Rosie on, there was no way I was getting out of this. And Rosie made the most of it, adding a petulant, "It's up to you, Donny. Whatever you say," before directing her band leader, "Hit it, John!"

After a verse, we ended the segment friends. Rosie even said, "I love you." Afterward, I apologized to Rosie, and she accepted. I even sent her flowers with a note to say again that I was sorry for what I'd said. But publicly, it was impossible for her to ignore the groundswell against me, and starting the very next day, Rosie made it a point to remind everyone of how badly I'd mistreated her. Before too long, she couldn't utter the words "Donny Osmond" without her audience erupting in a chorus of "boo"s. Over the next few weeks, she told her other guests what "that mean Donny Osmond" had done to her. In one of Rosie's versions, she told Gary Shandling, "I said, 'I love you, Donny,' he said, 'Rosie, you're a fat pig.'"

From a ratings and comedic standpoint, I totally understood why Rosie played it the way she did. And it was brilliant. My problem was that a lot of people didn't know it was a joke. The longer Rosie kept the gag running, the more I found myself explaining to people that I didn't really call her a fat pig, or even fat. I unthinkingly and foolishly made a remark suggesting that she was heavy, I'd tell them. But I'd done it without malice, and I'd apologized to her several times. But no matter what I said, my protestations and apologies were no match for Rosie's almost-daily recounting of the emotional trauma she'd suffered. Even the international press picked up on the story. I was a marked man. I would do anything, I told Rosie, anything, to show the world how sorry I was. How could Rosie refuse?

Marie had been booked to appear on Rosie's show. She called me and said, "I've been booked for two segments. Would you like to take the second segment and give Rosie an official apology?"

It was perfect. *Now*, I thought, *the whole world will see how truly sorry I am.* What I didn't know was that Marie was setting me up. My forthcoming comeuppance made as much news as the original faux pas, and while it was all in good fun, I admit being very nervous about what Rosie had in mind for me. But whatever she asked me to do, I vowed, I would. I sat backstage in the greenroom and listened as Rosie and Marie had a great old time talking about how mean I was. I expected a tough crowd, but this one was getting tougher by the minute. Rosie replayed a recording of my offensive remark and showed Marie a 1977 *New York Post* headline in which Marie claimed that I once called her "fatso." Going into the commercial break, the two of them were having a little too much fun as they tugged mercilessly on a purple Stretch Armstrong doll with a Donny doll head and multicolored loincloth. The audience roared as Rosie popped the Donny doll's head off. Backstage, I took a deep breath and waited for my cue.

Following the break, Rosie announced me, and as I walked on, my arms full of flowers for her, the band struck up "One Bad Apple" and the audience booed. A few even threw things at me. When I offered Rosie the bouquet, she said, "I guess it's okay for fat people to get flowers, huh?" Throughout my apology, Rosie affected the manner of a heartbroken teenage girl. She then reminded me, "I'm the Queen of Nice, Donny and you, on the other hand..." before pressing a button to replay the tape, which she did a few more times until people couldn't stop laughing. Then came my moment of truth. I knew I'd have to sing "Puppy Love," and that was okay. I'd even rehearsed it with the band and was prepared to perform it seriously, to prove how sincere I was. Then Rosie brought out a brown dog costume, complete with bouncy tail and big floppy ears. As Rosie and Marie helped me get into it, I said, "This is humiliation!"

"That's right. That's exactly what I was going for," Rosie quipped. Even showing her that I was wearing special purple socks embroidered with "Donny Loves Rosie" didn't warm her heart.

Standing by the piano, adjusting my "paws," I said, "And this is what my career has come to." I didn't sing more than a few words before Marie stopped me: "No, no! On the knee," she commanded, pointing to the floor. There's nothing like having your family behind you. Obediently, I knelt and started to sing.

Going into the bridge, I stood up and took Rosie in my arms for a slow dance. As I sang, "Someone help me," and began to dip Rosie, my mind was racing: Should I be a good, contrite guest and play it safe? Or should I resort to the evil plan that popped into my mind as Rosie began leaning further and further back in my arms? I was sorry for what I'd done, but not so sorry that I could resist pretending to lose my grip as I sang, "someone help me, help me, help me, please." Rosie and I both ended up on the floor. All I could do was lie there and struggle through to the end, as Rosie playfully pummeled me while shouting, "I forgive you!" The show was such a ratings hit that she remarked on a later show, "I'm now requiring all my guests to call me fat and then come back to apologize." Months later, I was asked by her producers to do a bit in an anniversary show that would resurrect my "mean Donny" image. By then, I felt the joke had gone on long enough and graciously turned them down.

Now, back to the helicopter. In a footnote to this story, it turned out I didn't even get to do exactly the helicopter stunt that led to the offending remark in the first place. In fact, the Federal Aviation Administration, the BYU administration, and all manner of local fire and police authorities were dead set against it. They believed it posed an unacceptable risk to the people in the stadium, so we reached a compromise. I would appear standing outside the helicopter as it circled the outside perimeter of the stadium. Then the copter would land outside the stadium, and I'd reenter in a red convertible. Perfect!

The night of the show, we took off from a nearby airport, about fifteen miles from the stadium. Everything was running like clockwork until we got word via radio that they were running behind schedule at Cougar Stadium. We could just kill some time buzzing around Provo. Why not? By this time hanging outside helicopters was so routine that I got bored and called Debbie, who was sitting in the stadium, from my cell phone. "Oh, hi, honey!" I shouted over the noise of the copter blades. "I'm just hanging around!"

When I finally made my grand entrance, over forty thousand people were screaming at the top of their lungs. It was such a rush. I loved it. But the question is, was it my last big stunt? Better ask Debbie.

Between getting a grip on my social phobia and going into my fifth year with *Joseph*, I was finally letting myself enjoy the success. Joseph would end someday, and my manager, Jill, set to work looking for other possible projects. Although the Canadian cast recording had gone platinum in Canada, and I'd been working on some songs in the recording studio, I knew better than to concentrate on recording. Still, I love making records; in 1998 I released *Christmas at Home*.

The subject of my getting back into television rose a few times, but it was an idea I initially took to the way a vampire takes to garlic. I wouldn't even hear of it, but I started to come around. I'd had a lot of fun hosting VH1's *Seven Days of '70s* that summer and *Here's Donny* the following year. One television producer who was interested in working with me was Peter Calabrese, who, coincidentally, had worked on *The Mike Douglas Show* when Marie and I cohosted back in 1974. We had numerous meetings with possible cohosts for my own talk show, one of which included Moon Zappa. I loved working with Moon, and despite what lots of people would assume was an "odd couple" pairing, we had a great chemistry and essentially the same sense of humor. I went to countless meetings, and people were very enthusiastic and had all kinds of ideas for me, but nothing materialized. Now and then, the word would come back that while people were interested in me alone, they also wondered if I'd consider cohosting with Marie. Unbeknownst to me, they were saying the same thing to Marie, but neither of us felt that the time was right. We'd each fought too hard to establish our own independence to go back.

Though I would be leaving *Joseph* someday, the end threatened to come sooner than I planned, when in the fall of 1996 I ruptured my vocal cords during a performance. Exactly why it happened, no one could say, but the stress of traveling to and from Utah every week and the fluctuations in air pressure and lack of humidity clearly played a role. We were in Boston, and I was singing the last note in the finale, flying over the audience, when I felt something pop in my throat. I tasted blood. It didn't hurt, but when I got backstage, I was spitting out blood. It was upsetting, but I didn't think it was so serious that I couldn't sing the following night. The lower notes came easily, but once I reached for something higher—nothing, so I had to cancel my performance.

The next day, I went to see a throat specialist, thinking it would be bad news, but nothing a little rest wouldn't take care of. I knew I was stressing my voice, but I also knew that I was singing correctly, so I wasn't really worried that I had nodules. That's probably why when the doctor delivered the diagnosis, I was shocked.

"You're not going to be singing for at least three months. One of your two vocal cords hemorrhaged so extensively that if you continue this way, Donny, you're going to damage your vocal cords irreparably."

All I could think was, *Just shoot me now.* How could I not sing for three months? Didn't he understand? But the look on his face let me know he wasn't interested in my objections. "Don't even whisper. Don't talk. Nothing. Get yourself a little blackboard and starting writing down everything you want to say."

I couldn't believe it. Just as I was learning to let go, to stop controlling everything around me, everything I'd built back up threatened to tumble down again. My family, the cast, and the crew were supportive and sympathetic, but some ticket buyers felt so cheated by my absence, Garth Drabinsky asked me to come to Detroit, where the show had moved. I took the stage almost every night to apologize, introduce my replacement, Sam Harris, and basically try to minimize the ticket holders' complaints. I could barely even talk, so I squeaked out a few words. After a couple of months of rest and therapy, I was able to return for the last three shows in Detroit in early October. To play it safe, I went back home only every other week, which was hard on all of us. By then I had a pretty good idea that I wouldn't be with the show much beyond spring 1997, so we knew it was a temporary situation. Still, as I missed Debbie and the boys more each day, I began to reconsider the benefits of a project that would keep me in the same place for a long time.

Marie's career had continued to grow through the 1990s. She garnered rave reviews for her musical theater work in *The Sound of Music* and *The King and I*, and I was so proud of her. I had a strange experience when I attended her debut in *The King and I* on Broadway in March 1998. I was visiting Marie in her dressing room when I realized that there was something so familiar about the place, it felt like I was having déjà vu. And then it dawned on me: This was the dressing room I'd used for *Little Johnny Jones*, sixteen years ago to the month. The reason I hadn't made the connection immediately is that the name of the theater had been changed. For a few seconds, I felt a little strange, but then I realized that the past was gone. It couldn't hurt me anymore.

As the end of my run in *Joseph* approached, I became understandably nostalgic. We gave what I thought was to be my last performance on May 25, 1997, in Toronto to a packed house. (There would be a limited, seven-week engagement in Salt Lake City, in January 1998.) I could barely get through "Close Every Door," and as I looked out in the audience, I saw hundreds of flames from cigarette lighters. I was so choked up, our conductor, Phil Reno, handed me a box of tissues and I blew my nose. (Of course, that was the photograph that ran in the paper the next day!) Then we started the song again. I gave a farewell speech thanking both my real family and my "show family," who'd both given me so much support through those triumphant and at times difficult five years. I would miss everyone, but I was going home, finally. I wasn't home for more than a few hours, though, before I kissed Debbie and the boys good-bye and was on a plane to Los Angeles for meetings about a possible television project with Marie.

chapter9

By the time I got to Los Angeles to start working on pilots for the new show with Marie, the idea for us doing a show like this had been floating around for a while. What finally clinched it for us, though, was a conference call we did with me in Toronto, and Marie in Los Angeles, with several top executives from Columbia TriStar Television, including Barry Thurston. When Barry asked, "What is the show all about?" Marie and I started talking like we always do, playfully cutting each other off, each of our ideas sparking suggestions from the other.

"I don't want to do a straight talk show, like everybody else," I said.

"We've got to have lots of entertaining guests," Marie added.

"The way I see it, three or four guests per show," I said. "With eclectic music."

"But, Donny, this is the way the music's got to be—" Marie interjected.

"No, no, no. It's gotta be my way," I replied, jokingly cutting her off.

I don't think Barry was as taken with any of our suggestions as much as he was impressed with how we related to each other. Even through a conference call, he could see the kind of relationship Marie and I have. We were mid–verbal volley when Barry said, "That's it. That's the show."

By the time we finished taping the pilot in June 1997, whatever reservations about getting back into television we had were gone. I left Los Angeles hoping there would be enough interest from television stations across the country that a new *Donny & Marie* show could work. But I wasn't counting on it. In fact, I had already tentatively accepted the lead in a production of Andrew Lloyd Webber's *The Phantom of the Opera*, to begin in September, back in Toronto with Livent. I was also thinking about other possible projects, perhaps producing films, and recording another album. For the first time in a long time, I wasn't running to prove myself to anyone anymore. I really didn't have to do anything if I didn't want to.

We were pleasantly surprised when television stations across the country enthusiastically signed on to air *Donny & Marie* in one hundred percent of the markets available. By August 1997, we had been told it was a go. When we found out that Dick Clark wanted to become our executive producer, Marie and I knew that the show could really be something special. By summer of 1998, the staff was put together, the new set built on the Sony Studios lot in Culver City, and we were ready to roll. Marie and I wanted our talk show to be different, and we made sure that music was an element. We also wanted to present a wide range of guests, not all of them famous celebrities, and we wanted to be sure that everyone had fun. To that end, I've been playfully hit in the stomach with a hairbrush by Sarah Ferguson, the Duchess of York, and I've kissed Larry King (who dances divinely, by the way). We've had the great pleasure of presenting musical stars of every genre, from Stevie Wonder to Garth Brooks, Mariah Carey to Snoop Dogg. And I've loved every minute of it.

Amid all the excitement, there were moments when I caught myself thinking about where it was all headed. It's not that I had second thoughts. Let's just say I gave things a lot of thought. My first concern was the impact the show would have on my family, which now included our fifth son—and my parents' fifty-first grandchild—Joshua Davis, born on February 16, 1998. Coming home each night and sitting down to dinner with my family was what I'd dreamed of during my last few years in *Joseph*. The most obvious solution would be to move everyone to California, but Debbie and I decided instead that I would continue to commute home every week and bring one of the boys with me whenever I could. Don was attending college, and Jeremy was in high school, Brandon would be very soon, and Christopher hadn't had to change schools since he'd started.

Most important, though, by the time the new *Donny & Marie* show began, Utah had become our children's home. They had their friends, they had their lives there. We had agreed years before that our children would not grow up "show business" kids, that we would protect them from the pitfalls of being children of a celebrity. I want my sons to be my children, never to feel like members of an entourage.

We've always drawn a clear line separating Dad from that guy everybody seems to know. We do not display my gold records or other commendations in our home, because we feel that home is a place for our children to shine. While I hope that Don, Jeremy, Brandon, Christopher, and Joshua will always be proud to be my sons, I want them to be proud of the man they call Dad. No matter how hard you work, success is fickle, acclaim fleeting. It's important for my sons—and, really, all children—to understand that there is no inherent moral value to show business success nor to many of the pursuits to which we adults devote so much time. When you have a name people recognize, you can use that to accomplish wonderful things, as my family has done through the Osmond Foundation, which oversees the Children's Miracle Network. Debbie and I want to be sure that our children know they don't have to be famous to be successful. In our home, we try to teach that "success" isn't defined by ratings or money earned, but by how you conduct yourself in the world. The accomplishments I hope my children choose to emulate, the ones I want them to measure themselves against one day, are the ones no one outside my family or my community ever sees, the days in my life that pass undocumented by a photographer or a journalist.

One day in church, a good buddy of mine jokingly said, "You know, Donny, in here you're nobody special." We laughed and I thought to myself, *You know, he's right*. But outside, in the world, the public may see things differently. For the children of celebrities, life in the parent's reflected glow can be harsh and unforgiving. In my neighborhood in Utah, nobody really makes a big deal of the fact that I'm Donny Osmond. Someone might wave at me in the supermarket, but I can go about my day without being stopped by strangers, which is nice. When we go anyplace as a family, we are usually left alone. If one of my children is playing a game or has a part in the school play, he is the star. Not me.

I know my sons take pride in my work, but they also paid a price. While we were all living in Chicago, for example, Jeremy's classmates greeted one of his presentations by singing "Go, go, go Jeremy" to the tune of "Go, Go, Go Joseph." One reason Debbie and I decided on Utah is that it's not so unusual to see or meet an Osmond there. Our sons could attend a high school where they had been preceded by their many older cousins, including a couple who were stars in their own right as members of The Osmonds Second Generation (all Alan's sons). We knew we'd made the right decision one day when Don told me, "No one cares that I'm Donny Jr. Everybody talks about my older cousins who were there before. It's not about you, it's about my cousins. I'm not just the son of Donny Osmond anymore."

Fortunately, all the boys have a great sense of humor and have gotten their share of laughs out of my career. (Besides, why should they be left out of the fun?) Once in Chicago, I came in to discover that Jeremy had papered my dressing room with old posters, albums, and other memorabilia. I was flattered and impressed that my son would spend his own money—until Jeremy revealed that the man he bought it from couldn't wait to get rid of the stuff! As I write this, Don is serving his two-year mission in England. Not long after he arrived, in the course of his mission work, he happened to ring the doorbell of a woman who had been an Osmonds fan as a young girl. She appeared to have been drinking, and Don had to do some quick talking to convince her he wasn't Donny Osmond, some twenty years younger, no less.

As a parent, you always think that you're raising your children. That's true for me, but there are also ways in which I feel my sons have taught me things no one else could. In my song "Only Heaven Knows," I wrote to my sons,

> *You help me understand.*
> *There's a life I don't know,*
> *And mine I can't let go,*
> *I couldn't if I tried.*
> *So I'm living through vicarious eyes,*
> *For times I've wanted to know.*
> *You're the mirror of a life*
> *That only heaven knows.*

I wanted them each to understand how much they've given me just by being here. They've taught me those great life lessons all children teach their parents—of patience, unconditional love, and sacrifice—but they've also given me pieces of the childhood I never had. I don't want to give the impression that I live vicariously through them, but I do see through their eyes a childhood I never had. And they have allowed me to keep alive a part of me that I hope never grows up. (As a matter of fact, we've even devoted an entire room in our home to Legos, where Christopher and I spend hours building intricate, unique designs. And I made sure the architects factored in connections for the zipline I envision running from a second-floor balcony to the future swimming pool. Note to self: Tell Debbie about the zipline.)

Beyond how the new show would change my personal life, as we settled into the day-to-day work of doing the show, I think both Marie and I considered what it would mean to be teaming up again. At first, I worried that people would assume that we were back together because neither of us had any other choice. Fortunately, for both of us, that was not the case. Still, inside me, there's always an instinctive reaction, almost like a reflex, to move forward, ahead, away from what I once was. It's not as strong as it used to be, but it's still there.

We weren't working together very long before Marie and I realized that things were different now. Under the pressure of putting together a new show, each of us have had moments when we wondered if we'd made the right decision. But now we find that we can talk things out. Even more important, I've grown to trust Marie's instincts and her decisions. It's nice to know that in any situation, I can turn to her and ask her advice or follow her lead and know that nine times out of ten, she'll be right. It's the one time I worry about (just kidding, Marie). Most important, though, working together now was a choice that we made—not something we felt we had to do for anyone else.

Almost a year into the show, I'm glad we made the decision. It's great to be working with my sister again. Yes, the hours are long, and it's very difficult at times, and the pressure is on. But I think viewers can see that we are genuinely having fun together and enjoy what we're doing. It's been twenty years since we taped the last episode of the original *Donny and Marie Show*, and it's good to know people still enjoy seeing us as we are today.

As I look back, I realize that despite how working together so much with my siblings may have pushed us apart at times, there is something about standing beside them onstage that also has the power to bring us together in new ways. Being back together with Marie marked the end of a journey I'd begun in 1994 when I took Debbie and the boys to Branson, Missouri. Branson is the newest entertainment spot in the world, and the home of the Osmond Family Theater, where my brothers now perform and where in 1996, theirs was voted the number-one show in Branson. How they came to Branson is interesting, because it was Jimmy's brainchild, inspired by, of all people, Andy Williams. Jimmy heard about Branson from Andy, who has his own theater there. With a population of only 3,700, Branson is a very family-oriented, Midwestern town. At the same time, it manages to attract about six million visitors a year, making it possible for performers to continue working steadily without traveling the country. Best of all, it put my brothers back onstage, where they belonged.

For all that I went through putting my recording career back together, my brothers had gone through some tough times, too. Like ninety-nine percent of all pop stars, my brothers eventually faced that moment when, through no fault of theirs, the hits just stopped coming. It's difficult to realize that even though you are making music just like you always did, the record buyers and the radio program directors have moved on to new sounds and new artists. It's nothing personal, of course, but it still hurts. Between my last album with my brothers, 1976's *Brainstorm* and

1984, the Osmond Brothers recorded three albums. The first, *Steppin' Out*, was produced by Maurice Gibb of the Bee Gees. The next two, 1982's *The Osmond Brothers* and 1984's *One Way Rider*, were in the country vein, and for a time it looked like they were heading in the right direction. From the summer of 1982 to the end of 1986, they placed eleven singles on the country chart, and their first, "I Think About Your Lovin'," went Top 20.

They continued to tour successfully through those years, but as their families grew, the touring began to lose its charm. Alan tells an amusing story of where and when he, Wayne, and Merrill decided to stop. "We were in a little trailer, getting ready to perform at the Hog Festival. There was lightning and mud about a foot deep and horse manure on the track between the audience and the stage. They're all standing in the rain with umbrellas waiting for us, then the lightning hit and the power went off. Wayne and Merrill and I just looked at each other and started laughing. And I said, 'You know what? It's time to go home.'"

By 1992, when Jimmy bought the Branson theater that would become the Osmond Family Theater, some of my brothers were going through difficult times. Alan had been diagnosed with multiple sclerosis, and Jay had discovered he wasn't entirely content being out of show business. Not long after they started in Branson, Wayne learned that he had a brain tumor. After undergoing surgery and treatment, he is cancer-free.

If I've learned anything over these years, it is that no matter what your view of your past may be, it still belongs to you. No matter what else my brothers turned their hands to, the fact was they were performers first. They sang as beautifully as ever.

Why should they have to give that up? After they'd worked hard all their lives, they deserved to continue doing what they do best.

Jimmy has said that there was something about Branson and the prospect of the family having its own theater that just felt right to him. From the day the theater opened, it has presented two shows a day, six days a week, ten months a year. My brothers' first shows—in September 1992—were very well received, and around 1993, most of the Osmond family—with the exception of Tom, Marie, and I—eventually came to spend at least part of every year in Branson.

As happy as I was for my brothers, however, I admit I appeared onstage in Branson a few times with mixed emotions. Although the success of *Joseph* had let me put some distance between the "goody-goody" family image I'd been trying to shake, it still bothered me to think that somewhere somebody might find out that I'd performed in Branson. It was, I realize, hypocritical of me to try and have it both ways. I personally had no problem with the cultural values of Branson. I was proud to see my brothers onstage again, singing for an audience that loved them for reprising "Side by Side," who didn't see anything corny in the dance routines or the saxophone number they'd first seen more than thirty years before. The cold truth was, I wasn't man enough to publicly embrace my legacy because I was still too worried about what "hip" people would think.

I'm sorry to say, my attitude was blatantly transparent to everyone in my family, and I know that I hurt them. The opening in 1992 was a golden opportunity for me to tell them how I felt, but I let it pass by. I sang onstage with them then, but my heart wasn't in the right place. I felt guilty about the message I sent them when I walked away from the group in the late 1970s. In my own way, I made it clear that I didn't need them anymore, that they represented something that I thought I wasn't anymore. Looking back, I see that they had a lot of patience with me. In some ways, they knew me even better than I did.

On December 1, 1994, Father and Mother celebrated their fiftieth wedding anniversary. Jimmy and my brothers, including Virl and Tom, planned to acknowledge this wonderful occasion with a special concert in Branson, and they invited me to join them onstage. I was hesitant at first, but once I heard all of their voices blending together on the old songs, I was overcome with emotion. It seemed like only yesterday that I laid in my bed, listening to my brothers practicing their harmonies until they drifted off to sleep. I was a toddler, and they were just boys. I looked beside me on the stage, and everyone was standing in their old places, but so much had changed. Virl was forty-nine, Tom, forty-seven, Alan, forty-five, Wayne, forty-three, Merrill, forty-one, Jay, thirty-nine, Marie, thirty-five, and Jimmy, the baby of the family, was thirty-one. We'd all grown older, but for that moment time stood still. I looked up to them, I admired them. I was proud to be among them.

Now it was time for me to grow up and stop worrying about what anyone else thought. Despite the distance I tried to put between who I am now and who I was before, singing with my brothers reminded me that time changes everything, but it is up to us to change our perceptions of the past. We are all different people, and we hold different views of what happened and why it happened. But what will never change are the moments we shared together. When I broke away from my brothers and from Marie, I couldn't imagine the day when the positive experiences would outweigh the negative. But that day did come, and I'm thankful that we were all there to celebrate it together.

It was not long after that show in Branson that my problems with social phobia reached the crisis point in Minneapolis. I don't want to suggest there was a direct cause-and-effect connection there. But I don't think it's complete coincidence that I was standing on that stage with my brothers at the start of what would be a long season of soul searching. Alan's and Wayne's health crises were a sharp reminder that we are all getting older, that the time to say what you feel in your heart is today. I feel that the time I spend with Father and Mother is especially precious. And I am so happy, because my relationship with each of them has grown closer. Whatever my siblings and I have accomplished, whoever we have become, I never forget that it all began with our parents and the very simple dreams they shared before any of us were born.

I don't mean to sound like someone's grandfather (though sometime in the next ten years, I probably will be, if you can picture that). As I try to tell my children—and as Debbie can already tell you, I'm sure—I don't have all the answers, but I do have some perspective I didn't have before. I've learned that, yes, life is just what you make it. It is a cliché, but most things that are true are. I found out that the struggles and setbacks weren't stones cluttering the smooth road to my dreams. They were the road, the unwished-for detours to those places I'd tried so hard to avoid and yet today am so grateful I got to see. I used to wonder how things would be today if I'd done this or if I'd done that, if that record had gone platinum, or if that show had triumphed on Broadway. I've wondered what kind of person I would be if only I'd succeeded every time, if I hadn't been the recipient of so many invitations to just quit and go home. I used to assume I'd be the same person I am today, only richer and happier. Today, however, I wonder if I would even recognize that guy.

Everyone tells us—and we all like to think—that if we achieve that one big goal, realize that single golden dream, everything else in our lives will come together. I believed that, and so when personal fulfillment didn't follow hot on the heels of hit records and sold-out tours, I wondered what was wrong with me. What I couldn't see then was that I'd invested more in making my dream come true than I'd invested in being true to myself. I gave more credit to attaining my goals than I gave to the person inside me who did the work. I'd perfected the art of perfectionism. I'd taken the criticism the world is too willing to offer to all of us. I put more faith in what others thought of me than in what I thought of myself. That's why when the dream stopped working, I felt so utterly lost and abandoned. I'd let the world tell me who I was when the world really didn't know.

Failure is a better teacher than success. The problem is, who in their right mind wants to sit in *that* classroom? And yet sooner or later, we all find ourselves there. If you're lucky, you graduate—not necessarily to success but to the realization that failure is an experience, not a personality trait; it's a noun for inanimate objects, not a word that applies to people.

It was only when I'd learned the lesssons of failure and started being a little more skeptical of success that the pieces finally did come together. Of course, it's easy to claim not to want what you can't have. Given my background, could I ever honestly say that I could be happy without ever having a hit record again? The answer is yes. For me, the proof came in December 1988, when "Soldier of Love" looked like a lost cause and my career was colder than ice. Even if I couldn't succeed at what I wanted the most, I would have found a way to be happy. From the outside, my life would be different in countless ways. But on the inside, the only place that really matters, I would be the same Donny, with the same wonderful wife and children, the same family, the same faith. I know I would still be, on my terms, a success. I don't think a day goes by that I don't remind myself of how easily it all could have never happened and how little it would take to undo everything again. The difference is that today I don't worry what would happen if it all went south again. I know everything would be just fine.

Every year, I give talks to many different groups. Whether I'm speaking to theater arts students in a college auditorium or to convicted felons in a prison, my theme usually boils down to: Believe in yourself. It is, I admit, a pretty well-worn piece of advice, the centerpiece of too many feel-good self-help books. But it's the one piece of advice—and, believe me, I'm an expert on receiving advice—that never failed me. Of course, it's not so easy to believe in yourself when everywhere you turn, there's someone ready to tell you why you shouldn't. The world would be a better place if we spent more time telling everyone we care about what they do right instead of what they do wrong, if we cheered them for simply running the race, whether they "won" or not. Sometimes it takes more heart to stay in the race than to win it. I am so glad that I never quit.

I think you can count yourself fortunate if you can look at your life and honestly say that if given the chance, you'd do it all again. With the exception of a few moments here and there, there's nothing in my life I would change. In fact, having come to the end of my story—so far, that is—and feeling very author-like, I feel I must pass on here some secrets for success.

> Treat everyone you meet as your brother or sister.
> Smile.
> Brush after every meal and see your dentist for regular
>   checkups.
> Perfect the art of not being perfect.
> Never drop your partner while dancing.
> Don't take the limo unless you have to.
> Remember: Any dream will do.
> When in doubt, order the club sandwich.
> Don't listen to anyone who tries to tell you who you are, or
>   who you should be.
> Turn off the power before handling live wires.
> Don't wear purple socks.
> Never forget and never disown your past.
> And never, ever change your name.

> Use them as you see fit. And good luck!

Epilogue

January 1, 2000

Now, I know this might seem confusing to you. Yes, you are reading a second ending to a book you thought you had finished, and you're probably wondering why. Let me explain.

As I write this, over a year has passed since I typed the last period in the last sentence and closed the book, so to speak, on my life story. So far. I remember hoping that people would read it and understand what I tried to say. I also remember thinking about it realistically, and putting on the final touches with a sense of relief (it's finally done!) and a fleeting sense of alarm. I expected some people to be surprised at how much I revealed about myself. I wanted readers to understand the challenges and the setbacks; I also wanted to show how I'd grown because of them, and share why I wouldn't change anything. I saw this as a chance to express who I really am without compromise or apology. And as committed as I was to that goal, I'd lived in show business long enough to know that I was taking a big risk. I accepted the possibility that readers might finish the book and decide they preferred the "old Donny" to the man I am today, or that I would be criticized for presenting my family as real people, not as the "perfect family" neither we nor any other family could ever be.

Each time I reread the manuscript, I sensed it growing away from me, taking on a life of its own. I knew that once it left my hands and went out into the world, I could not control how people would interpret it or what they would think of me. I was not afraid, though, for many reasons—including the process of actually writing the book. A little apprehensive, perhaps. Maybe a bit nervous. I opened my heart and I trusted my readers. And that trust has been rewarded countless times over in this past year. I can honestly say that this book was one of the best things that ever happened to me.

Early in the summer of 1998, we launched my national book tour. Because I was scheduled to fly to England to begin filming *Joseph and the Amazing Technicolor Dreamcoat* only days after I completed the tour, we crammed the interviews and appearances most authors would do over twenty or thirty days into a marathon (with weekends off for family) that took me to five cities in just over ten days. I admit, when I heard the words "book tour," I imagined something different, something quieter than a concert tour and less hectic than a bunch of ten-minute appearances at radio stations to promote a record. Little did I know. This was a marathon. From city to city, from television studio to radio station to book signing to interview, I discovered why several people had warned me that writing the book was the easy part. (And as I slaved to fill the blank screen with words to finish the book, I remember thinking, *You call this easy?*). Now I know. A talk show host myself now, it was interesting to be back in the guest chair (or, as we call it in the business, the hot seat) answering questions unlike any I'd ever been asked before. I won't lie and say that there weren't some difficult moments here and there. But I never left an interview regretting anything I'd said either there or in the book.

What made it all worthwhile, though, was getting to meet and speak to people who have been there for me through the years. From behind the signing table, my life seemed to parade before me in the form of old albums, magazines, videotapes, dolls, lunch boxes, photographs, and countless other relics of Osmondmania. If this book tour had a title, it would have to be "Guess What I Just Found in My Attic," because it was, hands-down, the most popular conversation opener of the tour, leaving "Are you wearing your purple socks?" a distant second. In the process of discovering what all of you have been keeping in your attics, I learned several important things: One is, there are way too many Donny and Marie dolls out there. I had to laugh when a woman showed me copies of my old albums that as a teenager she had kissed the lips right off. Fortunately, she was laughing about it, too. Appropriately, I also came away with an increased appreciation of my years in show business. I spoke with people of all ages. There was a lovely elderly lady who exclaimed, "I've been following your career since I saw you as a child on *The Andy Griffith Show!*" (I didn't have the heart to correct her.) And there was a teenager standing next to a middle-aged woman at one of my book signings, who glanced at the collection of my teen idol–era eight-tracks she held and asked in awe, "What *are* those?" The most fun, though, was talking to the kids who came with copies of *Mulan* in hand. I'm looking forward to the next tour, maybe thirty years from now, when I'll see those kids and *their* kids. It should be fun. And imagine what those eight-tracks will be selling for then. (Note to self: Check eBay.)

The best thing about the whole experience was coming face-to-face with the people who had made my career not only possible but also so fulfilling. I came away with a deeper respect for them as well as a more positive view of my earlier life. Through their kind words, they helped me realize that even in those times when being "Donny Osmond" was difficult for me personally, somewhere, someone had enjoyed what I was doing.

Once out, the book definitely did have a life of its own, a life that was essentially beyond my control. Fortunately, most of the media attention the book received was positive, but not everybody loved the book or me. But that's okay, too. What was most satisfying was the opportunity to talk frankly about my social phobia. I did it with the hope that someone who was feeling the way I once had might realize that they were not alone, that there was help for them. In the past year, I've heard from many people who have suffered in silence from some form of anxiety disorder. To my surprise, some were people I have known for many years, including famous celebrities even I never would have suspected.

In opening my life to the world, I also shared information about the people closest to me. Father, Mother, and Debbie had read the manuscript, so they knew the story I was about to share. In her wisdom, Debbie asked me—more than once, I should add—"Are you sure you want this much of your personal life out in a book?" I did. Father, whom I feared would be most affected, read it and supported me all the way. I thanked him and Mother for this before, but I will thank them again. While I never believed that my upbringing was in any way too strict considering the circumstances of our lives, not everyone who read this book agreed. A couple of interviewers chose to focus on that aspect of the story, to the exclusion of almost everything else. I defended my parents then, and I always will. By any measure, they did an amazing job; they are remarkable people. One positive result of the new television show's success dovetailing with the book's release was the sudden interest in our family from credible documentary series such as VH1's *Behind the Music*, MSNBC's *Headliners & Legends*, and the A&E *Biography* series. I felt each of these shows gave viewers a fuller picture of our family that, while not glossing over the rough spots, presented our story fairly and cast in a fair, positive light the crucial role our parents played.

Coincidentally, I was in the middle of writing this epilogue when we taped the *Donny & Marie* Christmas episode. Marie and I had arranged a family reunion, with all of our brothers together with us for this special show. I had promised Marie that I would never surprise her on our Christmas shows, but this was one time I had to break it, and for a good reason. Unbeknownst to any of my siblings, Father, Mother, and I had a plan. The three of us led (or misled) everyone else to think that our parents would not be able to attend the Christmas show. And everyone believed us. I snuck Father and Mother into town and kept them out of sight until the day of the show. In my introduction on the Christmas Eve show, I said the one thing I believe said it all: that these were the people who always made Christmas special for all of us. When Father and Mother surprised everyone and walked out onstage, each of us was overwhelmed with emotion. It was the first time in about seventeen years that all eleven of us had been on television together. More important to me personally was the chance to send the message that family is everything. Despite all the trials, the hardships, and the difficulties that we faced as a family, we remain strong. And even more important, we remain a family for whom the joy of loving one another has only grown with the passage of time. I've said it before, and I will say it forever: I owe it all to my parents.

After the book tour ended in June, I had three days back home with Debbie and the boys, then it was back to work. It had been over a year since I had agreed to star in Sir Andrew Lloyd Webber's film version of *Joseph and the Amazing Technicolor Dreamcoat*. I had not been onstage as Joseph since March 1998, and the thought of doing it again—for what would be the last time—brought mixed emotions. I was flattered that Sir Andrew had chosen me to play Joseph in the film and excited at the idea that one day my grandchildren would be able to see it. The six years I spent playing Joseph marked a pivotal period in my life, one that was both bitter and sweet. As I had come to understand and learn to manage my social phobia, it got easier to look back and acknowledge the pain and the terror I'd felt standing onstage. You might think you would just get over something like that, but even today, even when I'm "on" in public, there are moments when the memory of how out of control my life was can almost bring me to tears. It's not that I feel sorry for myself, or that the social phobia has made me more emotional. It's simply having the distance and the perspective to look back and realize what my life easily could have become had I not sought help. I can barely get out the words to describe it without choking back tears.

I was looking forward to playing Joseph, even though the loincloth—or, more accurately, the vision of myself in the loincloth—had been haunting me for months. Throughout the book tour, I was supposed to be getting in shape. Since last playing Joseph in March 1998, I'd witnessed my body gradually reshape itself, as the bulk that made up my once-impressive pecs and lats seemed to settle around my midsection. If I had five free minutes between interviews, I was doing sit-ups, push-ups, chin-ups—whatever it took.

At my first costume fitting in England, I was surprised to discover that my stage wardrobe for the film—the amazing multicolored coat, the golden Egyptian armor, and the loincloth—would be the same I'd worn onstage. They had been dug out of storage in Canada and shipped to England. The coat, which was the only costume item I'd worn from day one, had survived more than two thousand performances, and it was strange to put it on for what I knew would be the very last time. It was important to me to bring them home when the shoot was finished. I guess I'll store them somewhere in the house with my old tool belt, my unfinished electronic Heathkits, and a few other precious items from my past.

We filmed in England, at Pinewood Studios, an incredibly large and historical facility. With only five weeks to shoot, a new cast to get used to, and the challenge of modifying my technique to make my acting more natural for film, my work was cut out for me. It had been more than twenty years since I'd last acted in a film (and it's nice to know that the caliber of my film oeuvre has taken a quantum leap since *Goin' Coconuts*), and I had developed Joseph for the stage, not the camera. Acting for film demands an entirely different approach. Gestures, facial expressions, even the timing of lines must be more subtle and less grand. Where onstage you learn to play to the very last row that may be more than a hundred feet away from you, for film you must always remember that every "row" is the first row, at times just a foot or so away.

Although everyone knows that it's impossible for any film to re-create the experience of live theater, director David Mallet (best known for his pioneering rock videos for such artists as David Bowie, Billy Idol) brought *Joseph* to the screen in a way that captured the excitement of theater and the closeup emotional intimacy only film can achieve. Stage director Steven Pimlott, who had directed me onstage in *Joseph*, and Madeline Paul, who had been the resident director during all six years of *Joseph*, were also in England. Steven had once told me, "The theater is the place where people can dream in public," and this film captured the essence of a dream in colors so vivid they sometimes seemed illuminated from within. The numbers and sets were inspired by every major musical and artistic style from 1930s art deco musicals to 1960s swinging London and most of everything in between, including a hip-hop remix over the closing credits. We shot using six cameras simultaneously (as opposed to only one, which is typical), for example, which showcased the amazing work of Anthony Van Last, who'd also been the original choreographer of the Canadian stage production in which I'd appeared.

Overall, there was a lot of continuity between the stage production and the film. What was most dramatically different—and what took me a little time to adjust to—was the cast. With the exception of one actor, Jeff Blumenkrantz, who played Joseph's brother Simeon in the original cast, everyone was new to me. Among the featured actors were Joan Collins (the seductive Mrs. Potiphar), Maria Friedman (the Narrator), Sir Richard Attenborough (Jacob), Ian McNeice (Potiphar), and Robert Torti (Pharaoh).

Fortunately, despite the hectic shooting schedule for *Joseph*, there was time for other things. With Debbie and the boys, I went to visit our son Don, who was in the middle of a two-year mission for The Church of Jesus Christ of Latter-day Saints he had begun in late summer 1998. By then, it had been over a year since we had last seen Don in person, and it was wonderful to be together again.

Right before we began filming *Joseph*, in late July 1999, I took time off from rehearsals to go to Portsmouth, where a film crew was making a documentary of a local school's production of the play. I was honored to be a special guest, and during an assembly, I talked to the students about my experiences as Joseph. A few eight- to ten-year-olds asked for autographs; they knew me from *Mulan*. I could also see that a few of the teachers were fans, too, but from an earlier time. In moments like those, I do enjoy my celebrity and the experiences it affords me. Of course, you can always count on a child to give you that little reality check that keeps your feet on the ground. As I looked out across the assembled group of students, most of them staring at me and smiling broadly, I caught one little girl whispering loudly to her neighbor in a very, very British accent: "Donny Osmond? He used to be famous. I didn't know he was still alive!"

Once we completed filming *Joseph*, I returned to the United

States and dived right back into work on the upcoming second season of *Donny & Marie*. My sister and I did a brief but intense tour to promote the show (which is doing very well, thanks to you), then headed for Atlantic City to cohost the Miss America Pageant for the first time. Shortly after we had finished that, it was time to get back to work in Los Angeles.

In the course of an early staff meeting about the show, Marie told us about her problems with postpartum depression over the summer. Marie's baby, Matthew, was born right before I left for England. When I walked into her hospital room, I saw her holding Matthew, then just a few hours old, and together they looked almost angelic. Marie had not had an easy time giving birth; she was tired and wearing no makeup, yet I don't believe I've ever seen my sister more beautiful or more content.

When Marie told us about the postpartum depression she experienced while I was in England, I was concerned but not entirely surprised. Looking back, I had seen little signs toward the end of the previous season, but I had chalked it up to Marie being in the last stages of pregnancy. I—or I should say, Debbie—had been through five pregnancies, so I'd learned to roll with the moments when things seem a little tense. I am very proud of Marie for going public with her experience. In sharing her private struggles so openly, I know she's helped untold thousands of women who've suffered through the same difficulties realize that there is help for them. Not to suggest I could ever really know how Marie felt being burdened by depression during days that should have been among the happiest, I know that would be impossible. What I *could* understand was how it felt to feel utterly alone in your pain, how it felt to feel betrayed by your own emotions to the point that they overrode your common sense and your true feelings. Seeing Marie through this and through her separation, I was reminded again of how important family truly is and how deep the bond remains between us. Marie is a strong, thoughtful woman, and I know that whatever decision she makes comes only after much careful consideration and soul searching. She knows that I will always be there for her.

So this really is the end of the story. So far, of course. Since I've been so open about my life, more people than ever are offering me advice. The big—and welcome—difference is that no one's telling me to change my name anymore or suggesting I quit show business. Now I get so many kind suggestions from strangers about how to deal with my social phobia, I've come to think of the world as my therapist. In fact, if I'd known it would be like this, I'd have talked publicly long before!

One of the most liberating developments of the past couple years has been the ability to play with the image that I felt haunted me for so many years. I'm sure Marie and I turned a few heads when we appeared very out of character in a special fashion issue of *The New York Times Magazine* in late 1999. Marie was decked out in long bottle-blond hair, red five-inch heels, leopard-print top, and pants that turned her from, as the magazine wrote, "working mom to working girl." And me. Well, I'm not sure exactly who or what I was supposed to be. Suffice it to say that tight black leather pants, a silver sequined cowboy hat, an open black shirt, a black feather boa, mascara, and platinum-blond streaks and hair extensions all came into play. At the same time. And may I add, I think I made it look good.

For fun, I took a walk in that outfit one evening in Santa Monica, and the reactions I got were quite interesting. One teenage boy opined to a friend that I looked like "an old guy who's trying to be young." (I'd prefer to think of myself as a young old guy.) They were both shocked to discover that I was Donny Osmond, and they seemed to know who he was: "You mean the one from *The Partridge Family*?"

Yes, the next fortysomething years should be even more interesting. See you there. I may even write about it someday.

acknowledgments

This is going to be a humble and, I'm afraid, flawed attempt to thank publicly those who mean so much to me. If you don't find your name in these pages, know that you are in my heart.

Writing this book has been so cathartic. To revisit forty-one years and to try and articulate what I've experienced has been difficult but ultimately very rewarding. I appreciate the efforts of everyone who has helped me put the pieces together, especially those who relived with me some moments I would rather have forgotten. Having said that, I'm more convinced than ever after going through this process that I am a very lucky man who has been truly blessed.

The greatest blessing of my life is my wife, Debbie. From the start, I knew you were the one, and these past twenty-one years with you have proven that to me. Your love, patience, support, and wisdom have guided me in my life more than you'll ever imagine. You've shown me a path I never would have found on my own. Thank you for giving me five wonderful sons and for choosing me to share your life. I love you.

To Don, Jeremy, Brandon, Christopher, and Joshua, whom I love more than I can even begin to tell you: Thank you for your love, your support, and your understanding. Thank you for the joy of being your dad.

To my wonderful Father and Mother: I love and respect you so much. Each passing year deepens my appreciation of how difficult it must have been for you to raise nine children in such a crazy business. You taught us the principles and values that have enabled us to stay a close, strong, and loving family, and I'll be eternally grateful to you for that. You believed in us, and you sacrificed the security of a "normal" life so that we each could fulfill our dreams. You read my manuscript at every stage and encouraged me to tell my story as I saw it. It was a gesture of confidence, trust, and love I'll never forget.

To my Brothers and my dear Sister: Thank you for all the great times over the years. I'll never forget the harmonies, the routines, the work—oh, the work! But we did it, and I am so proud to be your brother. I've learned invaluable lessons from each of you, and I treasure your love and your friendship now more than ever before. I love you all, your spouses, and your children. (And a special thanks to Merrill and Alan for the title of this book, and the song from which it came.)

To my wife's parents, Avery and Marge Glenn, her brother Mike, and her sister Pam: Thank you for your love, your patience, and, most of all, your sense of humor to accept me as your crazy son- and brother-in-law.

To my longtime personal friends, who've hung in with me through it all: Sik Nik (Ritnaskow-ole'), Rob Dias, Bill Waite, Steve Hortin, Chad Murdock, Dean Hargrove, Harrison Payne, Karl Engemann, Allen Finlinson, Arlen Simon, Ann Jackson, Debbie Harrington, Ron Clark, Doug Pinkston, Joe Lake, Mick Shannon, Paul Peterson, Dave Rothstein, Annette Lei, Bob and Gail Ryan, Brad Weekes, Dave Cole, Mick Angus, Herb Karlitz, Rory Kaplan, Pat Custar, and Fred Judd.

I could have waited until I was seventy years old to write this book, but through my good friend Darrell Brown, I met my editor, Will Schwalbe, who convinced me to do it now. From the beginning, Will understood what I hoped to achieve with this, and he made it possible for me to write the book I wanted to write. Will introduced me to my wonderful coauthor Patty

Romanowski. I thank them both for working around my difficult schedule to make this book a reality. Patty now knows me better than most people do, and she still claims to like me. She warned me from the start that this was going to hurt sometimes, and it did. But I have thoroughly enjoyed the hundreds of hours we've spent on the phone.

To Jill Willis, my manager: Thank you for your wise and careful guidance through the years and for your sound advice. But most of all, thank you for your friendship during those difficult years. I value our relationship very much and look forward to many, many years together. To Eric Weissler: Everyone needs a good attorney, and, in you, I've certainly found mine. Thanks for helping put this book deal together. To Lewis Kay, my publicist: You're a blast to work with. You, too, Brad and Amy. I would also like to acknowledge Alan Mintz, my music attorney and the newest member of my team. I look forward to working with you. And a very special thank you to Rich Hill: I appreciate your friendship and all your help in putting this book deal together and seeing it through. I also thank you for bringing marketing whiz Greg Link aboard.

There are several people who have undertaken the unenviable task of keeping my day-to-day life running smoothly. To Pat Dresbach: Thank you for all the time and effort you devote on my behalf. You pulled together the clips, the tapes, the facts, and the perspective. And I can't believe you found all the pictures that I thought were long gone. To Julie Seagroatt: Thank you for the extra research and detective work you did. To Chris Hill, Dave Brewer, and all of those who contribute so much to D.O.I.N.: Thank you for your efforts and consideration. To Sheree Bradford, my assistant in Los Angeles: Thank you for keeping my agenda straight and helping clear the time so I could finish this, and for making me laugh on a daily basis. You're great. To Cathy Kinsella: Thank you for making available the resources of your *Osmond Family Trivia Book*.

Over the years I've come to realize I'm fortunate not only to have fans who have supported my efforts for so many years, but fans who are genuinely nice people as well. Thank you for being there.

I'd also like to thank the following people for the favors that sped this along: Rick Hall, Jann S. Wenner, Annie Leibovitz,

Phil Basha, Tana Osa-Yande, Halley MacNaughton, and the staff at Wordflow, Inc.

Over the years countless people have encouraged and supported my professional efforts. It would be impossible to name them all, but I would like to thank the following people for giving me crucial opportunities and support: Andy Williams, Jerry Lewis, Mike Curb, Carl Sturken, Evan Rogers, Garth Drabinsky, Dan Brambilla, Norman Zagier, and all of those at Live Entertainment. To Ray Chandler, Steve Quinn, Jeff Pluth, Bob Tevyaw, and the cast and crew who worked so hard on *Joseph and the Amazing Technicolor Dreamcoat*. To Sir Andrew Lloyd Webber, Tim Rice, Peter Gabriel, George Acogny, Lou Simon, Guy Zapolean, Jessica Ettinger, and everyone in radio who played my music. Thanks to Lee Dannay, Jeff Jones, Frank Rand, John Fagot, and everyone at Capitol Records and Virgin UK who believed in my music. Thank you, Pam Coats, Ruth Lambert, and everyone at Disney for the opportunity to work on *Mulan*. Thank you, Peter Calabrese, for your efforts. Also thanks to Jim Morey, Ray Katz, Bill Sammeth, Ged Doherty, Martin Serene, Steven Machat, Rick Smith, Joel Peresman, Norman Winter, Milton Katselas, Jocelyn Jones, Sid and Marty Krofft, Michael Lloyd, Roger Neal, Michael Pagnotta, and Jenifer Carr. More recently I'd like to thank everyone at Columbia TriStar Television for their continued support of *Donny & Marie*, especially Barry Thurston, Russ Krasnoff, Melanie Chilek, Steve Moskow, and especially Dick Clark. Thanks to John Feriter, Mark Itkin, and those at William Morris who put it all together. For their day-to-day work, thanks to everyone in the trenches at Sony Studio. Thank you, Charlie Cook, Maureen FitzPatrick, our producers, writers, Jerry Williams and our band, and everyone else who works so hard to make everything Marie and I do look so easy. We both appreciate you more than you know.

Finally, and above all, I want to thank my Heavenly Father and His son, Jesus Christ, for blessing me beyond measure.

Donny Osmond
www.donny.com